Language, Mind and Logic

Language, Mind and Logic

EDITED BY JEREMY BUTTERFIELD

University Lecturer
University of Cambridge

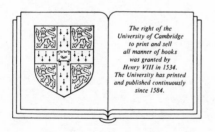

The right of the
University of Cambridge
to print and sell
all manner of books
was granted by
Henry VIII in 1534.
The University has printed
and published continuously
since 1584.

CAMBRIDGE UNIVERSITY PRESS

Cambridge

London   New York   New Rochelle

Melbourne   Sydney

Published by the Press Syndicate of the University of Cambridge
The Pitt Building, Trumpington Street, Cambridge CB2 1RP
32 East 57th Street, New York, NY 10022, USA
10 Stamford Road, Oakleigh, Melbourne 3166, Australia

Printed in Great Britain by
the University Press, Cambridge

British Library cataloguing in publication data
Language, mind and logic.
1. Analysis (Philosophy)
1. Butterfield, Jeremy   II. Series
149'.94   B808.5

Library of Congress cataloguing in publication data
Language, mind and logic.
Includes index.
1. Semantics (Philosophy) – Addresses, essays,
lectures.   2. Logic – Addresses, essays, lectures.
3. Knowledge, Theory of – Addresses, essays, lectures.
1. Butterfield, Jeremy.
B840.L36   1986   110   85 19511

ISBN 0 521 32046 1

Contents

Contributors

Jerry Fodor is Professor of Psychology at the Massachusetts Institute of Technology.

Anthony Appiah is Assistant Professor of Philosophy at Yale University.

David Papineau is Lecturer in History and Philosophy of Science at the University of Cambridge.

Harold Noonan is Lecturer in Philosophy at the University of Birmingham.

Jeremy Butterfield is Lecturer in Philosophy at the University of Cambridge.

John Perry is Professor of Philosophy at Stanford University.

Jane Heal is Lecturer in Philosophy at the University of Newcastle-Upon-Tyne.

John Skorupski is Professor of Philosophy at the University of Sheffield.

Edward Craig is Lecturer in Philosophy at the University of Cambridge.

Crispin Wright is Professor of Logic and Metaphysics at the University of St Andrews.

Charles Parsons is Professor of Philosophy at Columbia University.

Introduction

Our title echoes Ayer's *Language, Truth and Logic*, written fifty years ago. The analytic tradition in philosophy still sees the analysis of language and of logic as major branches of the subject. And it sees the analysis of language, aided by the techniques of formal logic, as an invaluable tool in tackling other philosophical problems.

But there has also been a change, reflected in our title by the substitution of *Mind* for *Truth*. In their enthusiasm for the analysis of language, and their proclaimed break with traditional philosophy, the logical empiricists seem to have hoped that such analysis could lead on its own to strong conclusions about truth. In particular, they hoped it could distinguish the kinds of discourse that stated facts from those that did not; thus rapidly settling many traditional problems, for example about the status of moral discourse. Of course they disagreed about where this distinction lay; and about how eliminativist one should be about discourse that did not state facts. Thus while Ayer hoped to distinguish the empirical propositions of everyday life and the sciences from meaningless metaphysics, Reichenbach hoped to distinguish within science between factual propositions and conventional, albeit meaningful, ones. But behind these differences, there was nevertheless this shared assumption in the power of such analysis to distinguish the factual from the non-factual.

Most analytic philosophers now reject this assumption. Admittedly, the distinction between factual and non-factual is all-important. But it probably cannot be drawn, and traditional problems cannot be settled, solely by the analysis of language: we cannot expect the philosophy of language to do our metaphysics or our ethics for us. As a result, all kinds of traditional problems – such as the nature of causation, perception, will, virtue and rights – have received over the last twenty-five years a more sympathetic, and more detailed, treatment than they got in the early decades of the analytic tradition.

In the revival of metaphysics, problems about the mind have taken centre stage. One reason for this has been the influence of materialism. The success of the natural sciences suggests that in some sense the material world they describe is all there is. And so mental phenomena pose problems: what precise version of materialism is true, and what account does it give of mind? There has also been the confluence of pragmatism, with its focus on action, with the analytic tradition's concern with language. This has resulted in a lot of work on the propositional attitudes: mental states like belief and desire that explain action and are apparently directed at propositions, as expressed in a that-clause.

The essays in this collection centre around two themes that have been very prominent in recent work on mind and language. The first is the question to what extent our account of mind must look beyond the individual subject to the environment. Features in the environment of course affect the mental states of the subject through perception; and are affected by such mental states through action. But putting aside such causal interdependence, are there ways in which, as a matter of logic, mental states require certain features in the environment? For example, does having a belief require speaking a language, and does every language have to be the language of a community? The second theme is the nature of content or representation, both for mental states and for language: in particular, what account can a materialist give of mental states or sentences having a content, by which they represent the world? Both these themes are discussed directly or at one remove in all the essays.

The first seven essays focus on propositional attitudes. Accordingly, the first theme is treated in a more specific form: how wide or narrow are attitudes? That is, how much or how little does their attribution entail about the world external to the subject? Broadly speaking, advocacy of narrow attitudes predominates. This is partly due to the influence of functionalism: the first three authors, Fodor, Appiah and Papineau are avowed functionalists, and functionalists have usually favoured narrow attitudes. Functionalism urges that an attitude is a mental state with a characteristic pattern of (largely causal) relations to stimuli, to behaviour and to other mental states. This pattern is called the functional role, or causal role. Since it is unique to the attitude in question, the attitude is said to be individuated by it. It is also meant to encapsulate our concept of the attitude. Thus it is part of our concept of the belief that it is raining that this belief should normally be caused by perception of raindrops, and should normally cause an agent who desires to be dry to stay indoors or take an umbrella; so these causal relations will figure in the belief's functional role.

Fodor explicitly tackles Putnam's and Burge's argument for wide attitudes. They use a Twin Earth thought-experiment to urge that two agents with the very same internal states can have different attitudes, owing to differences in their respective environments. We are to imagine a planet very like Earth except that the drinkable colourless liquid filling the rivers and lakes is not H_2O, but another substance. Let us call the planet Twin Earth and the substance XYZ. Suppose also that on Twin Earth there are twins or Doppelgangers of each of us here on Earth. These twins are to be as similar to us as they can be, compatible with XYZ's playing the role that H_2O plays on Earth. Thus we suppose that XYZ acts in their body-chemistry just as H_2O does in ours; and that a person and his or her twin have the same history of bodily stimuli, internal states and actions (described in ways that do not distinguish H_2O and XYZ). So if I say 'water is wet', so does my twin. But the beliefs we thereby express surely have different truth-conditions. Mine is about H_2O, his about XYZ. They are therefore different beliefs, despite our having the same internal states.

In reply, Fodor urges that we can and should save narrow attitudes by denying the 'therefore'. That is, we should think of truth-conditions as depending not only on the belief but also on the context in which it is held. In that way, my twin and I can have the same belief, albeit one with context-dependent truth-conditions.

Fodor, Appiah and Papineau also discuss the second theme, that of content or representation. Fodor argues that in order to assign contents to mental states, we must not make contents too sensitive to differences in functional role. He suggests we can base the assignment to a state on a combination of (a) its causal relations to external states of affairs; and (b) some aspects of its functional role. Appiah restricts himself to considering a computation-ally perfect subject: roughly, a subject who believes the logical consequences of what they believe. He argues that for such a subject we can base the assignment for belief-like states on (a). Papineau suggests the assignment needs the teleological idea of the external state of affairs that it is the state's function to be caused by. Both Appiah and Papineau also advocate a reduction of linguistic representation to propositional attitudes, using ideas derived from Grice and Lewis about the roles of intention and convention in language; and Papineau goes on to consider the problems posed for this programme by proper names.

Noonan and I complement Fodor's advocacy of narrow attitudes, though in rather different ways. We both use an adaptation of the Twin Earth thought-experiment to argue that attitudes should be narrow in the specific sense of not entailing the existence of any particular object. (Noonan calls such attitudes 'non-Russellian'; I call them 'object-independent'.) Noonan goes on to rebut Peacocke's and Evans' arguments for the contrary view. I go on to propose a conception of content that is designed to meet several constraints, one of them being that attitudes to such contents can be narrow in this sense.

Perry analyses how both wide and narrow attitudes contribute to explaining actions. He discerns a tension between our actions being often successful, and their being caused in a law-like way by our inner states. To account for actions' success, we use wide descriptions of actions, that is descriptions that entail statements about the world external to the agent; and we conceive attitudes as wide psychological states determining such actions. On the other hand, to account for actions' causes, we invoke narrow mental states, which Perry calls cognitions; these together with psychological laws determine actions as described in terms of bodily movements. Perry urges that we can and should use both wide and narrow psychological states, to explain actions under various descriptions; though he reserves the word 'attitude' for wide states.

Each of these first six papers advocates, or is compatible with, a functionalist account of attitudes. Heal challenges this consensus, suggesting an alternative account of action-explanation which she calls the replication strategy. It involves a kind of make-believe that one is the agent whose action is to be explained. Heal argues that this strategy does not collapse back into functionalism and that it can accommodate, in a way functionalism cannot, the open-ended nature of our idea of a rationally explicable action.

The last four essays deal as much with language as with propositional attitudes. For Skorupski the second theme, about the nature of content, is in the forefront. He argues that naturalism leads to two apparently opposed claims. First, it leads *via* the idea that our evidence, no matter how complete, is defeasible, to a distinction between truth and assertibility. It also leads to a view of understanding a language as a matter of responding appropriately to evidence, rather than participation in some non-natural realm of meanings. To make these claims compatible, we have to distinguish two ways in which a sentence represents: its semantic content and its cognitive role.

Craig takes up the first theme, about how individualist our account of mind can be. He scrutinizes the arguments for the claim that for inner states the notion of recurrence or sameness of kind is wrong. He finds the arguments wanting, even if we allow that this notion requires a consensus among a community. The reason is that this requirement does not prevent there being a consensus, of true belief if not knowledge, about people's inner states. He finally applies his results to criticize Kripke's exposition of Wittgenstein.

Wright and Parsons tackle two intimately related issues, alluded to by Skorupski and Craig: the nature of logical necessity, and of our cognition of abstract, in particular mathematical, objects. Wright argues against a certain kind of objectivism about logical necessity. He first rebuts the non-objectivist account implicit in Quine's *Two Dogmas*, on the grounds that it does not respect the convincing character of a proof. He then describes what it is for a statement to be factual; and argues that one can respect the convincing character of a proof, while denying that the necessity of the corresponding conditional statement is a matter of fact.

Wright admits that necessity might be factual, if we had a special intellectual faculty that was sensitive to it. Parsons takes up the idea of intuition, for the case of mathematical objects, specifically numbers. Parsons points out that discussion of intuitionism and other constructivist philosophies of mathematics has neglected this idea, centring instead on the idea of a mathematical sentence's meaning being its conditions of proof. He goes on to argue that this is a mistake: constructivism requires that numbers can be intuited.

All the essays in this collection are here published for the first time. Draft versions were presented at some meetings of members of the Thyssen Philosophy Group and their guests. On behalf of the Group, I would like to express our thanks to the Fritz Thyssen Stiftung, and its director Professor Dr Rudolf Kerscher, for their most generous financial support and encouragement.

JEREMY BUTTERFIELD

Cambridge
February 1985

Banish disContent*

JERRY FODOR

It is a curiosity of the philosophical temperament, this passion for radical solutions. Do you feel a little twinge in your epistemology? Absolute scepticism is the thing to try. Has the logic of confirmation got you down? Probably physics is a fiction. Worried about individuating objects? Don't let anything in but sets. Nobody has yet suggested that the way out of the Liar paradox is to give up talking, but I expect it's only a matter of time. Apparently the rule is: if aspirin doesn't work, try cutting off your head.

The latest of these cures for which there is no adequate disease is the suggestion that – largely on account of some semantic puzzles about content – psychological theory should dispense with the attribution of propositional attitudes. In my view, this is a *grotesque* proposal; both because we can't do without propositional attitude psychology and because it's far from clear that the semantic problems are as bad as they are alleged to be. The plan of this paper is to look very briefly at the first of these considerations and rather extensively at the second.

I. WHY WE CAN'T DO WITHOUT PROPOSITIONAL ATTITUDE PSYCHOLOGY

We can't do without propositional attitude psychology because, on the one hand, propositional attitude psychology works and, on the other hand, nothing else does. Propositional attitude psychology works so well that the mechanism is practically invisible. It is like those mythical Rolls Royce cars whose engines are sealed when they leave the factory; only it's better because it's not mythical. Someone I don't know telephones me at my office in Cambridge from – as it might be – Arizona. 'Would you like to lecture here next Tuesday?' are the words that he utters. 'Yes, thank you. I'll be at your airport on the 3:00 pm flight' are the words that I reply.[1] That's

---

* For useful discussions of earlier drafts of this work, I'm especially indebted to Ned Block, Tyler Burge, David Israel, and Ron McClamrock.

[1] *So* invisible is the mechanism that one may overlook such facts as that even the notion of a word belongs to commonsense intentional psychology and not to acoustics (say) or to physics.

I

all that happens, but it's more than enough; the rest of the burden is routinely taken up by theory. And the theory works so well that, several days later (or weeks later, or months later, or years later; you can vary the example to taste) and several thousand miles away, there I am at the airport, and there he is to meet me. Or if I don't turn up, it's less likely that the theory has failed than that something went wrong with the airline and the aeroplane is late. For these sorts of purposes, people are more predictable mechanisms than jets.

The point is that the theory from which we get this extraordinary predictive power is just good old commonsense propositional attitude psychology. That's what tells us, for example, how to infer people's intentions from the sounds they make (if someone utters the form of words 'I'll be at your airport on the 3:00 pm flight' then, with enormously high probability, he intends to be at your airport on the 3:00 pm flight) and how to infer people's behaviour from their intentions (if someone intends to be at your airport on the 3:00 pm flight then, with enormously high probability, he will produce behaviour of a sort which will eventuate in his arriving at that place at that time barring mechanical failure). And all this works not just with people whose psychology you know intimately: your closest friends, say, or the spouse of your bosom. It works with absolute strangers: people you wouldn't know if you bumped into them. And it works not just in laboratory conditions – where you can control the interacting variables – but also, indeed preeminently, in field conditions where *all* you know about the sources of variance is what commonsense psychology tells you about them. Remarkable. If we could do that well with predicting the weather, no one would ever get his feet wet. Yet the aetiology of the weather is surely child's play compared with the causes of behaviour.

Physics, by the way, doesn't begin to compete: though we can, by exploiting our knowledge of their psychology, routinely bring off these extraordinary predictions of the *behaviour* of 'intentional systems', there is no way – practically speaking – that we can hope to predict their *trajectories*. If you think of me as two hundred pounds (less in the jogging season) of peripatetic philosopher whose itinerary you've just been informed of, there are long odds you can predict where I'll be at 3:00 pm on Tuesday. Whereas, if you think of me as an equivalent mass of hydrocarbons which just produced a couple of seconds of local acoustic peturbation, nothing useful follows from any physical science we now have or can ever reasonably expect.

To be sure, that's just *commonsense* propositional attitude psychology; and it's mostly *implicit* commonsense propositional attitude psychology to boot. It might still be that, for scientific purposes, something other – something better – is required. After all, what we want in science is insight and explanation, not just prediction and control. It is now widely said that propositional attitude psychology is seen to be a 'stagnant' theory when viewed in the light of these desiderata. By contrast, what is not stagnant, what is said to be making scientific progress, is computational psychology, in which appeals to the attitudes are dispensed with. (See, for example, Stich 1983.)

I am, I suppose, as good a friend of computational psychology as the next chap; especially if the next chap is a philosopher. But that view of the current scene in cognitive science strikes me as a gross distortion. For, one can say in a phrase what it is that computational psychology has been proving so successful at: viz. *the vindication of generalizations about propositional attitudes*; specifically, of the more or less commonsense sort of generalizations about propositional attitudes illustrated a paragraph or so above. Thus, for example, we've got fragments of a theory of perception, and it makes clear how a computational system could regularly come to believe that P in causal consequence of its being visibly the case that P. Analogously, we've got fragments of a theory of language, and what it does is to make clear how, in a computational system, the intention to communicate the belief that P could eventuate, causally, in the production of an utterance that means that P. Or again, we've got fragments of a theory of memory; it explains how a computational system could come to believe that it was once the case that P in causal consequence of the fact that it was once the case that P. And so forth. The mental processes that such computational theories acknowledge are, no doubt, in some sense 'purely syntactic'; at a minimum, they're supposed to be specifiable without recourse to intentional idiom. But the generalizations that such theories account for are intentional down to their boots. Accordingly, computational theories of mental processes don't replace the commonsense story about propositional attitudes and their behavioural effects. Rather, what a computational theory does is to make clear the mechanism of intentional causation; to show how it is (nomologically) possible that purely computational – indeed, purely physical – systems should act out of their beliefs and desires.

I don't suppose that all that comes to much; I just wanted to remind you that – given standard principles of Scientific Realism – there is an enormous *prima facie* case for taking commonsense propositional attitude psychology to be more or less true. No doubt this case is less than literally conclusive. In principle, somebody might find overwhelming reason for rejecting intentional psychology; so overwhelming that rejecting intentional psychology would be rational even if we had no idea at all what to replace it with. (As, indeed, we don't.) But *overwhelming* reason is surely what rationality would require. If the sky opened up and God told us that there aren't any propositional attitudes, then I suppose that we would

3

have to believe Him. But it's not clear that a great deal less than that would do.

Having thus made clear where the burden of proof resides, let's look at the semantic puzzles about content.

2. PUZZLES ABOUT CONTENT: TWIN-EARTH

Is there anybody who *hasn't* heard? There's this place, you see, that's just like here except that they've got XYZ where we've got H_2O. In this place, there's someone who's just like me down to and including his neurological microstructure. The intuition that we're invited to have is that, in virtue of the hydrochemical facts and in spite of the neurological ones, the form of words 'water is wet' means something different in his mouth than it does in mine. And, similarly, the content of the thought that Twin-Me has when he thinks (*in re* XYZ, as one might say) that water is wet is different from the content of the thought that I have when I think that water is wet *in re* H_2O.

Suppose these intuitions are reliable; what follows? Well, on the one hand, my Twin and I are identical in physical constitution but, on the other hand, our thoughts have different truth conditions (i.e. what makes *his* 'water'-thoughts true is the facts about XYZ, whereas what makes my water-thoughts true is the facts about H_2O). So, it looks as though we have to say either (a) that thoughts don't have their truth conditions essentially (i.e. that two tokens of the *same* thought can have *different* truth conditions), or (b) that type-identity of thoughts doesn't supervene upon biochemical type-identity of their thinkers.

That, then, is the 'Twin-Earth problem'. Except that so far it isn't a problem; it's just a handful of intuitions together with a commentary on some immediate implications of accepting them. If that were all there is, the right response would surely be 'So what?' What connects the intuitions and implications with the proposal that we give up on propositional attitude psychology is a certain *Diagnosis*. And, while a lot has been written about the intuitions and their implications, the Diagnosis has gone largely unexamined.

Here's the Diagnosis: 'Look, on *anybody's* story, the notion of content (or "intention") has got to be a little problematic. For one thing, it is proprietary to the information sciences, and *soi-disant* "emergents" ought, at a minimum, to bear the burden of proof. At the very minimum, if you're going to have contents, you owe us some sort of account of their individuation.

'Now, prior to the Twin-Earth problem, there was some sort of account of their individuation; you could say, to a first approximation, that identity of intention depends on identity of extension. No doubt that story leaked

4

a bit: thoughts about the Morning Star look to be different in content from the corresponding thoughts about the Evening Star, even though their truth conditions are arguably the same. But at least one could hold firmly to this: "No difference in extension without some difference in intention." Conversely, it was a test for identity of intention that the extensions came out to be the same. And that was the best test; it was the one source of evidence about intentional identity that seemed surely reliable. Compare the notorious wobbliness of intuitions about synonymy, analyticity and the like.

'But now we see that after all it's not true that difference of extension implies difference of intention. Your Twin's 'water'-thoughts and your own are intentionally identical – assuming supervenience – but extensionally distinct. So unclear are we now about what intentional identity comes to – hence about what identity of propositional attitudes comes to – that we can't even assume that if two thoughts are intentionally identical they will be true and false together. The fact is, as we now see, we have no idea at all of what criteria of individuation for propositional attitudes might be like; hence we have no idea at all what counts as evidence for identity of propositional attitudes. (Given which, by the way, it is hardly surprising that propositional attitude psychology so rarely proves to be disconfirmed; once you abandon the extensional constraints, ascriptions of propositional attitudes are arbitrarily available for being gerrymandered.)

'*To summarize*: Inferences from difference of extension to difference of content used to bear almost all the weight of propositional attitude attribution. That was, however, a frail reed and now it has broken. The Twin-Earth problem is a problem *because it breaks the connection between extensional identity and intentional identity.*'[2]

Now, the Twin-Earth intuitions are fascinating, and if you care about the semantics of kind-terms you will, no doubt, do well to attend to them. But, as I've taken pains to emphasize, you need the Diagnosis to connect the Twin-Earth intuitions to the issues about belief/desire psychology, and – fortunately for friends of propositional attitudes – the Diagnosis rests

[2] Cf. Putnam (1983:148): 'Once we decide to put the reference...aside...far from making it easier for ourselves to decide whether the representations are synonymous, we have made it impossible. In fact, the first approximation we have to a principle for deciding whether words have the same meaning or not in actual translation practice is to look at the extensions. "Factoring out" differences in extension will only make a principled decision on when there has been a change in meaning totally impossible.' I'm not, however, claiming that Putnam actually endorses the Diagnosis I sketched in the text; I'm not sure whether he thinks that the Twin-Earth cases show that intentional Realists have to 'factor out the extension' from the individuation conditions on meanings. Such passages as the one I've quoted make it seem as though he does, but I can't find a place where he straight-out says it. My claim, in any event, is that without the Diagnosis, it's unclear that Twin-Earth considerations have any bearing at all on the facticity of propositional attitude ascriptions.

on a quite trivial mistake: THE TWIN-EARTH EXAMPLES DON'T BREAK THE CONNECTION BETWEEN INTENTION AND EXTENSION; THEY JUST RELATIVIZE IT TO CONTEXT.

Suppose that what you used to think, prior to Twin-Earth, is that intentions are something like functions from thoughts to truth conditions. Presumably, a truth condition would then be a function from worlds to truth values; condition TC takes world W onto the value T iff TC is satisfied in W. For example, in virtue of its intention, the thought that it's raining has the truth condition *that it's raining* and is thus true in every world in which it's raining and false in every other world.

I hasten to emphasize that if you don't – or didn't – like that story, its quite all right for you to choose some other; my point is going to be that if you liked that *kind* of story before Twin-Earth, you're perfectly free to go on liking it now. For, even if all the intuitions about Twin-Earth are right, and even if they have the implications that they are said to have, extensional identity still constrains intentional identity because *intentions still determine extensions* (relative to a context). If you like, intentions are functions from *contexts* and thoughts onto truth conditions.

What, if anything, does that mean? Well, there is presumably something about the relation between Twin-Earth and Twin-Me in virtue of which his 'water'-thoughts are about XYZ even though mine are not. Call this condition that's satisfied by {Twin-Me, Twin Earth} condition C (because it determines a Context). Similarly, there must be something about the relation between me and Earth in virtue of which my water-thoughts are about H_2O even though my Twin's 'water'-thoughts aren't. Call this condition that is satisfied by {me, Earth} condition C'. We don't know what sorts of things C and C' constrain, but causal relations of some kind are the current best bet and, anyhow, it doesn't matter much for the purposes at hand. Because we *do* know this: short of a miracle, it must be possible to satisfy C without satisfying C' and vice versa. How do we know that? Well, because short of a miracle, the following must be true: if an organism shares the neurophysical constitution of my Twin *and satisfies C*, it follows that its thoughts and my Twin's thoughts share their truth conditions. In particular, the following counterfactual is true: in a world where I am in my Twin's context, given the neurophysical identity between us, my 'water'-thoughts are about XYZ iff his are.[3]

But now we have an extensional identity criterion for intentions: two intentions are identical only if they effect the same mapping of contexts onto truth conditions. Specifically, your thought is intentionally identical to mine only if in every context in which your thought has truth condition TC mine

[3] Given shared context, the neurophysical identity of thinkers is, of course, sufficient but not necessary for the intentional identity of their thoughts. This is a matter we will return to.

has truth condition *TC* and vice versa.[4] It is worth noting that, by this criterion, my Twin's 'water'-thoughts are intentionally identical to my water-thoughts; they have the same intentional content even though, since their contexts are *de facto* different, they differ in truth conditions. In effect, what we have here is an extensional criterion for what is sometimes called 'narrow' content.(The 'broad content' of a thought, by contrast, is what you can semantically evaluate; it's what you get when you specify a narrow content *and fix a context*. This makes the notion of narrow content the more basic of the two; which is just what sensible people have always supposed it to be.)

We can now see why we ought to reject both of the following two suggestions found in Putnam (1975): That we consider the extension of a term(/concept) to be an independent component of the (to use Putnam's terminology) 'vector' that is the meaning of the term; and that we make do, in our psychology, with stereotypes *instead of* intentions. The first proposal is redundant since, given a context, intentions determine extensions; and we have – so far at least – no reason for supposing that there aren't intentions. The second proposal is unacceptable because, unlike intentions, stereotypes *don't* determine extensions *even* given a context. And, as the Diagnosis rightly says, we need an extension-determiner as a component of the meaning vector because we rely on 'different extension → different intention' for the individuation of concepts.

There are, no doubt, serious objections to the line that I've been pushing. For example, 'different extension → different intention' gives us only a necessary condition on intentional identity where what we really want is a biconditional. And if we try to parley what we've got into what we want, we run into the familiar troubles about thoughts that are extensionally identical but intentionally distinct. So, for example, it looks like – on the biconditional version – the thought that $2 + 2 = 4$ would come out to have the same intention as the thought that $3 + 3 = 6$. Not good.

However, these are just the old-fashioned, pre-Twin-Earth objections to the reduction of intentional identity to extensional identity, so they needn't concern us here. The main point to bear in mind is that if 'different extension → different intention' substantively constrains the attribution of propositional attitudes, then so too does this same principle when it is

---

[4] This condition has to be applied with some care when the thoughts are truly indexical (as some thoughts no doubt are). Thus specifying the context which – together with its intention – determines the truth condition of the thought that I am bored includes specifying the thinker of that thought.

  Somewhat similarly, 'visiting cases' suggest that Context must be four dimensional: what state of affairs makes your thought true or false probably depends on your history as well as your current surround.

  This is all much in the spirit of David Kaplan – or, at least, I hope it is – though, patently, he is not to be blamed for any of it. See also Fodor (1982).

relativized to context. So, if the worry about propositional attitudes is that Twin-Earth shows that extensions don't constrain intentions, the right thing to do about Twin-Earth is to STOP WORRYING.

Which is not, alas, to say that there is *nothing* to worry about.

First worry: It is one thing to have an (e.g. extensional) criterion for the intentional identity of thoughts (which, indeed, we do); it is quite another to be able to say what the intention of a thought is (which, indeed, we can't). What, for example, is the intention of the thought – or, as we might as well as well say, what is the *thought* – such that when I have that thought its truth condition is that H_2O is wet and when my Twin has it its truth condition is that XYZ is wet? Or, to put it another way (to put it, in fact, the old way) what is the *concept* WATER assuming that the concept WATER is not the concept H_2O?

I don't know the answer to this question, but I know how to find out: find out what (the word) 'water' means. Perhaps 'water' means something like 'the local, transparent, potable, dolphin-torn, gong-tormented..., etc. stuff one sails on'. If that is so, then the intention of my thought that water is wet (and of my Twin's thought that 'water' is wet) is that the local transparent, potable, dolphin-torn, gong-tormented..., etc. stuff one sails on is wet. My water thoughts are about H_2O because H_2O is the local transparent, potable..., etc. stuff in the context in which my water thoughts transpire (and similarly, *mutatis mutandis*, for XYZ in the context of my Twin's 'water'-thoughts). This would mean that a kind concept is some sort of implicit description after all, and it does leave one wondering just which description the concept WATER is. Just as it always used to.

But why does this question have to have an answer? Why, that is, does there have to be a way of expressing the intention of 'water' in English – or in Tw-English, for that matter – except as the intention of 'water'? Does English have to have more than one way of expressing every intention that it can express at all? Does every word (concept) that has an intention have to have a definition? (There is, of course, a way of expressing the intention of 'water' in, say, French: 'water' *veut dire l'eau*. But if you're worried about what the intention of 'water' could be – what it could be that picks out H_2O in the context Earth and XYZ in the context Twin-Earth – I don't suppose you will find this consideration comforting.)

I think this is all rather puzzling, but notice that it's a sort of puzzle that one has to face regardless of one's views about the Twin-Earth problem. So, for example, suppose you think that Twin-Earth shows that intention doesn't determine extension and/or that intention doesn't supervene upon neurophysiology. Still – and quite aside from all that – there's the following question: When my Twin says 'water is wet' what does what he says mean?

Not, presumably, that water is wet since, on the present assumptions, there is no reason to identify the intention of 'water$_{TW}$' (viz., of the Tw-English vocable that is pronounced like our word 'water') with the intention of 'water'. And not that XYZ is wet since my Twin will presumably take 'water is XYZ' to say something informative; something, indeed, which he might wish to deny. And not, for sure, H_2O is wet since there isn't any H_2O on Twin-Earth, and my Twin has never so much as heard of the stuff. It looks like either 'water$_{TW}$' means water (i.e. has the same intention that 'water' does) or its meaning is inexpressible in English. The moral seems to be: there is going to be a problem about saying what 'water' and 'water$_{TW}$' mean whatever view you take of the Twin-Earth problem. Or, to put it another way: the real problem is to figure out what 'water' means. You tell me what 'water' means and I'll bet that 'water$_{TW}$' means that too.

Second worry: Since intentional identity supervenes upon neurophysical identity, and since – given a context – there is no difference of extension without a difference of intention, it follows that the corresponding thoughts of neurophysically identical intentional systems in the same context are coextensive. Good. But, as I remarked above (see fn 3) you can have intentional (hence extensional) identity of thoughts without neurophysical identity of their thinkers. This suggests the following question: how much (and what kinds of) similarity between thinkers does the intentional identity of their thoughts require? This is, notice, a question one had better be able to answer if there is going to be a scientifically interesting propositional attitude psychology. For, generally speaking, the creatures that the generalizations of such a theory would have to subsume would not be anything like neurophysically identical; at a minimum they would differ as much as you and I differ from each other (at a maximum, they might differ as much as you and I differ from a silicon chip).

'What sorts of differences does intentional identity tolerate?' is the general form of the so-called 'collateral information' problem; and whereas I think that the Twin-Earth problem is, for the reasons I've set forth, something of a red herring, the collateral information problem is really very nasty and I don't know how to fix it; not, at least, in any detail. The next section is devoted to poking at the collateral information problem in the hope that something will come loose.

3. PUZZLES ABOUT CONTENT: COLLATERAL INFORMATION

Suppose Psmith (a neighbour, not a Twin) shares with me the belief that water is wet. And suppose we share all our other beliefs about water as well, except that he believes, and I do not, that cats like to drink water. This supposition looks to be OK; I mean, if it is possible that two people should have all their beliefs about water in common, it is also possible that two people should have all their beliefs about water in common except for the belief that water is something that cats like. On the other hand, the following is perhaps not OK: Psmith and I share all our beliefs about water except that he believes that water is animate and I do not. Here one feels inclined to say that if somebody really believes that water is animate, then he has a different concept of water and hence cannot, *strictu dictu*, be said to share one's belief that water is wet. In the first case, one feels inclined to say, having the belief that cats like(/don't like) water is *merely collateral* to having the concept WATER; whereas in the second case, one feels inclined to say, the belief that water is (in)animate *partially determines* the identity of the WATER concept that one has; sharing the concept WATER doesn't survive disagreement about things like that.

The philosophical point, however, is that it doesn't make the slightest bit of difference what one feels inclined to say about the examples. What is wanted is a principled way of drawing the distinction. Unless we have that, we have no way of determining identity and difference of intentional content in any case that falls short of a Twin case; in any case that falls short of neurophysical identity, that is.

This, of course, is just Quine psychologized. Quine puts it that you can't distinguish between theory and language. Putnam, drawing out the implications for computational psychology, puts it that you can't distinguish between concept and collateral information. In either case, the putative moral is the same: individual symbols (including mental representations) 'are meaningful in the sense of making a systematic contribution to the functioning of the whole language; they don't have "meanings", in the form of isolable objects, properties or processes, which are associated with them individually and which determine individual assertability conditions' (Putnam 1984: 1). But if mental representations don't have meanings, beliefs don't have contents. And if beliefs don't have contents, there are no beliefs.

Preliminary comment: The present problem arises whether or not you think there is a defensible notion of *narrow* mental content; that is, whether or not it is possible to preserve the intuition that my water-thoughts are somehow intentionally identical to my Twin's. You might, for example, take the view: 'save the truth conditions and cognitive science be damned; there is no kind of belief content that supervenes on the neurophysical identity of believers'. Even so, one must decide whether someone who believes that water is animate can have beliefs about water. If, as Quine and Putnam suppose, such questions aren't rationally resolvable, then the broad propositional attitudes go along with the narrow ones.

That would be all right with Putnam, of course; what he's stalking is the idea – which, by the way, he sometimes seems to suppose was invented at MIT – that an organism's behaviour should be explained by reference to its propositional attitudes. Putnam sees that belief/desire explanations presuppose some such notion as content, and it is precisely the explication of content that considerations of semantic holism are supposed to preclude. Putnam is cheerful in face of this conclusion; but, for the reasons set out at the beginning, this insouciance strikes me as unwarranted.

At this point, I want to float a diagnosis of my own. As far as I can tell, the arguments for semantic holism invariably presuppose some form of 'functional role' theory of meaning. If this diagnosis is correct, it comes down to a choice between the idea that behaviours are effects of beliefs and desires and the idea that meanings are constructs out of the functional roles of symbols; in which case, it seems to me that we ought to scrap the latter notion. For nothing that we believe about meaning is as likely to be true as most of what we believe about propositional attitudes. The rest of this paper will consist of variations on this theme.[5]

I take it that the argument from functional role semantics to semantic holism goes approximately as follows. First premise: Individual symbols 'are meaningful in the sense of making a systematic contribution to the functioning of the whole language'. Second premise: there is no principled distinction between aspects of a symbol's function that determine its meaning and aspects of its function that do not. Conclusion: Two symbols that differ in function at all must therefore differ in meaning at least to some extent. Similarly, *mutatis mutandis*, for concepts.

So if Psmith and I disagree at all in our beliefs, there is *ipso facto* some difference in the concepts that are the constituents of those beliefs. In face of this, we can say that nobody ever has the same concepts as anybody else, hence that the concepts 'concept' and 'conceptual identity' are unfit for serious scientific purposes; or we can say that the question when concepts are shared must be answered by fiat, hence again that the concepts 'concept' and 'conceptual identity' are unfit for serious scientific purposes. In either case, Q.E.D. We're not, in short, intended to infer from the identification of meanings with functional roles that there might be some way of saying which distinctions among roles correspond to distinctions

---

[5] Putnam says, in 'Meaning Holism', that whereas Frege taught us that the unit of meaning can't be smaller than a sentence, Quine took the case a step further, showing us that it can't be smaller than a theory. The present reading is that Quine thereby effected *a reductio ad absurdum*, demonstrating that there must be something wrong with the idea that what you believe determines what you mean.

among meanings. On the contrary, the idea is that because there is no principled way of individuating functional roles, there can be no principled way of individuating meanings either.

Now, in my view, both premises of the Quine/Putnam argument are false. But while the second premise is only false *strictu dictu*, I'm inclined to think that the first is false, root and branch. So let's start with it.

Neither Quine, nor Putnam, nor – to my knowledge – anybody else, has provided serious arguments for the identification of meaning with functional role, and I suspect that the main argument is simply a lack of alternatives.[6] This suggests a tactic for dealing with meaning holism arguments; namely, don't grant the theory of meaning that they presuppose.

It's not, after all, as though functional role theory offers a particularly plausible reconstruction of meaning. On the contrary, there is lots to be said against it; for example:

– it invites meaning holism and hence scepticism about meaning. Thereby tending to refute itself.

– it underestimates the inertia of content. By the inertia of content, I mean the fact that concepts can be shared by organisms whose overall psychological organizations differ in quite radical respects. So, for example, intuition strongly suggests that the concept WATER can be shared by me and Blind Me. Landau and Gleitman have some lovely data which suggest that a great many spatial concepts can be shared by me and Blind Me too; see Landau and Gleitman (forthcoming). This sort of fact looks to present serious problems for functional role theories of concept individuation. For example, the *causal* roles that their concepts of water enter into must surely be very different for an organism like Blind Me, which never infers the presence of water from what it sees, than for an organism like me, that makes such inferences routinely. Yet the *functional* roles of their concepts will have to be the same if identity of functional roles is necessary for concept identity.

---

[6] It may be that semantic holism, which is a dubious doctrine of sceptical import, gets some reflected glamour from *epistemic* holism, a much more plausible doctrine, and one to which Realists about propositional attitudes – or about anything else – may perfectly well accede. Roughly, epistemic holism is the view that whole theories are the unit of *confirmation*; by contrast, semantic holism is the view that whole theories are the unit of *meaning*. There is no obvious reason why the former doctrine should be taken to imply the latter, though Quine and Putnam are famous for having sponsored both. (On the other hand, you *can* infer a holistic account of meaning from a holistic account of confirmation if like Quine and sometimes Putnam you happen to be a verificationist. For a verificationist, the meaning of an expression is identified with the means of its confirmation, so if the latter is holistic it follows that the former must be too. That is a very good argument against being a verificationist, in case another such happens to be required.)

The obvious reply is that the properties of causal relations that make for sameness and difference of functional role are very abstract indeed. Well, maybe; but there is an alternative proposal that seems a lot less strained. Namely that if Blind Me can share my concept of water, that's not because we both have mental representations with identical abstract causal roles; rather, it's because we both have mental representations that are appropriately connected (causally, say) to water.

– *prima facie*, functional role semantics is question-begging if functional role is taken to include inferential role and hopeless if it's not.

I take it that the first half of the putative dilemma is patent. It is all right to speak informally of the inferential role of a concept as determining its functional role. But, *strictu dictu*, for purposes of semantic theory, all one has at hand is the causal role of mental representations *syntactically individuated*. Assume more than that and the theory is going to take for granted precisely what most needs doing: namely, the reconstruction of the semantical notions in a vocabulary that is neither semantical nor intentional.[7]

The other half of the dilemma, however, is that if functional role *is* a syntactic notion, it's awfully hard to see how the functional role of a representation could determine what it means. There are widely publicized considerations which suggest that you can't get semantical properties out of symbols just by piling up their syntactical ones.

To summarize: once you have functional role semantics you are well on your way to meaning holism (and hence scepticism about the contents of propositional attitudes). For, their functional roles – unlike, notice, their causal attachments to the world – aren't, even in principle, things that symbols can have severally. But who says you have to buy functional role semantics? Looked at the other way: if there is nothing serious against mental content except meaning holism, and if meaning holism is plausible only if functional role semantics is assumed, then all that the enthusiast for mental content need do to shift the burden of argument is to show that alternatives to functional role semantics are not out of the question. (My friend Ned Block says that one shouldn't be interested in shifting the burden of argument; one should be interested in *truth*. From each according to his ability is what I say.)

---

[7] This is not, by the way, particularly a problem about the semantics of *mental* representations: the corresponding point holds for functional role theories of the meaning of expressions in English. So, if you really think that the meaning of a word is a construct out of its use, and if you want this doctrine not to be question begging, then you had better have a nonsemantical and nonintentional notion of the individuation of uses. This is one – not the only – reason why Wittgensteinians have to be behaviourists; it would be no good individuating uses by reference to, say, actions since action is itself an intentional notion.

So now I want to try to shift the burden of argument. I've thought a lot about how to organize this discussion, and decided on balance not to. I shall simply set out, in no particular order, some questions that come up if one thinks about a theory that is Realist about content but does not take the notion of functional role as fundamental in semantics. I should say that the line here is in broad agreement with the semantical and ontological views of Barwise and Perry (1983) and with the suggestions of Dretske (1981) and Stampe (1977). I don't know that any of them have advertised their views as antidotes to semantic holism of the Quine/Putnam variety, but that is what I'm now about to do.

QUESTIONS AND ANSWERS

We begin with an easy question. (Discussion of the hard questions is postponed indefinitely.)

Q1: Functionalism in the philosophy of mind teaches that believing that such-and-such is a functional state; for, it argues, since dualism and type physicalism are false, functionalism is all that's left, and whatever is all that's left must be true (see, for example, Fodor (1968) where this line of argument is pursued interminably). But functional states are *ipso facto* individuated by their functional roles, are they not? So how can you be a Functionalist in philosophy of mind and not be a functional role theorist in semantics?

A1: The (usually tacit) assumption that Functionalism in philosophy of mind somehow comforts – or even implies – functional role semantics is responsible for no end of confusion. In fact, the best you can get from Functionalism is that what makes something a belief is its functional role. Functionalism does *not* certify that functional role makes a belief the belief that *P*.

This is important for the following reason. Imagine a quite crude semantic theory which holds that it is *being caused by water* that makes something a water-belief. It might be objected to such a theory that there are many things that are caused by water that are not water-beliefs: mudslides, hydroelectric power and the growth of strawberries are examples that suggest themselves. But this objection is frivolous. Mudslides, hydro-electric power and the growth of strawberries do not have the functional roles which (if Functionalism is true) it is essential for beliefs to have; *a fortiori* they are not beliefs; *a fortiori* they are not water-beliefs. The interesting proposal is that, given that something *does* have whatever functional properties beliefs have to have, what makes it a *water*-belief is the character of its causal attachment to water.

Q2: If only attachment to the world counts for something being a water-belief, then people could have all sorts of crazy beliefs that are, nevertheless, water-beliefs; they could believe that water is *animate*, for example.

A2: Alchemists had the following crazy belief: they believed that mercury is alive and grows from seeds. Contrary to what functional role theory implies, we have no doubt, in practice, about the content of their belief. What they had was the crazy belief that mercury is alive and grows from seeds. Functional role semantics systematically underestimates the inertia of content; see above.

Q3: You say that nobody bothers to argue for functional role semantics; but that is surely untrue. Consider: it's important to have a semantic theory that slices mental states thin enough; a theory that allows us to distinguish beliefs about the Morning Star from beliefs about the Evening Star, beliefs about closed triangulars from beliefs about closed trilaterals, and so forth. But since the Morning Star *is* the Evening Star (since all closed triangulars are closed trilaterals and vice versa) a theory that makes content out of 'relations to the world' can't slice the mental states thin enough to distinguish thoughts that are in fact distinct. In short, there must be something more to the content of mental states than their extensions, and what could this something more be if it isn't functional role? Even friends of mental content frequently find this sort of argument persuasive, hence 'two factor' theories of representation: a more or less causal factor gets the representations attached to the world, and a functional role factor distinguishes between representations that are extensionally equivalent but nonsynonymous. What, to put this in the form of a question, is wrong with that?

A3: What is wrong with that is that it leads to meaning holism, a doctrine without which we have decided that we can do. Anyhow, the thinness of slice argument, though interesting, isn't conclusive. Consider the triangular/trilateral case: one could take the view that the property of being a closed triangle is simply different from the property of being a closed trilateral. On this view, the corresponding concepts differ in content because they express different properties. The way to slice mental contents thin enough is by postulating thin enough properties.

Q4: That seems to me to be a question-begging sort of semantic theory; it says what a symbol means by taking for granted what the symbol denotes; and denotation is itself a semantic relation.

A4: We need a theory of what it is for a (mental) symbol to have the extension it does (a theory of Contexts, to use the vocabulary introduced above). Here is a first approximation to such a theory: A symbol S denotes an entity D just in case under certain sorts of circumstances, tokenings of S are causally contingent upon D. (Which sorts of circumstances count depends, *inter alia*, on the ontological status of D. In the case where D is a property, for example, S denotes D just in case, under the appropriate circumstances, the instantiation of D brings about the tokening of S.) Skinner was roughly right after all – except, of course, for the learning theory and the behaviourism.

By the way, this sort of theory of denotation is far more plausible for mental representations than for the expressions of a natural language since the tokenings of the latter – but not, presumably, of the former – are contingent upon the motivations, linguistic competences and communicative intentions of the speaker who utters them; in fact, on a whole range of 'pragmatic' variables. Thus, for example: suppose Psmith notices that Mary's hair is on fire – and hence, perforce, thinks: 'Mary's hair is on fire' (thereby tokening the Mentalese expression whose truth condition is that Mary's hair is on fire). Whether Psmith then *says* 'Mary's hair is on fire' (thereby tokening the English expression whose truth condition is that Mary's hair is on fire) depends, *inter alia*, on whether he thinks that Mary (or some other suitably situated auditor) would be interested to know that Mary's hair is on fire. (See Grice (1975) for an indication of how complex these sorts of pragmatic considerations can become.) In short, the causal chain that connects the tokenings of mental representations to events which satisfy their truth conditions is typically shorter than (indeed, is typically a proper part of) the causal chain that connects the tokenings of English sentences to events which satisfy their truth conditions. That is the principal reason why it is mental representations, not English sentences, that are the natural candidates for being the primitive bearers of semantic properties.

Q5, Q6, Q7, Q8: I hardly know where to begin. Let's go back to the thinness of slice problem. First worry: Heaven only knows how you are supposing properties to be individuated; but with the best intentions in the world, it's not obvious that the property of being the Morning Star is distinct from the property of being the Evening Star; and I simply do not believe that the property of being Cicero is distinct from the property of being Tully. So (Q5, Q6) how are you going to distinguish the belief that the Morning Star is wet from the belief that the Evening Star is wet? Or the belief that Tully was wet from the belief that Cicero was wet? Still worse, you have a fatness of slice problem to worry about too. It's plausible that the property of being water is the property of being H_2O. So (Q7) how are you going to keep the thought that water is wet distinct from the thought that H_2O is if you hold – as you appear to do – that identity of denotation makes identity of intention?

And finally, property Realism as a solution to the thinness of slice problem sits badly with a causal theory of denotation; since every tokening of closed trilaterality is going to be a tokening of closed triangularity (Q8) doesn't every causal chain that traces back to the one *ipso facto* trace back to the other? Note that counterfactuals won't pull this apart; no causal chain *could* trace back to a tokening of one property without tracing back to a tokening of the other because 'all closed triangles are closed trilaterals and vice versa' is necessary.

A5: On the other hand, I didn't say I had a working semantic theory. It is well to emphasize about here that nobody – functional role theorists definitely included – has a working semantic theory. I'm arguing the narrow case that a more-or-less denotational theory isn't *known* to be out of the question. Well, it isn't.

In fact, I propose to argue a narrower case still: to get meaning holism out of functional role semantics, you need to assume that just *any* aspect of functional role can be a determinant of the semantic properties of a representation (this is, in effect, the second premise of the Quine/Putnam argument reconstructed above). For, if some aspect of functional role is *a priori* irrelevant to meaning, then representations which differ in that respect may nevertheless be semantically equivalent; and meaning holism is the doctrine that you can't have a principled notion of semantic equivalence for representations whose functional roles differ at all. So the present suggestion is that extension plus *a little* functional role might do to determine meaning. We'll see how this works as we look at the examples.

To begin with, if you take 'the Morning Star' and 'the Evening Star' as *descriptions* it seems reasonable to say that they express different properties and that that's why the belief that the Morning Star is wet differs in content from the belief that the Evening Star is wet. The hard problem is what to say about the reading which takes these expressions to be *names*. So Q5 reduces to Q6.

A6: The problem about names is, as just remarked, a hard problem; even if there is a property of being Tully – which property the word 'Tully' expresses – it is not plausibly distinct from the property of being Cicero. But the expressions 'Cicero' and 'Tully' can't be semantically equivalent since, as Frege pointed out, the thought that Cicero is Tully is informative.

The obvious suggestion is that 'Cicero' means something like 'the person called 'Cicero'' whereas 'Tully' means something like 'the person called 'Tully''. Or, to put this more in the present terms, the obvious suggestion is that 'is Tully'(/'is Cicero') expresses a certain linguistic property, viz. the property of beng called 'Tully'(/'Cicero'). But, as Kripke has insisted, the obvious suggestion won't work; though it explains how 'Cicero is Tully' could be informative, it implies that 'Cicero was called 'Cicero'' is a necessary truth. Which, in fact, it isn't. So now what?

The path of wisdom would be to repeat that this is a hard problem, emphasizing that it is hard for *everybody*. For, even if you propose to pull 'Cicero' and 'Tully' apart by reference to their functional roles – and quite aside from the holism issues about which bits of their functional roles count for their meanings – you're still left with the question that nobody can answer: what *do* 'Cicero' and 'Tully' mean if, on the one hand, they're not synonyms and, on the other, they don't mean anything linguistic?

The course of wisdom, as I say, would be to shut up and leave this alone. Still, how about this: 'Cicero' and 'Tully' are synonymous but differ in presupposition (slightly like 'and' and 'but'; more like the demonstratives 'he' and 'she'. The present doctrine is that proper names are, as it were, 'dedicated' demonstratives: your name is a demonstrative pronoun that you get to keep for your very own). 'Cicero was wet' says, in effect, HE WAS WET and presupposes that he was called 'Cicero'. 'Tully was wet' says that HE WAS WET too, but it presupposes that he was called 'Tully'. That is, 'Cicero was wet' and 'Tully was wet' differ in semantic value because the former is not-true unless the relevant Roman has the (linguistic) property of being called 'Cicero', whereas the latter is not-true unless that same Roman has the (different) linguistic property of being called 'Tully'. 'Cicero is Tully' is informative because, although it doesn't *say* that the guy who was called 'Cicero' was called 'Tully', it carried the information that he was (see Dretske 1981, Barwise and Perry 1983). 'Cicero was called 'Cicero'' fails to be necessary because, uttered in a world in which Cicero was called 'Psmith' it would be (not false but) not-true.[8]

If that won't work, perhaps something else will.

A7: I think the way to fix the fatness of slice problem is to let in a moderate, restricted and well-behaved amount of functional role. The point about the formulas 'water' vs 'H_2O' is that, though they – presumably – express the same property, the second is a complex, built out of expressions which themselves denote hydrogen and oxygen. I do want to let into meaning – over and above denotation – those implications which accrue to an expression in virtue of its compositional semantics; that is, in virtue of its relations to such other expressions as occur as its morpho-syntactic constituents. This is to say that the distinction between the concept WATER and the concept H_2O is that you can have the former but not the latter even if you lack the concepts HYDROGEN and OXYGEN.

The point to emphasize is that letting in that much functional role does

---

[8] We – in this world – can, of course, say truly that Cicero is not called 'Cicero' in a world in which Cicero is called 'Psmith'. That is, the presupposition of our use of 'Cicero' to refer to Cicero in some possible world is that Cicero is called 'Cicero' here in our world.

This seems to be a general point about presuppositions: they need only be satisfied in the 'home' world (as contrasted with entailments which, of course, must be satisfied in *every* world.) Thus, if there were a King of France it would be all right for us to say what we can't say now, things being what they are; viz. that the King of France might have been a commoner. In short, we can use an expression with an existential presupposition to pick out an individual in a world in which that presupposition fails, so long as it doesn't fail here.

not, in and of itself, raise the collateral information problem. True, having the concept H_2O requires more than just having a concept that denotes water; it requires that you know about hydrogen and oxygen. But it doesn't, thus far, open the flood gates. It doesn't, for example, constrain your views about what cats like to drink since neither 'cat' nor 'drink' is a morpho-syntactic constituent of 'H_2O'.

A8: Much the same point applies. Tokenings of the concept CLOSED TRIANGULAR trace back to triangles via tokenings of the concept ANGLE; whereas tokenings of the concept CLOSED TRILATERAL trace back to triangles via tokenings of the concept SIDE. Notice that though not even counterfactuals can pull closed triangulars apart from closed trilaterals, there is no problem about pulling apart ANGLES and SIDES *tout court*: lots of figures have more of the one than they do of the other, for example. (This suggests that you couldn't have nonsynonymous but logically equivalent primitive expressions; that if two representations are logically equivalent but non-synonymous, at least one of them must be complex. Is that true?)

Q9: What are you going to do about 'bachelor' and 'unmarried man'; surely these *do* express the same concept even though one is built out of constituents that don't appear in the other? Are you going to say that somebody could have the concept BACHELOR but not have the concept UNMARRIED MAN?

A9: I'm going to say that there are some cases of word-to-phrase synonymy; cases where a word happens to express the same concept that a phrase does. Word-to-phrase synonymy is a linguistic accident; one which, in fact, almost never occurs. It would be a waste of effort to worry about it.

Q10: On reflection, I am inclined to doubt that your proposal has even the virtue claimed for it: that it does, in fact, avoid meaning holism. For, after all, you're prepared to admit that the causal route from things happening in the world to the tokening of a mental symbol may sometimes run via tokenings of other concepts (cf. TRILATERAL and SIDE). So it turns out that world-symbol connections are like functional roles after all: symbols have their attachments to the world en bloc. Don't we, then, have the holism problem all over again?

A10: This mistakes the spirit of the proposal, which is that, fundamentally, what matters for denotation is the covariation of symbol tokens with denotation tokens. In particular, the inferential route that effects the covariation usually doesn't matter. The exceptions acknowledged to this principle are, from this point of view, merely technical. They involve *only* cases in which the semantic value of an expression is determined by the semantic values of its morpho-syntactic constituents.

Let me tell you – by way of making the spirit of the proposal clear – a story about what was wrong with verificationism. Verificationism was the idea that the meaning of an expression could be identified with whatever route connects the use of the expression with its denotation. So, for example, there's something that connects our use of the word 'star' with stars: a causal chain that starts with light leaving stars, passing – maybe – through telescopes, falling on our retinas, and eventuating, finally, in utterances of 'star'. The verificationist idea was that it's that sort of thing that constitutes the meaning of 'star'.

Now, there is something right about this: namely, that tokenings of the verification procedures for 'star' have stars on one end and 'stars' on the other; when they work, verification procedures connect terms with their denotations.

On the other hand, there is also something wrong with it. Namely that verification procedures connect terms with their denotations in too many ways. Think of the routes via which stars can determine tokenings of 'star': via telescopes; via just looking; via looking at reflections in a puddle; via inference from astronomical theory; via inference from astrological theory; via inference from what somebody happened to say, via paintings of stars in a museum, via just thinking about stars..., etc. The point is: these different routes do not determine different semantic values for 'star'. The moral is that *the route doesn't matter (much)*; what determines that 'star' means star is *that* the two are connected, not *how* the two are connected. *It's the covariance that counts.*

Similarly for concepts of course. It may be that my concept of water is, from time to time, connected to water via my concept of cat; (I believe that water is what cats like; I find that my cat likes this; I infer that this is water). But that's not what makes my concept of water a water-concept. What makes it a water-concept is that its tokenings covary with water tokenings under appropriate circumstances. It doesn't matter (much) by what route the covariance may be achieved; we get meaning by quantifying over the routes from a symbol to its denotation.

Q11: Covariation is no help. At best – and barring accidents – my beliefs about stars will covary with star tokenings *only when they are true*. Other times they'll covary with fireflies. If you really think that covariation 'under certain circumstances' makes meaning, you must have in mind circumstances that are frequently – not to say typically – counterfactual. You wouldn't, by any chance, like to say something about what these circumstances are?

A11: No. The collateral information problem isn't real, but it's the reflection of a problem that is. The real problem is: what sorts of covariations establish denotation? That not every causal route from the world to a symbol establishes a semantically relevant covariation is patent;

even if the wind regularly traces 'wind' in the sand, these 'wind'-tokenings don't denote the wind (or anything else). And, as you say – as Plato said, for that matter – there is a worry about how symbols(/beliefs) can be false. These are hard problems; but at least they're the *right* problems.

Q12: How about properties? You rely a lot on distinctness of properties for coping with thinness of slice arguments. Would you like to give us some idea about how you suppose properties to be individuated?

A12: No. Everybody has a problem of individuation to face. I don't know how to individuate properties; functional role theorists don't know how to individuate functional roles. It is nonetheless a substantive issue whether this problem should be faced in the semantics or in the ontology. I am assuming that it should be faced in the ontology.

Q13: What about necessary connections? If functional roles don't determine meanings, how do you account for the necessity of the relation between, say, being a father and being male?

A13: Everybody has a problem about necessary connections. It is nonetheless a substantive issue whether this problem should be faced in the semantics or in the metaphysics. I am assuming that it should be faced in the metaphysics. There is a lot that we do not know about necessary connections, but of one thing I am practically certain: for the most part, they aren't linguistic.

I concede, of course, that having the concept FATHER involves, *inter alia*, having a concept that denotes a property that is necessarily connected with the property of being male; hence that believing that Psmith is a father is believing something that entails that Psmith is male. What I deny is that having the concept requires acknowledging the entailment. On the contrary; all it requires is having a concept whose tokenings covary, in the right way, with tokenings of fatherhood.

Q14:

Imagine that there is a country somewhere on earth called Ruritania. In this country...there are small differences between the dialects which are spoken in the north and in the south. One of these differences is that the word 'grug' means silver in the northern dialect and aluminium in the southern dialect. Imagine two children, Oscar and Elmer...alike in genetic constitution and environment as you please, except that Oscar grows up in the south of Ruritania and Elmer grows up in the north of Ruritania. Imagine that in the north...pots and pans are normally made of silver, whereas in the south [they]...are normally made of aluminium. So [both] children grow up knowing that pots and pans are normally made of 'grug'.... But if the word 'grug' and the mental representations that stand behind the word...have the same content at [the initial] stage, *when do they come to differ in content?* By the time Oscar and Elmer have become adults, have learned foreign languages, and so on, they certainly will not have the same conception of grug. Oscar will know that 'grug' is the metal called 'aluminium' in English...and Elmer will know that the metal called 'grug' in his part of Ruritania is the metal called 'silver' in English. Each of them will know many facts which serve to distinguish silver from aluminium and 'grug' in the south Ruritanian sense from 'grug' in the North Ruritanian sense...Moreover this change...is *continuous*. (Putnam 1983).

What about Oscar and Elmer, then?

A14: The difference in extension between Elmer and Oscar's use of 'grug' doesn't, in and of itself, betoken a difference in the intentional content of their mental states; when they start out – when, intuitively speaking, they have the same beliefs about 'grug' – theirs is just a Twin-Earth case: different extensions because of the difference in contexts; but the *same* intentions because there's the same mapping from contexts onto truth conditions realized in each of their heads. As they get older, the patterns of covariation change; for, whereas at first tokenings of 'grug' would covary with either aluminium or silver for both children, by the end only silver can control 'grug' for Elmer and only aluminium can control 'grug' for Oscar. *Just* when the change happens depends on which counterfactuals have to be true for there to be the right sort of covariance – the semantically relevant sort – between tokenings of 'grug' and tokenings of the metal that it denotes. There is, however, no reason to suppose that this question presents a *principled* difficulty; or that its application in the Oscar/Elmer case is of any special theoretical interest.

The controlling consideration, as usual is this: intentions differ only when they are different functions from contexts to truth conditions. We will know how to apply that principle when we have a theory that tells us what it is about an organism and a context that determines how the organism's intentional states are semantically evaluated in that context (e.g. what truth conditions its beliefs have in that context). When we have the theory, we will be able to say exactly when Oscar and Elmer's mental states began to differ in intention; or there will be something wrong with the theory.

Q15: Are you quite finished now?

A15: Yes, thank you, I believe I am.

REFERENCES

Barwise, J. and Perry, J., 1983. *Situations and Attitudes*, Cambridge, Mass.: MIT Press.

Dretske, F., 1981. Knowledge and the Flow of Information, Cambridge, Mass.: MIT Press.

Fodor, J., 1968. *Psychological Explanation*, New York: Random House.

Fodor, J., 1982. Cognitive Science and The Twin-Earth Problem, *Notre Dame Journal of Formal Logic, 23*: 98–118.

Grice, H. P., 1975. Logic and Conversation, in Syntax and Semantics, vol. 3, ed. P. Cole and J. L. Morgan, New York: Seminar Press.

Landau, B. and Gleitman, L., (forthcoming). *The Logic of Perception in a Blind Child*, Cambridge, Mass.: Harvard University Press.

Putnam, H., 1975. The Meaning of 'Meaning', in *Mind, Language and Reality: Philosophical Papers*, vol. II, Cambridge: Cambridge University Press.

Putnam, H., 1983. Computational Psychology and Interpretation Theory, in *Realism and Reason: Philosophical Papers*, vol. III, Cambridge: Cambridge University Press.

Putnam, H., 1984. Meaning Holism, unpublished, Harvard University.

Stampe, D., 1977. Towards A Causal Theory of Linguistic Representation. *Midwest Studies in Philosophy*, 2: 42–63.

Stich, S., 1983. *From Folk Psychology to Cognitive Science*, Cambridge, Mass.: MIT Press.

Truth conditions: a causal theory*

ANTHONY APPIAH

INTRODUCTION

It once seemed a good idea to suppose that to know the meaning of a sentence S is to know under what conditions S would count as true; and thus that truth conditions *were* meanings; see for example, Davidson (1967). Alas, as is now well known, truth conditions on their own will not do. For if we identify the meaning of a sentence with its truth conditions, then all necessarily equivalent sentences will end up inconveniently saddled with the same meaning: truth conditions are not enough.

One response to this fact is to say this shows that truth conditions simply aren't any use as the central semantic notion. But I think this is to give up too early in the game. And there is another standard response, exemplified in David Lewis' (1970) paper 'General Semantics', which offers the hope of a more conservative solution. Rather than identifying the meaning with the truth conditions, Lewis suggests, we should identify it with an ordered pair of which the truth conditions are but one component.

That second component is the syntactic structure of the sentence. Lewis observes at various points that we can give finer or coarser grain to our account of meaning by including more or less syntactic information in our specification. But he writes as if there is no principled way to decide how much we should include: the notion of meaning is, he implies, not definite enough for us to be obliged to do it any particular way. To those of us with more definite views about meanings, this is likely to seem arbitrary.

* I am extremely grateful to all the participants at the Thyssen Philosophy Group meeting at Evesham in April 1984, for their many helpful comments on an earlier version of this paper; and especially to Jeremy Butterfield, who not only participated actively in the discussion but also gave me extensive notes, on the original and on a revised version of the paper, which showed how carefully he had read my work; to John Perry, whose many comments were extremely stimulating; and Hugh Mellor, who discussed all these matters with me, both at the Thyssen meeting and when he supervised my dissertation. Jeff Poland and Barbara von Eckhardt discussed the first draft of this paper with me in detail in the Spring of 1983: I am grateful for all their help. This paper was revised while I held a Morse Fellowship: I wish to thank the Morse Committee for the opportunity for a year free of teaching, and Clare College, Cambridge, for providing me with a home while I exercised that freedom.

This standard response seems to me to be in another way arbitrary: it doesn't say *why* we need this second component, taking it as enough of an argument that it conforms to some of our intuitions. There is, however, a cognitive psychologist's answer to this question, which suggests, I think, how we can justify the second component.

> Grasp of the meaning of a word *does* indeed lie in knowing its contribution to the truth conditions of sentences in which it occurs. But truth conditions have actually to be computed: processes go on in our heads which take a heard sentence as input, assign it a syntax, and finally give it truth conditions. Only then is it understood. These processes take time; and even where the truth conditions of two sentences are the same, they may differ substantially in the amount of computation that it takes to work them out; see Fodor (1976). That is why two sentences with the same truth conditions may have different functions in the lives of speakers.

And the suggestion is that the key notion behind our intuitive concept of meaning is that of a sentence's functional role – a thesis comfortably reminiscent of the familiar (though less than transparent) doctrine that meaning is use.

One kind of obscurity in this doctrine derives from the uncertainty as to which features of the way a sentence is wielded constitute elements of its use. And one way to lighten the obscurity, at least where we are talking of sentences used in assertion, is to say that we are really interested in those aspects of use determined by what *beliefs* the sentences express. Functional role will enter again here; for we can individuate beliefs, it is nowadays claimed, by way of their functional roles. A mapping from declarative sentence-tokens to the functional roles of the beliefs they expressed, would do pretty well as a theory of declarative meaning.

I do not think that, as yet, this notion of functional role is anything like precise. But, so it seems to me, if we can make it more precise, this answer has a good prospect of being right. It tells us why meanings are more than truth conditions, while leaving truth conditions a central role. It suggests, too, where we must look to find what else we need: for we want just enough extra to allow us to distinguish the different functional roles of the beliefs that sentences express; see Fodor (1976).

Functionalism in psychology is now familiar territory. Functionalist theories of mental states look to individuate them by their causal antecedents and consequences within and without the mind; see for example, Fodor (1976), Dennett (1978), Lewis (1972). Suppose we had such a functionalist theory of beliefs. Then, if we wanted a theory of the truth conditions of English sentences, we might suggest with Fodor, that what speakers do is, in essence, to map predicates and names in English into 'predicates' and 'names' in Mentalese, the 'language' of the inner representations that constitute our beliefs, and then use the internal equivalent of a truth theory to derive the Mentalese 'sentence' which states the truth conditions of the English sentence.

But why drag in truth? After all, if understanding a sentence is a matter of finding an interpretation for it, then why won't the Mentalese translation do as the interpretation? Before we had functionalism, we had truth conditions as the best bet; now we have the functional role of the beliefs expressed. What, in a functionalist framework, would motivate dividing functional role in two, leaving the truth conditions, on the one hand, and something like syntax, on the other?

This paper has three projects, and answering this question is the first. Once it is answered, we shall be in a position to carry out the second: which is to say what, other than truth conditions, we need to fix the functional roles of beliefs. That will make the third project easy: for, relying on the thought that knowing what a (declarative) sentence means is knowing what belief it expresses, I shall also be able to offer the outlines of a semantic theory that gives sentences both truth conditions *and* something like the structural features that Lewis suggested. But now this bipartite theory will not be arbitrary. For it will be bipartite because we have a bipartite account of beliefs.

The rest of the paper is itself bipartite. In part 1 I deal with the necessary general features of a functionalist theory of the mind. I begin with a reminder of decision theory's picture of beliefs and desires (1.1), and go on to develop this picture in a way that makes sense of the claim that these states are representations (1.2). Truth conditions, along with the formal features that make states of belief and desire representational, are sufficient, I'll suggest, to individuate those states. Part 2 deals with truth in this functionalist and representational framework. I suggest, first, how this *mélange* of representational and functionalist theory might allow us to make sense of a basic intuition about truth conditions: namely, the intuition that a truth condition for S is a condition sufficient for the success of actions explained by the belief that S (2.1). But what we get from this intuition is not the classical notion of a truth condition; for it allows for conditions which are necessary and sufficient for truth but not *logically* necessary and sufficient (2.2). I call this kind of truth condition a 'causal truth condition'; and I show how to build out of functionalist materials the distinction between causal truth conditions and classical truth conditions,[1] and explain how it arises (2.3).

In order to be able to proceed with truth conditions as my central concern I shall take a rather dogmatic attitude on some other interesting questions.

---

[1] When I need to distinguish the classical truth condition, I'll call it a 'logical truth condition'.

Where I do so, I shall refer to an account and some arguments already available in the literature which support my dogma. Still, some of what I say will have to be sketchy; but I believe that we need the broader perspective if we are to make progress with truth conditions. I think that the general conclusions I want to draw about truth conditions do not depend on the details of my account of beliefs, though it is easier to develop these points in the context of a particular account.

I. DECISION AND REPRESENTATION

1.1 Ramsey's decision theory
The kind of functionalism I propose to rely on is what Shoemaker calls 'analytical functionalism', whose project is one of conceptual analysis.

The analytical functionalist seeks to extract his definition [of a given mental state] from a 'theory' consisting of...conceptual truths about the relations of mental states to inputs, outputs and other mental states (1982: 104).

So the functional roles of mental states are the *a priori* truths about their causal roles in the life of the agent. It is a familiar fact that decision theory, in its descriptive guise, characterises the beliefs and desires of agents by saying what actions someone with certain degrees of belief and desire would perform. It declares that agents will act so as to maximise a function of degrees of belief and desire called 'expected utility'; see Ramsey (1978), Jeffrey (1965). That is what makes decision theory functionalist. The causal role of beliefs and desires is fixed by the way degrees of belief and desire interact to produce action. Given a pair of functions that characterise an agent's partial beliefs and utilities, we are able, therefore, to predict what that agent will do – provided, of course, that the theory is correct. Now, as is also well known, Ramsey argued that degrees of belief must have the shape of a probability function (hereafter 'p-function'), because

(I)f anyone's mental condition violated these laws his choice would depend upon the precise form in which the options were offered to him, *which would be absurd.* (Ramsey, 1978:84; emphasis mine.)

This may seem, to begin with, to be a good idea; it is what is at the root of so-called 'Dutch Book' arguments; see Mellor (1971). But if we look at how the theory actually works out we can see why Ramsey thought that it was only a 'useful approximation' (1978:76). For decision theory, particularly in its purest form, with degrees of belief corresponding to a p-function, and well-behaved utilities, makes extremely stringent demands. Take degrees of belief, which will concern us in this paper.

If degrees of belief behave like probabilities, so that we might as well write the degree of belief that S, for any S, as $p(S)$, then every logical truth has a degree of belief, if any, of 1. Translated into more familiar language, this means that everyone should be certain of every logical truth they entertain.

This consequence is outrageous; no one should want a theory which characterises agency in such a way that it requires that the agent be incapable of logical error. If we are to suppose, therefore, that Ramsey was right to start with decision theory, we must remedy this glaring deficiency.

Let me give this problem a name: I'll call it the 'problem of logical perfection'. It is the problem of avoiding the clear implication of any attempt to use decision theory descriptively that every agent is logically perfect. And it is in solving *this* problem that it helps to take account of the fact that beliefs are representations. Let me say why.

1.2 Representations

To see the force of the claim that beliefs and desires are representations, let's begin by comparing them with those other paradigm representations, sentences of natural language. Sentences are regarded in traditional grammar as having two distinct kinds of characteristics: namely, syntactic characteristics and semantic ones. It is taken for granted that sentences with identical semantics – sentences which 'mean the same' – need not have identical syntax. Thus, for example, 'John loves Mary' and 'Mary is loved by John' are naturally regarded as having the same content, as far as truth is concerned, since one is true iff the other is. And having hit on the idea of *content* it is natural to describe the respects in which the two sentences differ as differences of form; natural, that is, to see differences of syntax as differences of form.

So to talk of beliefs and desires as representations is to suggest that these states, like sentences, have both form and content. The form of a belief is to be conceived of, on this view, as analogous to the syntax of a sentence. Nobody is likely to want to argue that the form of every belief is exactly isomorphic with the syntax of the sentence which expresses it. For two sentences, of different form, can plainly express the same belief: active sentences and their passive transformations frequently do this. And the same sentence can express two different beliefs: which is why sentences can be ambiguous. Nevertheless, sentences which express the same belief are naturally held to be identical in meaning, even where they differ in their syntax; and if a sentence can express two different beliefs then, plausibly, it has (at least) two meanings. Provided we find for each unambiguous sentence a belief, individuated by more than truth conditions, for it to express, then we have a good chance of saying what it means.

Because my account of belief is functionalist I shall have to say how one might characterise both form and content in terms of their causal roles. Note that I do not use 'form' for the features of beliefs other than their truth conditions because I take over-seriously the thought that these states are like sentences. Some beliefs are probably encoded in states which are more like images than sentences. It is because 'form' contrasts with 'content' that I use the term: the formal features are just those features which are needed to fix functional roles, over and above their truth-conditional content. So anyone who worries about the possibility that I am committed to a view of the mind as a 'syntactic engine', can substitute throughout 'feature other than content' for 'form'. Indeed, I prefer to call the form of a belief its 'computational structure', which is enough of a jargon-word to avoid unnecessary associations. When I say that the form of a belief is analogous to the syntax of a sentence I mean that the former and the latter share this property: each is a feature of the representation's functional role other than its truth-conditional content.[2] So now I need to fill out this notion of computational structure, and to show how it helps solve the problem of logical perfection.

We may suppose, to begin with, that agents whose partial beliefs and degrees of desire are to work in the sort of way envisaged in decision theory, must have both form and content to their beliefs and desires. To assign these representations a computational structure is to suppose that decisions result from operations which take the computational features of representations as input, and produce, as output, states whose computational features are a function of those of the input states. The computational structure of a belief or desire is just an abstract property of it which allows us to make generalisations about its relations with other representational states: generalisations, in the first instance, about how the presence of a state is likely to affect the production of others. If this representational view is correct, truth conditions plus computational structure will do to individuate beliefs and desires; and if the meaning of a sentence is the belief it expresses, together truth conditions and computational structure will also give us meanings.

I do not propose to provide an idiom for describing computational structures: all I need to rely on, in this paper, is the fact that given this notion, we have an extra feature over and above its truth conditions by which to individuate any representational state. Thus, for example, we may allow that there is a difference between believing that Mary is present and believing that it is not the case that she is not present – even though these

[2] Here I have been helped by Jeremy Butterfield's observation that psychology and linguistics might want to fine-grain content in different ways (this volume, p. 92); and more generally by points made by him, John Perry and John Skorupski at the Thyssen seminar.

beliefs have the same truth conditions – because one of these beliefs has as part of its computational structure two negatives more than the other.[3]

Computation, on this view, is a real mental process: it is carried out in us, we have discovered, by our central nervous systems. Like all processes, it takes time. It can go wrong – errors of computation can occur; and it can fail to be completed – when, for example, we are distracted. Consider, then, the process of calculating what action to perform. We suppose that if all necessary computations are completed, then the agent will come to be in a state of preferring some options to others, and that he or she will do that available action which ranks highest. If the computations are without error as well as complete, then that action will be the one with the highest expected utility. There are thus two barriers to agents' actions displaying their preferences as computed by the pure decision theory: first, there may be errors in the computation; secondly, some necessary computations may not be carried out. With this much agreed, I think we can solve the problem of logical perfection.

Let me state my solution starkly: I claim that:

> decision theory characterises the relations between degrees of belief, strength of desire and action, in computationally perfect agents (what I shall call, from now on, 'CPAs'). That is, it characterises the behaviour which actual agents (with the appropriate concepts)[4] would exhibit if they applied each one of the computations which they are physically capable of applying, instantaneously and without error.

Let us call the class of computations the agent can perform the agent's set of *feasible computations*. Then, for example, amongst my set of feasible computations is one which takes me from the belief that Mary is coming to the belief that it is not the case that she is not coming. And I am capable of applying this computation to any belief, provided it is not too structurally complex. This fact is reflected in the decision theory by the theorem $p(S) = p(\neg(\neg S))$. It is the fact that I can apply this computation – even if errors of brain or mere structural complexity will sometimes produce the wrong answer – that makes this theorem a proper reflection of what I would do if computationally perfect.

If, however, there are no feasible computations which go from S to R, or vice versa, then there is no reason why our theory should treat the belief that S and the belief that R identically. And it does not. Let us call the

---

[3] And, once more, the presence of negation doesn't mean that it has to be like a sentence: an image of a cat on a mat with a cross through it could have the computational structure of a negative belief built into it through the presence of the cross, provided the cross functioned in the appropriate way.

[4] By the possession of concepts here I mean only whatever capacities are involved in being able to have beliefs. There is no commitment at all to any capacity for linguistic expression.

axioms and rules of inference which characterise the computational capacities of some agent the *proof theory* for that agent.[5] And let us call the class of p-functions which an agent could reach from his or her present p-function by way of a sequence of feasible computations, that agent's *feasible p-functions*. Suppose an agent's feasible p-functions are defined over a system of representations of the form of the propositional calculus; and that their proof theory includes propositional logic. Then it will be true that $p(S) = p(R)$ for every feasible p-function defined on S and R, iff S and R are tautologically equivalent. The axioms and rules of inference of the proof theory in effect state constraints on what computations agents can perform with their representations. As classical propositional logic stands to classical decision theory, so each agent's proof theory stands to his or her utilities and degrees of belief.

We can now say what it is on our theory for a representation S to have a representation R as a logical consequence, for an agent, A. It is for A to be capable of computations which would guarantee, if applied without error, that A would believe that R at least as strongly as A believes that S. More precisely, using the fact that if S entails R, $p(S)$ is at most $p(R)$, we can say that R is a logical consequence of S iff the agent is capable of computations whose carrying out would guarantee that $p(S)$ is at most $p(R)$ in every feasible p-function. But if, in the agent's proof theory, there is no proof that R follows from S, nothing stops A from arriving at a p-function where R has a lower probability than S. So, in particular, R is *a priori* true (following from the empty set of beliefs) iff any CPA who had the concepts necessary to have the belief that R, would believe that R to degree 1.

This theory already affords us some relief. An account of belief that treats beliefs with the same truth conditions identically, will be obliged to allow that every one believes (say) Gödel's theorem; see Field (1978:15).[6] That is just the problem of logical perfection. But we can now see that this consequence only follows if the agent is capable of computations leading from things he or she actually believes to Gödel's theorem; and that it still does not follow unless the agent has actually carried out those computations.

Admitting this much will still not quite do, however, to save decision theory from plain inconsistency with the facts. For Gödel's theorem follows from things every number theorist knows, by familiar principles of inference,

---

[5] The proof theory *characterises* the agent's capacities. There is no commitment to the agent's using its axioms and rules of inference; only to its being true that the agent would believe all the theorems of the proof theory, if computationally perfect. Thus, suppose in the proof theory of some agent, we use, instead of a standard rule like inferring a conjunction from the pair of its conjuncts, two rules: $A,B \vdash \neg(\neg A \vee \neg B)$ and $\neg(\neg A \vee \neg B) \vdash (A \ \& \ B)$. This will do the job; even if, as seems likely, the standard rule is more like the one the agent actually uses.

[6] Field actually uses the Banach–Tarski theorem as his example; but the point does not depend on the result being unfamiliar.

a grasp of which is presumably constitutive of knowing what numbers are. Thus, if Mary knows what numbers are, and so knows what rules of inference are permitted, she can still be proved to assign probability 1 to Gödel's theorem. So if she has any belief about the matter at all, Mary, as number theorist, has to be certain that Gödel's theorem is true: even before she has ever seen a proof. Whereas, in fact, someone who knows any number theory is likely to find a proof of it rather surprising; more surprising than someone who knows no number theory at all.

We are now in a rather difficult situation. For if we do not assign this number-theoretically informed agent a p-function in which the theorem has probability 1, then we shall not be able to derive a preference ranking that is transitive, from her probabilities and utilities. If we do assign Gödel's theorem probability 1, however, we shall have to explain how it is that she can appear not to believe it.

I propose to adopt the former course, allowing that agents may have beliefs that S and that R, where S and R are logically equivalent and $p(S)$ is not the same as $p(R)$. But, I suggest, there is a way of doing this which makes the decision-theoretic approach neither vacuous – because CPAs don't exist – nor merely normative.

The first essential is to adopt a strong conception of the distinction between the agent's actual and the agent's potential beliefs and utilities. The *actual* representations are states of an agent which play a part in the causal determination of his or her behaviour. Potential states are states which could be produced by computations feasible for agents, which take their actual states as input. (Note: the potential states of the agent are not all the states that he or she could have had; they are only those states derivable from actual states by feasible computations. Thus, if I didn't have the concept of an aeroplane then I would have no potential beliefs about aeroplanes, in this sense; even though, in another sense, since all that is required is that I acquire the concept, I *do* have such beliefs potentially.) I propose we say that agents act so as to try to maximise actual expected utility: where this means that they try to perform the action of bringing about some state of affairs that S, where S has a higher utility than the other actual representations of available actions.[7] Only actual states play any part in the causation of action.

As is well known, decision theorists have shown that, given a preference ordering of the right kind, probability and utility functions exist – see Jeffrey (1965); that the existence of these functions guarantees that the preference ordering is of the right kind is more obvious and equally well known. But I have just, in effect, conceded that a preference ordering of the right kind

---

[7] If two representations have the same utility, the agent chooses one of them. This is a tricky 'Buridan's ass' problem, which I do not want to try to solve here.

will not generally exist for actual agents. So now we face the problem of explaining why we suppose that agents have probabilities and utilities which sometimes perform in the way decision theory requires; granted that the only reason we had for this was the assumption that the agent's preferences were transitive, complete and so on.[8]

The answer to this question is as follows: it is a part of our conception of the functional role of beliefs and desires that, if agents were computationally perfect, they would act in the way decision theory requires. So, for example, decision theory tells us what it is, in part, to believe to such and such a degree that snow is white, by saying what agents with a belief of that degree would do, given all their other beliefs and desires, if they carried out all the computations necessary to calculate expected utility. Agents will not be computationally perfect, but the states which determine their actual behaviour can still be characterised by how they would manifest themselves, given computational perfection. Analogously, the actual velocities of real gas molecules, which explain their less-than-ideal actual behaviour, may nevertheless be characterised as the velocities which would, if only gas molecules were perfectly inelastic point masses, produce the ideal gas laws predicted by the simplest version of kinetic theory.

Can we now reasonably credit actual agents with proof theories strong enough to enable them to derive, say, Gödel's theorem from beliefs about natural numbers? I want to insist that we can, for two reasons. First, the claim is weaker than it may initially appear. The route between a class of beliefs and its consequences may be indefinitely long and complex; and it might be that the agent could not carry them out in sequence because of limitations on memory, for example. Secondly, the notion of logical consequence in the theory is a descriptive notion, and it must somehow be possible to ground logical relations between the beliefs of agents, in facts about their mental structures. It is difficult to think of any requirement weaker than the one I have offered which will do this.

That, then, is the picture. It is obvious that, given states with computational structures, we can account for some deviations from logical perfection. For computational errors may occur. Similarly we can see how deviations can arise because relevant computations may not be carried out. It is easy to construct examples of this sort of thing: suppose Mary, who, as we say, knows perfectly well that there is a quicker route from her college to the

---

[8] Nothing I say is meant to rule out the possibility that subjective p-functions are 'fuzzy', so that the probabilities of some representations should be given an interval measure. This will be so if, for example, the agent's actual preference ordering contains too little information to determine the metric. I do rule out that an agent might assign one and the same S two distinct (for intervals: disjoint) probabilities; but cf. also Appiah (1985).

library, goes by a slower route. Here the explanation may be that she has not brought to bear one of her beliefs, and has therefore wrongly computed that the slower route is more desirable.

To a first level of approximation, then, the expected utility, which is assigned by decision theory to a certain outcome as a function of known degrees of belief and strengths of desire, is the value that would be assigned to the representation of that outcome in an agent if he or she carried out all necessary calculations without error. Or, more precisely, since all agents will in fact have inconsistent beliefs, we can interpret degrees of belief (and desire) in terms of the contribution they *would* make to determining the expected utility, if the agent *did* have a coherent preference ordering.

This does *not* mean that we now have a theory which can treat anything at all as an agent by regarding all deviations from predicted behaviour as computational errors. For computational errors have to be deviations from the normal functioning of the physical system that embodies the functional states. It follows that in calling something a computational error, we are committed to there being some explanation of it. A deviation from normal functioning is a deviation from what is prescribed by the functionalist theory. But this is not circular. For what this means is that if people's behaviour deviates from what decision theory requires, this must be the result of some independently verifiable causal intervention with the functioning of their minds. What's normal is what happens without such interventions.

I have been explaining how an account of a CPA can be related to the behaviour of actual agents: in part 2 of this paper, I will show what role truth conditions play in the life of the CPA.

2. TRUTH AND CAUSALITY

2.1 Defining 'truth'
Since decision theory characterises the behaviour of CPAs, it treats beliefs which are logically equivalent – having the same truth conditions – as if they were the same belief. So that, conversely, identity of decision-theoretic properties for beliefs should suffice to fix truth conditions.

In fact, this is not quite true. What is true is that those representations that are assigned the same probabilities and utilities in every probability and utility function fall into equivalence classes of representations with the same truth conditions. (There will be at least a pair of such classes for each truth condition, one for beliefs, one for desires.) So far, that is, the theory assigns a complex structure of relations between beliefs and desires and their associated measures.

Though this structure is guided by our recognition of the truth conditions – that is why $p(S)$ has to be $[1 - p(\neg S)]$ – it does not say what those truth conditions are, until they are related to the effects of perception and the effects on action. That is, the formal structure of decision theory fixes the truth conditions of beliefs and desires only when supplemented by what I shall call 'input' and 'output' claims. Input claims are truths about the relations between events outside agents and whichever events inside agents they cause; truths which play a part in fixing the functional roles of the interior events. Output claims do the same job for whichever events outside agents are caused by internal events. Insofar as they are relevant to fixing the functional roles of beliefs, input claims are about what goes on in experience; output claims are about action. And until we have these claims, there is nothing to connect the equivalence classes of representations with things outside the agent, truth conditions or anything else.

Once we know both how events outside agents give rise to changes in their probabilities and utilities, and how the state of the world outside agents affects which of their tryings-to-act will produce successful actions, then we have a functionalist account of the behaviour of the CPA. Given these input and output claims, we should know how events outside the agent would lead to changes in the agents probabilities and utilities; given a knowledge of these changes we could tell what actions the agent would try to perform; and given knowledge of which tryings would be successful, we should know what the agent would do.

From now on, then, let us suppose our functionalist decision theory to be supplemented by the input and output claims necessary to say how changes in the external world produce changes in the p-function, by way of sensation and perception, and how intentions, desires and tryings-to-act relate to action. Then this supplemented decision theory should be sufficient to fix the truth conditions of representations.

Can we say, in a general way, what makes a condition a truth condition? If we start by asking ourselves a simpler question, I think we shall find that we can. Let us begin, then, by asking why we want our beliefs to be true. The obvious suggestion is that if all our beliefs were true then the actions we undertook on those beliefs would satisfy our desires; and the obvious extension of this, when we act, as decision theory requires, on degrees of belief, is that the truth of the beliefs we act on will make the action more likely to satisfy our desires. But what, in this extended case, is it to act on a belief: when my $p(S) = p(\neg S) = 0.5$, for instance, do I act on the belief that S or the belief that not-S?

We might be tempted to say that someone acts on the belief that S iff he or she both

36

(a)   acts having calculated the expected utility of the action on the partition $\{S, \neg S\}$; and

(b)   has a high degree of belief that S

But because we are dealing with CPAs, we cannot use (a). For a CPA will get the same expected utility for an action on every partition[9], so that this suggestion would have agents acting on *every* belief that satisfies (b). And (b) is wrong on other grounds also. For consider the case below, where Mary contemplates the action A and calculates the expected utility on the partition $\{S, \neg S\}$:

p	S	$\neg S$		u	S	$\neg S$
A	0.9	0.1		A	-1	20

Now suppose that the action A, whose utility we can call $u(A)$, has highest utility. Then she will do A, and she has a high degree of belief that S. But she would clearly prefer the outcome in which it is not the case that S. For $u(A \& \neg S) \gg u(A \& S)$. So, on this definition of what it is to act on a belief, it would not be true to say that her action is more likely to satisfy her desires if the belief she acts on is true.

What is required, I think, for the notion of acting on S is that believing S to whatever degree you do, you do A; *and* that you would desire to do A more if you believed S more. That, I think, captures the intuition that S's being probable makes the act more desirable than it would otherwise be.

But another condition is required for acting on a belief: namely that you think that S is fixed, independently of your action. Otherwise S is not part of the background of belief for the decision, but part of what the action is directed at achieving. So I suggest the following definition:

ACT: a CPA performs act A on the belief that S iff,

(a)   that agent does A, and

(b)   he or she believes that whether or not S is causally independent of whether or not he or she does A; and

(c)   if the agent believed that S more strongly, he or she would also desire more strongly that A.

ACT looks as though it has the right properties. For in the case just considered, if the agent's degree of belief that S had been greater, $u(A)$ would have been less, not more. So, in this case, we should say that the agent is acting, not on the belief that S, but on the belief that not-S. But it is very odd to say that Mary is acting on the belief that not-S, when in fact she believes that S more strongly than she believes that not-S. What we can say,

---

[9] This is true on Jeffrey's theory; it need not be, on a causal decision theory. But on *any* theory there will be too many partitions which satisfy this condition.

however, is this. Provided that we mean by 'coming to believe that S more strongly', an agent conditionalising on the partition $\{S, \neg S\}$, where $p'(S)$ is greater than $p(S)$,[10] then

> E: It is true that an agent would desire that A more strongly if he or she came to believe that S more strongly, iff $u(A \ \& \ S) > u(A \ \& \ \neg S)$.[11]

We can now state one way in which truth and success in action are connected:

> TRUTH: the truth condition of the representation S of an agent is that condition whose holding is necessary and sufficient to guarantee that, for every action A, if he or she were computationally perfect and performed A on the belief that S, then the outcome would be that one of the two possible outcomes he or she preferred.

TRUTH is a truism. If you act on the belief that S, so that evidence for S would increase the utility of your action, then, if S is true, the outcome will be: S and you did A. And you will prefer that outcome, of course, because, as I've said, $u(A \ \& \ S)$ is greater than $u(A \ \& \ \neg S)$, which latter is what would have been true if S had been false. TRUTH is a truism because, if you would want to do A more if you believed that S more, it must be that you'd prefer a world in which S and you do A, to a world in which $\neg S$ and you do A. But TRUTH still gives us connection, however trivial it may seem, between representation and reality; and that is all we need.

Or rather, almost all we need. For though TRUTH is true, it still does not give us a functionalist account of truth. For the functional significance of the fact that an outcome is preferred by an agent depends not on its being preferable but on the agent's recognising that a preferred outcome obtains. If I lift the switch, acting on the belief that the light will go on, then my future reactions will depend not simply on whether the light goes on, but on whether I come to believe that it is on. To make TRUTH into a functional account of truth we should have to say how the fact that an outcome is one

---

[10] Conditionalisation is the process in which an agent's p-function is altered by changes originating in some partition of his or her beliefs. I favour Jeffrey's method; see Jeffrey (1965).

 To get E, we must also assume that the agent thinks that whether or not S is causally independent of whether or not he or she carries out the action, so the expected utility of A is $u(A \ \& \ S)p(S) + u(A \ \& \ \neg S)p(\neg S)$. For reasons discussed in Appiah (1981: 33–52), it follows, if we use conditionalisation, that the utility of $(A \ \& \ S)$ after acquiring evidence for S, is the same as it was before acquiring it. This much given, the algebra is easy. (I ignore here – as elsewhere – problems that arise if, like me, you favour a causal decision theory; see Appiah (1985).)

[11] If an agent does A, where $u(A \ \& \ S)$ exceeds $u(A \ \& \ \neg S)$, we would naturally call this 'acting on the belief that S', only if he or she also had a high degree of belief that S; if he or she had a low degree of belief that S we should more naturally call it 'acting in the hope that S'. But since the distinction does not matter here, in ACT, I call them both acting on the belief that S.

an agent prefers to another will affect his or her future dispositions to action. And to do this we should need to say how the fact that a preferred outcome obtains will affect the agent's beliefs about what is the case. We should need, in other words, to rely on input claims: claims about how the holding of a certain condition would lead to changes in the mental states of agents; in particular, their beliefs.

It is essential to see that this feedback loop could not be specified just by saying directly what the effects of agents' attempts at action will be on their states of belief: the reference to the world is not an optional extra. It is a crucial element in the specification of the mental states that the route from attempts to act to the satisfaction of desire should go through the world. It is true that sometimes, as when we turn our heads to look at a clock, part of the *object* of our action is to produce a change in our beliefs: we wish to come to believe that the time is whatever the clock says it is. But in general the objects of our actions are external states, and it is part of what it is for a state to be a state of desire that it leads in certain contexts to the agent's changing the world in certain ways. The consequences for action of the fact that peoples' desires are satisfied will depend on whether they recognise them to be so; that is why we need input claims.[12]

Though I cannot say in detail how this would actually be done, I can say something about how an account of CPAs should assign truth conditions to beliefs. As we have seen, this would be done, in part, by way of input claims relating beliefs and their truth conditions. Thus, for example, we might have an input claim of the following form:

1. When agents with the concept *red*, who are conscious and whose eyes are open, are presented with a red thing in normal lighting, they will come to have a high degree of belief that something in front of them is red.

The details of this formulation should not be taken too seriously. All I want this suggestion for is to make plausible the view that there will be truths which are, at a higher level of abstraction, of the form:

2. If it were the case that S; and the agent became appropriately causally related with the state-of-affairs in virtue of which it is true that S; then, given computational perfection, that agent would increase his or her degree of belief that R to near 1

where R is any representation whose truth conditions are that S. Truths of this form will help fix the truth conditions of R: for at least part of what

[12] Even in the case where what people are trying to change is their own beliefs, they must come to believe that their beliefs have changed before they recognise they have achieved their desires. So this case is an instance of, not an exception to, the general rule that action aims first at changing the world – in this case a state of the agent's mind – rather than at changing his or her beliefs. This was pointed out to me by Hugh Mellor.

it is to be a belief with R's truth conditions, is to be a belief which would, in certain circumstances, be caused by events occurring when it is the case that S.[13]

Now 1 is about a visible property of middle-sized objects. But sentences of the general form of 2 are not restricted to dealing with beliefs for which the truth conditions are that something should have a certain 'observational' property. For we conceive of agents as causally located in the world with all its properties. Thus, *if*, for example, there is an electron hitting the screen; and *if* that causes a certain scintillation; and *if* Mary is before the screen; and *if* Mary has appropriate beliefs about electrons; then she will come to believe that an electron has hit the screen. This complex conditional is also of the form of 2. And there are many more, known to all of us with the necessary concepts, which help fix the relations between something's being the case and an agent's believing it to be the case. And these truths will help to fix the truth conditions of the belief.

In the definition TRUTH I speak of an agent's doing A. In order to connect doing A with the mental states of the agent we shall need to know under what circumstances agents trying to perform actions will actually succeed. Corresponding to input claims of the form of 2, we shall have output claims also. The details are for the development of a functionalist theory; I have said enough, I think to give the general idea. I have certainly said enough to make clear the problems I want to discuss now.

2.2 Causal truths

I propose now to introduce the distinction I promised in the introduction between a causal truth condition, one causally necessary and sufficient for truth, and the more familiar notion of a logical truth condition. I need to do so because one might think that the definition, TRUTH, in 2.1, defines truth conditions as *causal* truth conditions. If that were right, then I should be wrong in claiming to have explicated the notion of truth condition that is needed, along with computational structure, to individuate beliefs and fix meanings. For, as we saw in 1.1, it is logical truth conditions which are functionally equivalent in CPAs.

I shall start by explaining how the problem arises; and I'll then go on to show how we can make sure we get the notion of a *logical* truth condition out of what is, nevertheless, an essentially *causal* functionalist theory. So, first, let me set the problem up.

Whether we consider input claims, of the form of 2, or output claims, their general form is of a claim that a relation obtains between four things: an agent, a set of conditions, the state of affairs that S, and a state of the agent

[13] There are, of course, problems in the application of 2 to the cases of general beliefs, *a priori* beliefs and existential beliefs; which I discuss towards the end of chapter 5 of Appiah (1985).

with the truth conditions of S. And that relation is causal. It holds because of causal relations between mental states and other states which are not mental. That the relation holds *a priori* does not show that the underlying facts are not causal: what is *a priori* is that the existence of things which satisfy that causal relation makes it true that there is a certain functional state; what is *a posteriori* is that there are any things which satisfy the causal relation.

Now causal relations, like all relations, are extensional; and this fact has important consequences for our account of truth conditions[14]. Call the sentence, 'Something before the agent is red', RED. Suppose that (all and only) red things emit in the wavelengths, w, so we can call them 'w-emitters'; then it will follow that

> 1. When agents with the concept *red*, who are conscious and whose eyes are open, are presented with a w-emitter in normal lighting, they will come to have a high degree of belief that something in front of them is red.

Because causality is a relation, we can substitute 'is a w-emitter' for the co-extensive term 'is red' in 1. And indeed, all the truths about the causal role of a belief in which reference is made to red things will correspond to truths in which reference is made to w-emitters. If it is a necessary and sufficient condition for *that a is F* to be the truth condition of a belief, that a and the property of being-F stand in certain causal relations to tokens of the belief, then, surely, we must conclude that RED's truth conditions are that something before the agent emits in the range of wavelengths w? This seems to be a reflection of the fact that causation is extensional. Insofar as our theory of truth conditions is causal, it will apparently assign to beliefs (and desires), as 'truth conditions', states of affairs which are true whenever the beliefs are – not out of logical necessity, but simply as a matter of fact.

In fact, however, this does not follow at all. For our functionalist theory individuates mental states by their functional roles: that is by *a priori* features of their causal role. And though it is true that, if 1 is true and red things are w-emitters, 1′ is true: it is not the case that if 1 is *a priori* true and red things emit in those wavelengths, 1′ is *a priori* true. The truth conditions of the representation are fixed by the *a priori* truths of the form of 2 (and similar output claims) which form part of the theory, not by every truth of one of these forms.[15] We can draw one conclusion immediately. Claims 1 and 2

---

[14] That causal relations are thus extensional does not mean that causal explanations are extensional also: the fact that the ball passed through a point 20 metres to the left of the pine tree doesn't explain why it broke the window, even if its passing through that point was its passing through the window; see Anscombe (1969).

[15] In a functionalist framework, it might be objected, there is no space for the *a priori*. But, as I said in 1.2, S is *a priori* true just in case any CPA who had the concepts necessary to have the belief that S, would believe that S to degree 1. Functionalism can explicate the *a priori*, and so can make use of it.

were offered in conjunction with TRUTH; which said, roughly, that a truth condition was a condition necessary and sufficient for success. But if 'necessary and sufficient' meant '*causally* necessary and sufficient' we would have failed to explicate the notion of a logical truth condition which I claimed, in 1.2, was what we needed for meaning. The lesson is clear: 'necessary and sufficient' had better mean '*logically* necessary and sufficient', if we want to define logical truth conditions.

2.3 Truth conditions: logical or causal?

If we want to understand the distinction between causal and logical truth conditions, it will help to have before us a case where, for some belief, we know the former, but not the latter. In a concrete case, we shall see what the distinction really amounts to. Consider, for this purpose, the case of a dog. Let's call him Charles. Suppose that Charles has special vision; his eyes are sensitive to emission of electro-magnetic radiation in a certain range of the ultra-violet. Let us call things that emit (or reflect) light in just that range of frequencies 'ultra-violet'; and likewise let us call the light they emit (or reflect) 'ultra-violet' also. Sometimes a thing is before Charles' eyes and we switch on a source of ultra-violet light. Suppose the room is otherwise unilluminated. Then we see nothing. But, as we can confirm by looking at the room with an ultra-violet sensitive camera, Charles goes about roughly as he does when the room is normally illuminated. Of course, he bumps into things that are transparent to ultra-violet, just as we should expect.

There is no doubt that Charles is having experiences, and, on the account of belief I have proposed, there is no doubt, either, that he is forming beliefs; including beliefs that things are the colour that ultra-violet objects look to him. For there is a system to his preferences and the behaviour consequent upon them, that can be captured by probability and utility functions, subject to computational error. In the end, then, after watching Charles for some time, we shall be able to give a functionalist account of the beliefs he forms when presented with ultra-violet objects. This theory will entail (something like):

> UV: Charles believes-something-is-R if an object before him is ultra-violet, *ceteris paribus*. Further his belief-that-something-is-R is true iff that thing is ultra-violet.

Now the first thing to insist on here is that, despite having a well-defined theory of Charles' state, and having a grasp of its causal truth conditions, we do not know its logical truth conditions. To know *that*, we should have to know something of the form:

> The belief-that-something-is-R is true iff that thing is R.

42

And the reason why we do not know the truth conditions of the belief-that-something-is-R is simple: we don't have the concept of *being-R*. That is why I called the state 'the belief-that-something-is-R'. For, for us, it is an unanalysable primitive notion: it is not one we can decompose into a relation between an agent and being-R. For the only conceivable candidate for 'R' is 'ultra-violet': and we know that this is wrong, because we can distinguish the belief-that-something-is-R and the belief that something is ultra-violet, functionally. The latter, but not the former, plays a causal role in our minds; the former, but not the latter, functions in Charles'.

Consider, for the sake of comparison, a belief of which we *do* know the logical truth conditions. For someone who has the concept of the belief that something is red, it is *a priori* that that belief is true iff that thing is red. And it is only possible to come to think this,[16] if you have the concept *red*. Consequently, only someone with the concept *red* can have the concept of the belief that something is red. *Mutatis mutandis* for R (as Charles might think!)

Our relation to Charles is, then, like the relation between someone who is blind and someone who is sighted. Suppose again that red things are all (and only) w-emitters. Then a blind man could know that I have beliefs-that-something-is-S which I form on the basis of visual exposure to things that w-emit, and which are true iff those things do w-emit. But he cannot, not having the capacity to form any beliefs that something is red at all, believe that I sometimes believe that things are red.[17]

So far I have been talking about what is known (or knowable) about our functional states for anyone with our concepts. Here is one way that the distinction between knowing *causal* truth conditions and knowing logical truth conditions, can be explained in the context of my theory. To know the logical truth conditions of a representation, R, it is not enough to know the causal truth conditions; it is necessary further to represent them to yourself by way of the very same concepts that R contains. And that, I claim, is what we cannot do for Charles' belief; and the blind man cannot do for ours.

There is something rather curious about this situation. Our notion of a truth condition – that which is shared by every computationally equivalent belief – turns out to be compounded of two elements, at least from the

[16] As a result of computation: which, recall, is what is required for it to be *a priori* for you.

[17] It would be extremely misleading to say that what the blind man lacks is a piece of information – say 'what redness is'. For that would suggest he might acquire the information that redness is…, where the dots are replaced by some concept-word. Whereas, of course, the only proper candidate here would be 'redness' (or a synonym): and learning *that* would be acquiring a capacity – colour vision – and not a piece of information. The same goes for the concept that Charles has: we just lack that concept, not a piece of information.

perspective of a functionalist theory which is fundamentally causal. On the one hand, there is the causal truth condition, a notion which makes good sense in the context of a functional theory; on the other is a constraint on the way in which agents must represent that causal truth condition to themselves if their knowledge of that causal truth condition is to be knowledge of the logical truth condition. Indeed, we might feel that looked at from a functionalist perspective, the notion of a truth condition which is not just a causal truth condition is just a tremendous muddle. Why not stick with the notion of a causal truth condition, while making sure to put into the functionalist theory, the very interesting, but surely separable fact, that anyone with the concept of the belief that S must be able to specify that causal truth condition by way of the very concepts which make up the belief that S?

But there is another way of seeing the matter that makes clear what the real significance of the truth condition is. I mentioned, at the beginning of 2.1, that beliefs could be separated out into equivalence classes consisting of members with the same truth condition. In CPAs any member of this class has the same causal role as any other. Not only are they all always true together – that condition is satisfied by the members of classes of beliefs with the same causal truth condition – but, in a CPA, they will be caused in the same circumstances. This condition is not satisfied by beliefs with the same causal truth conditions in general; it is obviously false, for example, that the belief that something emits at the appropriate wavelength is caused when and only when we see something red. (Indeed, as this case suggests, it is obviously false of perceptual concepts generally.) And the identity of causal role, with respect to decision theory, of beliefs with the same logical truth condition is one that may be seen to justify the importance which that notion has played in the philosophy of language and of mind.

Let me conclude by summarising how this bears on the topic of meaning. Declarative sentences express beliefs. To know the meaning of a token declarative sentence is to know what belief it expresses in the context of its utterance. Beliefs have truth conditions; and if we were CPAs, these conditions would individuate beliefs, and would be meanings. But because we are not CPAs, we cannot individuate sentence-meanings by giving the truth conditions of the beliefs those sentences express. We need also to know their computational structures. Furthermore, no amount of computational improvement will get you from the belief that something is red to the belief that it is a w-emitter. And so, if we were CPAs, it would be logical truth conditions, not causal ones, that would be meanings.

BIBLIOGRAPHY

Anscombe, G. E. M., 1969. Causality and Extensionality, *Journal of Philosophy 66*: 152–9.
Appiah, A.,1981. Conditions for Conditionals, Cambridge University PhD Thesis.
Appiah, A., 1985. *Assertion and Conditionals*, Cambridge: Cambridge University Press.
Butterfield, J., 1986. Content and Context, this volume.
Davidson, D., 1967. Truth and Meaning, *Synthese 7*: 304–23.
Dennett, D., 1978. *Brainstorms*, Brighton: Harvester Press.
Field, H., 1978. Mental Representation, *Erkenntnis 13*: 9–61.
Fodor, J., 1976. *The Language of Thought*, Brighton: Harvester Press.
Jeffrey, R. C., 1965. *The Logic of Decision*, Chicago: University of Chicago Press.
Lewis, D., 1970. General Semantics, *Synthese 22*: 18–67.
Lewis, D., 1972. Psychophysical Laws and Theoretical Identifications, *Australasian Journal of Philosophy 50*: 249–58.
Mellor, D. H., 1971. *The Matter of Chance*, Cambridge: Cambridge University Press.
Ramsey, F. P., 1978. *Foundations*, ed. D. H. Mellor, Cambridge: Cambridge University Press.
Shoemaker, S., 1982. Some Varieties of Functionalism. *Mind, Brain and Function*, ed. J. I. Biro and R. W. Shahan, Brighton: Harvester Press.

Semantic reductionism and reference*

DAVID PAPINEAU

My aim in this paper is to discuss the difficulties raised for a certain kind of reductionist position in semantics and philosophy of mind by the workings of proper names. In the first half of the paper I shall elaborate the various interlocking theses that together make up the reductionist position in question. Many issues will inevitably be treated rather sketchily, but my primary concern is not so much to defend the reductionist position as simply to lay it out and give some idea of why I find it attractive. In the second half I shall then turn to questions about the reference of proper names. This will involve my treading fairly clumsily across some very well-cultivated philosophical ground. For this, too, my apologies – but, again, my aim is not to improve on previous refinements but merely to explore the options open to my kind of reductionism.

I

The semantic reductionism I have in mind is, in the first instance, of the familiar Gricean-conventionalist sort, which seeks to define meaning, for sentences, in terms of such psychological notions as belief and intention. (See Schiffer 1972, for a detailed elaboration of this programme.) But it could also be called reductionist in a further, secondary, sense. Somebody who wants to define meaning in terms of belief and related notions has an obligation, albeit one that is not always recognized, to say something further about these defining concepts – at least to the extent of showing that they are adequate to play the requisite definitional role. And in this connection I shall be discussing various aspects of the functionalist approach to belief – which, although the term is normally reserved for something stronger, is certainly a kind of reductionism about belief.

It will be helpful to start by giving some reasons in favour of being a Gricean in the first place. For there is an alternative, non-reductionist approach to the concept of meaning which rejects any attempt to give an

* I would like to thank Jeremy Butterfield for his suggestions for improving earlier versions of this paper.

explicit definition of meaning, and instead regards it as sufficient to give an implicit definition, via a general account of the form to be taken by an empirical theory of meaning for a natural language and of how to test such a theory in practice. (Compare the way in which one might, in dynamics, say, give an implicit account of the notion of force, by explaining what a theory specifying the forces present in certain circumstances would look like, and explaining how one might empirically test such a theory of force.) I take this non-reductionist approach to meaning to be implicit in the writings of Donald Davidson (see the essays in Davidson 1984). But it has perhaps been most clearly expressed by John McDowell (1976, 1980), and in consequence I shall call it the 'neo-Davidsonian' view of meaning. Note that this approach to meaning offers the option (not of course open to the Gricean) of explaining the notion of belief in terms of the notion of linguistic meaning: since one has an analysis of meaning that does not invoke the concept of belief, one can then, it seems, analyse believing that p as a disposition to utter a sentence which means that p, or as something along such lines.

However, complications arise for the neo-Davidsonian view, and in particular for the relation between belief and meaning, as soon as we look more closely at the question of how we test an empirical theory of meaning for a given language. The simplest answer is based on the 'principle of charity': given that the data consist of actual utterances made by the speakers of the language, prefer that theory which maximizes the number of such utterances that come out true. (Throughout this paper I shall be making the familiar simplifying assumption that all sentences are indicative.)

But there are obvious objections to the principle of charity. Is it really an ideal in a theory of meaning to represent, as far as is possible, all utterances as true? Is the reason for putting the principle in terms of maximization rather than total truth, and allowing that some actual utterances might have to be deemed false, simply that in practice the data turn out not to allow total truth? Something is clearly wrong here. False utterances aren't just 'noise', an upshot of the fact that the actual data won't yield an entirely smooth fit to a systematic theory of meaning for the language in question. For people often say false things as the specific result of believing false things. And insofar as a particular community is particularly prone to do this on particular topics, we surely ought not to have it as a desirable aim that a theory of meaning should make the relevant utterances come out true.

For this reason it is fairly generally accepted that a 'principle of humanity' ought to replace the principle of charity. Suppose we view a theory of meaning as an interpretative tool for going from the utterance of indicative sentences to the attribution of beliefs to the speakers of those sentences. (If someone asserts s, and the theory says that s means that p, then conclude the speaker believes that p.) The principle of humanity is then the idea that we should test a theory of meaning by considering whether it is plausible for the relevant speakers to have the beliefs the theory leads us to attribute to them. On this conception, then, it is by no means a demerit in a theory of meaning that it leads us to deem certain speakers to be saying something false, provided, that is, that we can satisfactorily explain how they have come by a false belief on the matter in question. What a theory of meaning has to maximize is not the truth of utterances but the human explicability of the beliefs behind them. (See in particular Grandy 1973.)

This switch from charity to humanity is significant. It shows that the notion of belief is at least to some extent independent of the notion of meaning. Certainly the switch precludes the neo-Davidsonian from any full-blooded analysis of belief in terms of meaning, of the kind briefly mentioned above: for if our access to the notion of meaning is via an account of how an empirical theory of meaning works, and if, as it now turns out, such an account in turn makes essential use of the notion of belief, we are clearly no longer in a position to turn round and explain away the concept of believing that p in terms of the concept of a sentence meaning that p.

It is worth being a bit more specific about the way in which the switch to humanity demands a certain meaning-independence in our notion of belief. What the switch shows is that our grasp of a given belief-type is not exhausted by the idea of a state which simply 'registers' the truth-conditions of the sentence that expresses it, that is, by the idea of a state which is (by and large) present when those truth-conditions are. For the principle of humanity hinges precisely on the fact that for some beliefs at least we have a reasonably clear grasp of what circumstances other than their truth-conditions are likely to give rise to them. If this were not so, we would have no handle by which to judge whether attributions of false beliefs were plausible or not. All such beliefs would have to be seen alike as aberrant 'noise' to be minimized as far as possible by a good translation, and humanity would collapse back into charity.

These points about the relative independence of belief and truth-conditional meaning are reinforced by the further consideration that false belief is not the only source of false utterance. As well as the falsities that result from misinformation, there are those that result from insincere and unliteral intentions. A further refinement of the principle of charity is required to deal with these sources of falsehood. And the fact that we are capable of being so further refined shows that we have yet further systematic abilities to identify people's psychological states even in cases where those states diverge from the states indicated by the meanings of their words.

Still, showing that we have a grasp of belief that transcends its linguistic manifestation in various ways does not yet establish that we ought to reverse the Davidsonian approach, and adopt the Gricean strategy of defining meaning in terms of the belief a sentence expresses (where 'expresses' gets spelt out as a matter of conventional expectations as to what beliefs speakers will be trying to get across). Perhaps belief and meaning are mutually dependent notions, neither of which can be reduced to the other, and so perhaps the right resting place for analysis should still be an implicit definition of meaning, albeit one which happens to invoke the notion of belief along the way.

But it seems to me that we ought at least to ask what reasons there are for avoiding the Gricean reductionist path. It is true that it is not essential, in physics, to have a reductionist analysis of the notion of force. But such reductions are nice if you can get them, and it would have been a great achievement if, say, classical physics had been able to show that all forces, including gravitational and electromagnetic forces, could be reduced to action by materal contact. Similarly, if we could reduce semantics to psychology, this would certainly be something worth doing.

There is, as it happens, a rather good reason for being suspicious of Gricean reductionism, albeit one that it is surprisingly rarely spelt out in anti-reductionist writings. Philosophical puzzlement about meaning comes, in the first instance, from the mysterious circumstance that words *represent*, that mere marks on paper and intrinsically arbitrary sounds can stand for things other than themselves. A satisfactory philosophical definition of meaning ought to explain this mystery. (The kinetic theory of gases would not give us much of a reduction of the notion of macroscopic temperature if it simply explained it in terms of the temperatures of microscopic particles.) But, if we stop to think about it, is there not just as much of a puzzle about how *beliefs* represent, about how they manage to stand for things other than themselves?

Of course this is only a puzzle on some conceptions of belief. If we were still adopting the line that the notion of belief is to be explained in terms of the notion of meaning, and were explaining the latter in terms of how an empirical theory of meaning worked, then we would indeed have a kind of story which accounted for the representational powers of belief. But if we want to explore the alternative course of defining meaning in terms of belief, we need a notion of belief that will stand on its own feet, and consequently need to say something about where its representational powers come from.

Perhaps one reason why anti-Griceans have not often pressed this point (and have instead concentrated on largely irrelevant epistemological considerations) is that both traditional dualist and more modern conceptions of belief tend to obscure the lacuna. Certainly people who are prepared to swallow that beliefs are made of some distinctive mind-stuff, which, though not itself existing in space, can interact with things that do, are unlikely to baulk (though they ought to) at the attribution of just one more ineffable power to beliefs, namely that of being able to reach out and stand for things other than themselves.

And I suspect that the functionalist approach to belief (which I take to be the most promising modern candidate for the basis of a Gricean reduction) has also, if in a rather different way, tended to hide the obligation to explain the representational powers of belief. Of course, if the functionalism in question is 'methodologically solipsist', in the sense that the causal structure with respect to which beliefs and other psychological states are identified is one which begins (on the way in) with stimuli at the sensory peripheries, and stops (on the way out) with bodily movements – if, to repeat, the functionalism is one which works with such a truncated causal structure, then it is obvious enough that there is a problem in accounting for the representational powers of beliefs, for this kind of functionalism will have left the states of affairs represented by all (non-introspective) beliefs quite out of the story altogether. But just this consideration yields a natural (albeit, as I shall shortly argue, confused) motivation for functionalists to extend their causal net beyond the bodily peripheries, to the characteristic 'external' causes of our mental states. For it seems that if functionalists do extend their causal net, they have a natural enough answer to the problem of representation: namely, that the state of affairs represented by a belief is simply its 'characteristic' cause, or 'typical' cause, or something along such lines. And, correspondingly, it seems natural enough for the opponents of Griceanism to suppose that there are no real problems of representation for a (non-solipsistic) functionalist, and to turn therefore to less fruitful lines of criticism.

But, as I said, all this seems to me confused. I agree that functionalism ought to extend its causal net beyond the bodily peripheries. But I think that this is for reasons largely irrelevant to our present concerns and nothing directly to do with representation.[1] I would argue that even if we do allow the causal net to spread out, functionalists are still left with the problem of explaining representation (and anti-Gricean opponents ought to press them on it). For representational relationships are not by any means the same thing as causal relationships, nor is it at all obvious how one might go about explaining the former in terms of the latter.

A good way of bringing this out is to return to an observation made earlier, in connection with the principle of humanity: namely, that for many beliefs we have a perfectly clear idea (it is, one might say, part of our

---

[1] See my 1985 for comments that bear on this issue.

common-sense psychological theory) of how those beliefs can arise in circumstances other than their truth-conditions. Thus, to take a simple example,
it is no more surprising that someone confronted by a good imitation
papier-mâché tree should come to believe there's a tree there than that
someone confronted by a real tree should believe this. (It wouldn't count
against a translation which took such a person to be saying *there's a tree there*
that what they were looking at was only an imitation.) Again, we are quite
familiar with the fact that somebody looking at a red object is likely to
believe that it is green if they are (unknowingly) viewing it in sodium
lighting. And so forth.

The point of these examples is this. Functionalism identifies a belief-type
as a state which will be produced by any of a certain range of causes (and
which will, in conjunction with other mental states, give rise to certain
effects). We are now supposing that these causes include external circumstances as well as peripheral ones. But, even so, once we actually attend to
the range of external circumstances which will give rise to a given belief-type,
we see that it includes circumstances other than the belief's truth-condition,
other than the state of affairs the belief represents. No doubt there is in the
end going to be *some* philosophical story which will distinguish the belief's
truth-conditions from its other, 'deviant' possible causes, and indeed I shall
briefly mention the story I favour in a moment. The point I am making
here is simply that in itself functionalism (construed straightforwardly as the
claim that beliefs are whatever entities fill the causal roles our common-sense
psychological theory postulates for beliefs) does not even offer the outlines
of such a tale.

It is an increasingly familiar suggestion that there are two components
of the notion of belief – on the one hand belief-as-the-bearer-of-a-causal-
role, and on the other belief-as-the-representer-of-some-state-of-affairs (see
Putnam 1978, part 3; McGinn 1982). What the above argument in effect
shows is that functionalism is strongly committed to this two-component
view – if only in the backhanded sense that it gives us a notion of belief that,
in the first instance at least, leaves the representational component out of the
picture altogether.

Perhaps a brief observation on terminology will be helpful here. I am
assuming functionalism is not (or at least ought not to be) 'solipsist', in the
sense that the net in terms of which causal roles are identified extends (or
ought to extend) beyond the bodily peripheries. But at the same time what
I have just argued is that functionalism is 'solipsist' ('purist', 'narrow') in
a rather different sense. For even if the attribution of a functionalist belief
to somebody implies the existence of something outside the believer
(*something* must have caused the belief), it does not imply the existence of
entities of the kind we intuitively think of the belief as representing (for just

that belief could, according to the functionalist, have been produced by a quite deviant cause).

What then should functionalists say about representation? If they are not going to ignore the very thing about belief that makes it philosophically interesting, they need to go on from the initial analysis of beliefs-as-bearers-of-causal-roles to say something about their representational powers.

Some functionalist sympathizers have attended to this problem. One suggestion (originating with Hartry Field (1978), and discussed also by Brian Loar (1981), and Colin McGinn (1982)) is that the pairing of beliefs with truth-conditions should be explicated in terms of the passing of information between individuals. People generally take the beliefs of others, or the words that express those beliefs, as indicators of further states of affairs. Thus if I hear a competent English speaker utter the words 'It is raining outside', I shall in general conclude that it is raining outside. What we are doing here – and it is clearly very important to us that we have this ability – is viewing each other as 'instruments', viewing each other's beliefs and utterances as 'readings' which carry information about various states of affairs. But of course readings have to be interpreted, instruments have to be calibrated. So the suggestion is that the pairing of beliefs and utterances with truth-conditions, the conferring of the familiar representational powers, is just such a calibration, a way of pairing words and the world which will best serve our interest in moving inferentially from the former to the latter.

The trouble with this, it seems to me, is that it puts the cart before the horse. The pairing of beliefs with truth-conditions is being accounted for in terms of its usefulness in allowing us to draw inferences. But drawing inferences is itself a matter of forming beliefs. Indeed, when I infer that it is raining from somebody's uttering 'It is raining', what I am doing (or at least so I presume) is putting myself in the same belief-state as they are in. But what's the point of my forming beliefs in this way? It is true that, insofar as my informant's belief is generally present only when a certain state of affairs obtains (its 'truth-condition'), then so will mine only be present in those circumstances (and so indeed will that of anybody else who in turn 'catches' the belief from me). But what's the point, for any of us, of gearing our belief-forming practice to this constraint, of having beliefs only when their 'truth-conditions' obtain? It can't just be a desire for social conformity, a desire that we should all have the same beliefs in the same circumstances. Surely the fact of the matter is that it is a good idea for any individual person, quite independently of their informational relationships with others, to have beliefs as far as possible only when their truth-conditions obtain. And surely any explanation of why it is advantageous to adopt a certain practice for inferring beliefs from other people's beliefs will therefore be derivative on a prior account of why this is a good idea in the first place.

Of course once we raise the question of why an individual's beliefs should be geared to truth-conditions there is an obvious enough answer: namely, that if you have true beliefs your actions will succeed. It is because the 'calibrational' approach quite leaves out this connection between the truth of belief and the success of action that it seems to me to fail to get to proper grips with the concept of representation. Perhaps we can remedy the situation, then, by analysing truth directly in terms of success: the truth-conditions for a belief are circumstances the obtaining of which guarantees the success of actions informed by that belief. This suggestion is, I think, a lot less silly than it seems to many people. But unfortunately it, too, fails to get to proper grips with the problem of representation. For the notion of success is itself at bottom a representational notion, and to invoke it in an analysis of representation is to be guilty of circularity.

Let me spell the point out. It is not enough, for an action to succeed, that any old satisfactory effect ensue. What needs to result is some specific circumstance which will fulfil the desire behind the action. But fulfilment, for a desire, is a notion closely analogous to that of truth for a belief, and one which is quite as much left out of account by a purely functionalist approach to desires as bearers-of-certain-causal-roles. The functionalist understanding of, say, a desire for a drink of water, will involve a range of characteristic effects of that desire, and these effects will indeed include the drinking of water; but they will also include the exercising of the throat muscles, or (imagine the agent is at a party and mistakes a glass of gin for one of water) getting a mouthful of gin. And it will not be at all obvious what there is in the functionalist story to pick out the first effect from the others as the fulfilment condition of the desire.

The principle that truth guarantees success indeed places a constraint on the joint explication of the notions of truth for beliefs and fulfilment for desires. But something further needs to be added before we can break out of the representational circle.

I think the trick can be done if we adopt a teleological approach to the issue. Functionalism views beliefs and desires as components in a postulated cognitive mechanism. But by looking exclusively at the causal *structure* of that mechanism it fails to capture the representational features of the components. We need to ask further about the biological *purpose* of those parts. Take beliefs first. The reason it is appropriate to think that the state that can be produced both by trees and by papier-mâché mock-ups is a representation of the former and not of the latter, is that it's in the presence of trees, and not in the presence of imitations, that the belief is supposed to be there. And this is 'supposed' in the biological sense, in the sense that the behaviour prompted by the belief state will be biologically advantageous when there are trees present, but not, in general, when there are only imitations around. Similarly with desires. What makes the desire in the above example a desire for water, and not for gin or throat-muscle exercise, is again that it is the former result, but not the latter ones, that the desire is supposed to produce. And once more this is 'supposed' in a biological sense – it is getting water, as opposed to gin or throat-muscle exercise, that is advantageous for the individual in question.

There is much more to be said in elaboration of this teleological suggestion. For a start, there is the complication, slurred over in the last paragraph, that beliefs only direct behaviour when acting in conjunction with desires, and vice versa. And then there are general questions about how teleological thinking is to be interpreted, which will obviously affect the specific suggestion that representation is a teleological notion. But it would take us too far afield to pursue these issues; I shall content myself here with three comments. (For further development see my 1984.)

First, it might be thought that a teleological analysis of representation is already contained in the functionalist approach to psychological notions. ('You are advocating that we should focus on the functions of beliefs and desires. But isn't that precisely what the functionalists have been saying all along?') But this is simply a bad pun. Perhaps this terminological ambiguity has led some people to suppose that functionalism in the philosophy of mind is concerned with the purposes of psychological states (and perhaps this in turn has obscured some of the difficulties surrounding the notion of representation) – but there is certainly nothing in the classic statements of functionalism, as the view that beliefs and desires should be identified via their roles in a causal structure, which requires that such states should be identified in terms of their functions, in terms of their biological purposes.

Secondly, it is worth being clear that the teleological explanations I want to focus on are not the familiar explanations of actions in terms of the beliefs and desires behind them. My concern is rather with the question why the dispositions to form beliefs and desires are there in the first place, and I want to explain this in terms of their characteristic effects. The interesting thing is not your drinking a glass of water because it will quench your thirst, but rather that you believe it will quench your thirst because that has the advantageous effect of getting you to drink it.

And thirdly, my suggestion here should be distinguished from that made by Daniel Dennett in various places (1978, 1981, 1982), where he argues that belief–desire psychology will be applicable to any biological organism, whatever its internal cognitive structure, because evolution will somehow have ensured that what the organism does will be teleologically appropriate to its circumstances. That's as may be (though I have my doubts). But my suggestion here, on the contrary, involves taking belief–desire psychology seriously, as a theory of our actual and imperfect cognitive mechanisms, and *then* considering the biological function of the various components of that mechanism.

II

I turn now to questions of reference. So far I've been implicitly taking it for the most part that belief-types, and correspondingly the states of affairs they represent, are more or less unstructured: most of my examples haven't involved anything more sophisticated than basic feature-placing beliefs ('red', 'a tree', etc.) But of course this is over-simple. The functionalist approach surely wants to allow that beliefs, conceived as causal-role types, are made up of various components which, when combined in various ways, make a systematic contribution to the overall causal role. And correspondingly, when we turn to representation, we would expect the truth-conditions of such complex beliefs to be made up of elements and according to a mode of composition which are functions of the components and the structure of the belief (*qua* causal-role type) in question.

I want to focus, in what remains, on simple subject–predicate beliefs. I shall suppose that as causal-role types such beliefs are composed of a 'referring component', somehow concatenated with a 'predicate component', and I shall suppose that what such a belief represents is the instantiation of some property by some spatio-temporal particular. And I shall suppose moreover that the spatio-temporal particular in question is a function of the 'referring component' and, possibly, of the context the agent is in. (That is, other beliefs involving the same referring component will have the same – or, more generally, contextually corresponding – spatio-temporal particular in their truth-conditions.)

All these supposings are of course matters which, in the context of the functionalist approach I am adopting, require some kind of justification. But perhaps I can let that pass, and move straight on to more familiar questions about the nature of the relation between referring components and the particulars they refer to. What does the view of representation I have outlined in the first section imply about the reference relation?

There is perhaps a temptation here, especially if we concentrate on beliefs acquired more or less directly from observation, to conclude that the particular referred to should be deemed to be that item in the believer's environment that was the *cause* of the belief in question. After all, won't it be the properties of that particular rather than of any others that the belief in question will most accurately register? And so doesn't it seem sensible to suppose that the biological function of such a basic subject–predicate belief is to carry information about the particular that was causally responsible for it? Which, of course, given the teleological analysis of representation, implies that what such a belief refers to is the particular that caused it.

But this would be too quick. It ignores the fact that a belief involving a given referring component will only give rise to actions, and hence serve any biological purpose, when acting in concert with other beliefs and desires involving the same referring component. For instance, my believing that a certain chair is comfortable will only affect my actions insofar as I also believe, say, that it is the same chair as that chair in the corner, and so that by moving so-and-so I shall be able to sit in it, and only insofar as I also desire to be comfortable, and therefore to sit in that chair. In the limiting case this surrounding context of attitudes may simply involve keeping continuous track of some nearby particular that one wants to do something to. But even here the same moral will apply. Namely, that the biological purpose of a given subject–predicate belief is tied up with the purposes of other beliefs and desires involving the same referring component – and that therefore the purpose of such a belief is not so much to get right the properties of the particular that caused it, but to get right the properties of the particular which will cause other beliefs, and be affected by other desires, involving the same referring component. Or, to put the point in more familiar terms, what counts is not so much the particular that caused the belief in question, as the one that the believer will reidentify as the same one again.

This line of thought could obviously be developed at some length. In particular, things need to be said about the 'updating' of beliefs occasioned by the presence of indexical elements in referring components. (Cf. Butterfield, this volume, p. 91f). But I shall skip this. After all, there is nothing very surprising in the suggestion that the particular picked out by a referring component is the one the believer will respond to recognitionally. The natural way to think of a referring component is in terms of a mode of presentation which embodies (a) some qualitative information (which may be explicitly articulatable in a linguistic description, but might simply consist of some inarticulatable perceptual image) and (b) an indexical indication of the 'direction' in which the referent is located (which indication might of course be given by specifying the referent's relation to some other indexically located particular). Thus, for example, one could have referring components along the lines of 'The self-employed plumber who lives next door', or 'The woman with blue eyes who used to read the news on television'. In such cases it is natural to suppose that the referring component refers to that unique particular, if any, which (a) satisfies the qualitative information, and (b) lies in the indicated direction. But this then is just the particular that the believer will – with the help of any necessary tracking of the particular's spatio-temporal career – be disposed to reidentify as the same again. And so to this extent the account of reference suggested by the functionalist–teleological approach to representation seems to be just what is called for by our most obvious intuitions on the subject.

The trouble is, however, that the functionalist–teleological approach seems to force a similar account on us with respect to referring components expressed by proper names. And that, of course, is something few philosophers nowadays would be happy with. Consider people who sincerely assert 'NN is tall', or who can accurately be described as believing that NN is tall. The reductionist about meaning and belief maintains that sentences express belief-types, and that belief-types are bearers of causal roles. So the reductionist will have to attribute to such people a causal-role belief-type containing a referring component corresponding to the name 'NN'.[2] But what could such a referring component consist of if not a mode of presentation embodying qualitative and indexical elements? ('The woman with blue eyes who used to read the news on television', etc.) And so it seems that the reductionist ought to deem people who hold that NN is tall to be referring to the individual picked out by the relevant mode of presentation – for, as just pointed out, that is the individual they will reidentify as NN.

But, notoriously, it doesn't seem to work like this. Since Kripke's 'Naming and Necessity' (1972) it has generally been conceded that the claim NN is tall is not about the person that members of the community will recognize as the bearer of the name (even supposing there is such a person) but rather about the person who in some sense is the originating source of the use of the term 'NN'.

This then is a difficulty for the reductionist position I outlined in section I. The reductionist seems committed to the view that 'NN' stands for the particular that best fits the qualitative-plus-indexical constructions of the community. But Kripke and intelligent reflection show us that this view is wrong. In the rest of this paper I shall explore various ways in which the reductionist might try to deal with this difficulty.

One suggestion (I shall call it the *special case suggestion*) would be simply to admit that the general reductionist approach doesn't work for proper names, and to give them special treatment. Thus, the reductionist might say,

[2] Here I am assuming the 'disquotational principle' (cf. Kripke 1979) according to which somebody who sincerely, competently and literally utters an indicative English sentence —— thereby shows themselves to have the belief that ——. The reductionist could of course go some way towards resolving the difficulties raised by proper names by simply denying the disquotational principle; for then oddities about the conventions governing the direct linguistic use of names wouldn't automatically translate into oddities about what happened when those names were used to attribute beliefs. But the disquotational principle is so central to our practice of belief attribution that the reductionist can scarcely deny it outright and leave it at that.

consider any socially significant particular – a person, or town, or building, or racehorse, or football team or whatever. There is no reason to suppose that there will be any one referring component, common to all members of the community which succeeds in picking out the particular in question. Different individuals will have different qualitative and indexical 'fixes' on the particular, and consequently different referring components for it. Others might have no such component at all, or at least none that actually succeeds in picking out the particular in question. Given all this diversity, we can see why it makes sense to use proper names as we do – to have standardized terms for significant particulars, and to hold speakers using those terms to be talking, not about those particulars (if any) they would recognize as bearing the terms, but rather about the particulars which lie at the source of their use of the terms. For the existence of standardized names means that people can pass on information about a given particular without having to undertake the often awkward job of establishing identities between explicit descriptive–indexical referring expressions. And no doubt the specific convention that such names should be held to pick out the source of their use can be accounted for in terms of the fact that conformity to *this* convention, rather than to some alternative, will tend to ensure that the information that gets passed around using proper names is maximally reliable.

Again, much more needs to be said. But what matters for our present purposes is not how the details are filled out, but simply that some such story about the social rationale for our practice with proper names might be given. For once we have such a story the reductionist can reasonably admit that there is no single belief- (as-causal-role) type expressed by the words 'NN is tall', and correspondingly admit that when we say of two people that they both believe NN is tall, there need be, strictly speaking, no belief-type common to both of them; the reductionist can admit this, and yet maintain the general view that sentences express beliefs and belief-types are causal roles. For in the light of such a story it is open to the reductionist to maintain that there are special social reasons why the direct use of proper names does not conform to the general rule; and why the attribution of beliefs such as NN is tall should be regarded as a manner of speaking, which does not attribute belief-types as such to the believers involved, but rather indicates what they would *say* (and what linguistic conventions they would be answerable to) if the beliefs they actually held prompted them to utterance.[3]

But let us now look at this special-case suggestion a little more closely.

[3] In a sense the special-case suggestion does deny disquotational principle, for it maintains that the attribution of beliefs by means of proper names isn't strictly speaking an attribution of beliefs, but only a manner of speaking. But it does at least give some account, even if only a Pickwickian special-case story, of the 'proper-name beliefs' that we ordinarily take speakers to be manifesting by the direct use of proper names.

Has not the reductionist conceded too much? That is, doesn't the special-case suggestion imply that there is, after all, a common causal-role type behind the use of a term such as 'NN'? The special-case suggestion had it that people who use proper names are held to be talking about the originating source of the use of the name. But held by whom? The natural answer seems to be: by (the majority of) the members of the relevant linguistic community. But doesn't that then imply that the linguistic community *does* associate a common referring component with the name 'NN' – namely that corresponding to the description 'the origin of the use of 'NN''? Admittedly competent members of the community will differ in what *other* information they associate with the name. But surely the special-case story implies that somebody who didn't even grasp that uses of 'NN' were answerable to the causal source of that name just wouldn't be understanding the term as a name.

This suggestion (let us call it the *compromise* suggestion,[4] since it is a kind of compromise between the old 'description' theory of reference and the modern 'causal' one) does, it is true, make many people uneasy. For a start, there is the objection that it is implausible to credit lay speakers with a grasp of some sophisticated causal theory of reference. However, while there would indeed be something wrong with crediting lay speakers with the explicit ability to articulate such a theory of reference, all that the compromise suggestion requires such speakers to have is an effective ability to pick out, as the referent of a given name, that particular that is the origin of the use of that name. And there seems to me to be plenty of evidence that speakers have at least this ability. In particular, there are the intuitions they characteristically display in response to Kripkean stories about pseudo-Homers and pseudo-Gödels – which intuitions, after all, are the basis for philosophers accepting the causal theory of reference in the first place.

Then there is the worry that the compromise suggestion implies that the name 'Margaret Thatcher', say, is synonymous with the description 'origin of the use of the term 'Margaret Thatcher'', and thereby seems to rule out the perfectly good possibility that Margeret Thatcher could have been christened by some other name. However a reductionist will know nowadays what to say to this complaint. That the name 'Margaret Thatcher' is introduced via a description doesn't make it necessary that Margaret Thatcher fits that description. For the name 'Margaret Thatcher' is, as a name, a rigid designator, while the description in question is not (cf. Kripke 1972, *passim*).

But, the complaint might be pressed, does not the compromise suggestion at least imply that 'Margaret Thatcher is the source of the term 'Margaret

4 Cf. Plantinga (1978).

Thatcher'' is in some sense analytic, and therefore knowable *a priori*? But this consequence is one which presumably ought indeed to follow from the compromise suggestion. For the suggestion is precisely that everybody who has the referring component expressed by 'NN' will understand it primarily as equivalent to the-originator-of-'NN''s-use, and so *will* know *a priori* that NN is the source of 'NN''s use. (Though see Schiffer 1977, for doubts about such contingent *a priori* truths.)

There is however a more solid objection to the compromise suggestion. So far I have been assuming that the name 'NN' will only be used to attribute beliefs to people who are themselves familiar with the term. But of course they are not the only people to whom we will want to attribute beliefs of the form NN is such-and-such. I might tell you that Jack thought that Jill, whom he met at the party, was very attractive – although, I continue, he doesn't yet know that she's called 'Jill', because nobody got around to introducing them properly. But then I can scarcely maintain that the referring component of Jack's belief is adequately expressed by the description 'the causal origin of the use of the name 'Jill'' – for in this story Jack needn't have any ideas about the name 'Jill' at all.

Indeed, though I skipped over it, this kind of case would obviously pose a problem for our original special case suggestion as well. According to the special case suggestion, belief attributions made using proper names shouldn't be understood as attributing real (causal-role) beliefs to the people in question, so much as indicating how they would linguistically express their actual beliefs (whatever those were). But if Jack doesn't know Jill's name, we can scarcely be attributing linguistic dispositions involving the term 'Jill' to him when we say that he thinks Jill is attractive.

At this point the reductionist might be tempted to try a rather different tack. Suppose we abandon the compromise suggestion's attempt to find a causal-role type common to all NN is such-and-such believers, in the face of those people who have the belief but are unfamiliar with the name. Might it not still be argued that there is *something* in common to the causal-role types of those people to whom such an attribution is made? Namely, that though they don't all involve the same referring component, they all involve *some* referring component that picks out NN.

On this suggestion (let us call it the *belief-as-representer* suggestion) proper-name attributions would not attribute, nor would proper-name sentences express, beliefs as such, beliefs as specific causal-role types, so much as an equivalence class of beliefs, namely that class of beliefs which share the relevant truth-condition involving NN.

This belief-as-representer suggestion is in a sense something of a retreat to the earlier special-case suggestion, in that both suggestions imply that proper-name beliefs are distinct only in so far as they represent distinct states of affairs. That is, both suggestions imply that proper-name beliefs can be adequately individuated by ordered *n*-tuples of the relevant particulars and relations. But the belief-as-representer suggestion is not a total retreat, in that it still conforms to the general functionalist–teleological approach in explaining what picks out those particulars as relevant. On the special-case suggestion the reference of a proper name was fixed quite independently of which modes of presentation happened to be involved in speakers' causal-role types: it was the causal history of the use of the name that fixed reference, not the thoughts of the relevant community. The belief-as-representer suggestion, on the other hand, goes along with the idea that the basic notion of a belief is the notion of a causal-role type, and that the referents of such beliefs are fixed by the qualitative-plus-indexical features of the modes of presentation involved: the distinctive aspect of the belief-as-representer suggestion is simply that proper-name belief attributions do not discriminate as finely as actual causal-roles, but merely specify a belief as a member of a class of causal-roles which share a certain truth-condition.

How much consolation does this offer the reductionist? The belief-as-representer suggestion is at best a very weak form of reductionism, and I shall return in a moment to the question of whether it requires the reductionist to concede too much. But there are other problems to be dealt with first: weak as it is, the belief-as-representer suggestion is open to a number of objections.

For one thing, it is difficult to see how to avoid the consequence that all belief attributions using proper names will be transparent to substitution by co-referring names.[5] Perhaps this is acceptable, with apparent counter-examples to be explained away as abnormal cases. But then there is the more telling point, already mentioned briefly in connection with the special-case suggestion, that some of the people to whom we want to attribute beliefs of the form NN is such-and-such have referring components that don't actually succeed in picking out NN at all. After all, one of the more striking morals of 'Naming and Necessity' was that someone could believe that Quine was a great philosopher, without having enough descriptive information to distinguish Quine from anybody else (or indeed, while having information that would lead him or her to *mis*identify Quine). When we say that people like this believe that NN is such-and-such we can't even be saying that they have *some* causal-role belief which represents the relevant state of affairs – for the functionalist–teleological approach implies that the

---

[5] Schiffer (1977) avoids this difficulty by reading proper names as indexical belief attributers, with the specific mode of presentation being attributed to the believer somehow being fixed by the context of utterance. While this seems a little too strong to me, Schiffer's position is similar in spirit and in most other details to the one I end up with in this paper.

belief in their head represents something quite different from that state of affairs.

In the face of this difficulty the reductionist might be tempted to settle for some kind of special case strategy after all. True, we have now seen that belief attributions involving proper names cannot in general tie people to the referents via the conventional responsibilities incumbent on their linguistic dispositions – for such attributions can work with people unfamiliar with the name. But perhaps there is some different kind of special story, which doesn't hinge essentially on the believer using the name 'NN', but which will still succeed in tying believers to NN even though that is not what is picked out by the causal-role beliefs in their heads.

However, there is a much more general reason why it is desirable for the reductionist to avoid special case arguments. Namely, that it is by no means clear that proper names are so special after all. Much recent work (see in particular Kripke 1972; Putnam 1975; and Burge 1979) makes it clear that natural kind terms – like 'elm', 'gold', 'tiger', 'arthritis' – share many of the features of proper names. In particular, this work shows that all the difficulties that the reductionist faces with proper names will arise in just the same way with natural-kind terms. *Prima facie* the truth-conditions of beliefs expressed or attributed by means of natural-kind terms seem to depend, not on what causal roles are instantiated in the believers' heads, but rather on general conventions relating to those terms' uses. This can't be avoided by resorting to some 'compromise' suggestion, for there are people who have the beliefs but are unfamiliar with the term. (An observant rustic could know that badgers were nocturnal, and many other things about them, without knowing what they were called.) And it doesn't seem that a belief-as-representer suggestion will go through, because of people who have the beliefs but will misidentify members of the kind. This means that the reductionist who treats proper names as special cases is clearly going to have to treat natural-kind terms as special cases too. But this surely won't do. It would require abandoning reductionism not just with respect to the referring components in the proper-name beliefs, but with respect to both referring and predicative components in a wide range of beliefs. Such reductionism as survived would scarcely be worth the name.

What then is the reductionist to do? Perhaps the following offers a way out. (What I say from now on is intended to go both for proper names and for natural-kind terms.) Do we ever attribute proper-name beliefs to people who are *neither* familiar with the name *nor* possessed of some non-linguistic qualitative-indexical component which picks out the referent? As a first approximation I would say not: why ever should we attribute the belief that NN is tall to a believer whose referring component fails to pick out the

63

referent, unless the believer is familiar with the term 'NN'? An immediate qualification is needed, however, to deal with people who are familiar with another name for the same referent: Kripke's (1979) Pierre can surely believe that London is nice even before he learns English and while he knows nothing else about the place, given, of course, that he is familiar with the term 'Londres'. So I would propose, as a general principle, that somebody who believes that NN is such-and-such must either (a) be familiar with the name 'NN', or with some other name, possibly in a different language, the causal origin of which is also NN, or (b) have some non-linguistic qualitative-indexical component that picks out NN.

This suggests that the belief-as-representer proposal might be defensible after all, provided that we do not forget that the referring component 'originator of 'LL''s use' (where 'LL' is either 'NN' itself or some co-originating name) can function as one of the members of the equivalence class of referring components attributed to someone when we say that they believe that NN is such-and-such. Indeed one would expect that such a referring component is the kind that most believers will have.

Why should someone who thinks of NN as 'the originator of 'LL''s use' ('LL' as above), but is otherwise inclined to misidentify the referent, be deemed to be possessed of a referring component that picks out NN? Why say NN is picked out, rather than the particular that gets misidentified? The relevant consideration here seems to me the relative importance of the different strands in the individual's referring component – does the individual acquire most of his or her beliefs about NN from linguistic communication involving the relevant name, or are more derived from observation and other kinds of first-hand investigation? In the latter kind of case (and remember it is a *mis*identifier that is in question) I don't in fact think we are inclined to attribute the relevant proper-name beliefs. (Imagine that John is familiar with the name 'Quine', and perhaps even knows it names a philosopher. But somehow he gets the name attached to a local academic, whom he knows well enough by sight, and indeed bumps into quite often. Do we want to say that John believes that Quine goes to the 'Dog and Duck' to play darts every Thursday?)

So the belief-as-representer suggestion can perhaps be made to stand up. How much comfort it offers the reductionist is another question. The idea, remember, is that everyday belief attributions only give us real beliefs indirectly, via a specification of the states of affairs they represent, rather than directly, via a specification of their causal roles. The picture is thus that, behind the crude attributions allowed us by ordinary language, there are more subtle distinctions amongst real psychological states. And it is at this level of more subtly distinguished real psychological states that the phenomenon of representation is to be explained and the representational powers of sentences ultimately to be accounted for.

But should we not be suspicious of this picture of subtle real beliefs lying behind the crude everyday attributions? If everyday thinking about belief proceeds naturally at the cruder level, then what good grounds are there for postulating this structure of causal roles and cognitive mechanisms behind it? One can of course construct various models along such lines, but if we are to take them seriously then surely they should relate to the practice of everyday attributions which give substance to our concepts of belief and other psychological attitudes in the first place. Are we not simply being offered an abstract framework for a reductionist position, without being shown how to fill in the pieces and make the framework do some work?

However, there is no reason why the reductionist picture of our cognitive workings should stand or fall with the range of distinctions made in everyday attributions of belief. The reductionist can perfectly well maintain the belief-as-representer account of our crude everyday practice of belief attribution, and yet argue that there are independent reasons for acknowledging the existence of finer distinctions amongst beliefs than are recognized by that practice. The English sentence 'John believes that NN is tall' may well tell us nothing about John's referring component beyond the fact that it picks out NN. But other things, in particular the idiosyncrasies of what he says and does, could still require us to distinguish between John's belief and those of others similarly describable.

My aim in the second half of this paper has been to consider how a reductionist can best analyse claims like 'John believes NN is tall'. I have argued in favour of a version of the belief-as-representer suggestion for such claims. Showing that there are distinctions amongst beliefs beyond those registered in such everyday claims is a further task for the reductionist. But there is no reason to suppose that this task will be a difficult one.

REFERENCES

Burge, T., 1979. Individualism and the Mental, in *Midwest Studies in Philosophy*, vol. IV, *Studies in Epistemology*, ed. P. French, T. Uehling, and H. Wettstein, Minneapolis: University of Minnesota Press.

Butterfield, J., 1986. Content and Context, this volume.

Davidson, D., 1984. *Inquiries into Truth and Interpretation*, Oxford: Clarendon Press.

Dennett, D., 1978. *Brainstorms*, Brighton: Harvester Press.

Dennett, D., 1981. Three Kinds of Intentional Psychology, in *Reduction, Time and Reality*, ed. R. Healey, Cambridge: Cambridge University Press.

Dennett, D., 1982. Beyond Belief, in *Thought and Object*, ed. A. Woodfield, Oxford: Clarendon Press.

Field, H., 1978. Mental Representation, *Erkenntnis 13*: 9-61.

Grandy, R.,1973. Reference, Meaning and Belief, *Journal of Philosophy 70*: 439–52.

Kripke, S., 1972. 'Naming and Necessity', in *Semantics of Natural Language*, ed. D. Davidson and G. Harman, Boston: Reidel.

Kripke, S., 1979. A Puzzle About Belief, in *Meaning and Use*, ed. A. Margalit, Boston: Reidel.

Loar, B., 1981. *Mind and Meaning*, Cambridge: Cambridge University Press.

McDowell, J., 1976. Truth Conditions, Bivalence and Verificationism, in *Truth and Meaning*, ed. G. Evans and J. McDowell, Oxford: Oxford University Press.

McDowell, J., 1980. Meaning, Communication, and Knowledge, in *Philosophical Subjects*, ed. Z. van Straaten, Oxford: Clarendon Press.

McGinn, C.,1982. The Structure of Content, in *Thought and Object*, ed. A. Woodfield, Oxford: Clarendon Press.

Papineau, D., 1984. Representation and Explanation, *Philosophy of Science 51*: 550–72.

Papineau, D., 1985. Social Facts and Psychological Facts, in *Popper and the Human Sciences*, ed. G. Currie and A. Musgrave, The Hague: Martinus Nijhoff.

Plantinga, A., 1978. The Boethian Compromise, *American Philosophical Quarterly 15*: 129–38.

Putnam, H., 1975. The Meaning of 'Meaning', in *Mind, Language and Reality*, Cambridge: Cambridge University Press.

Putnam, H.,1978. Reference and Understanding, in *Meaning and the Moral Sciences*, London: Routledge and Kegan Paul.

Schiffer, S., 1972. *Meaning*, Oxford: Oxford University Press.

Schiffer, S., 1977. Naming and Knowing, in *Midwest Studies in Philosophy*, vol. II, *Contemporary Perspectives in the Philosophy of Language*, ed. P. French, T. Uehling and H. Wettstein, Minneapolis: University of Minnesota Press.

Russellian thoughts and methodological solipsism

HAROLD W. NOONAN

In his book (1982) Gareth Evans argues for the existence of a category of what he calls *Russellian* thoughts – thoughts about a particular object, or particular objects, which would not be available to be thought at all if that object, or those objects, did not exist. He differs from Russell himself in maintaining that such thoughts can be about ordinary material objects. Hence, if Evans is right, and if reference to such thoughts is sometimes essential to the psychological explanation of intentional action, it follows that *methodological solipsism* of the type recommended by J. A. Fodor (1980) must be an error.

Methodological solipsism has also been attacked by Christopher Peacocke (1981), taking a line closely akin to that of Evans.

In what follows I defend methodological solipsism against these attacks. This does not mean that I think methodological solipsism is correct. I do not. But I think that the attacks of Evans and Peacocke are misdirected, and that mixed in with the errors of methodological solipsism is an important truth which they have failed to appreciate. The aim of this paper is to extract and defend that truth.

I

The term 'methodological solipsism' was introduced by Putnam (1975:220) for the assumption that 'no psychological state, properly so called, presupposes the existence of any individual other than the subject to whom that state is ascribed'. As Putnam goes on to say, to make this assumption is to adopt a restrictive programme – a programme which limits the scope and nature of psychology to fit certain mentalistic preconceptions, or, in some cases, to fit an idealistic reconstruction of knowledge and the world. And, he adds, only if we assume that psychological states of the type allowed by methodological solipsism (*narrow*, as opposed to *wide*, psychological states) have a significant degree of causal closure is there any point in embarking on such a programme. Of course, this must be right, but there is a further point that needs stressing. We think of our psychological states, properly so called, in particular of our propositional attitudes, as explanatory of our intentional actions. Consequently the assumption of methodological solipsism would be merely a pointless stipulation of a new meaning of the expression 'psychological state' if reference to psychological states in any but the narrow sense were ever essential to an adequate psychological explanation of an intentional action. The methodological solipsist is thus committed to believing that this is not so, and it is (a refinement of) this thesis with which I shall mainly be concerned.

There are a great many more points to be made, and distinctions drawn, for a proper understanding of methodological solipsism (see my 1980). However, I shall pass over these and come immediately to my reason for thinking that, however weakly formulated, methodological solipsism must be false. The reason, to put it in a nutshell, is simply that it seems to be a clearly intended implication of Putnam's definition of methodological solipsism that an attribution of a narrow psychological state is compatible with its subject being the only object in the world, and this is also how methodological solipsism is understood by Fodor.[1] But then the methodological solipsist thesis that only narrow psychological states need be referred to in the explanation of action must be false. For an agent's *rational* actions have to be explained by reference to his *thoughts*, but what thoughts are possible for one is not independent of the feature of one's external environment; for example, one could not have the thought 'the bank is open' in a world without banks, or money or any form of trade (cf. Geach (1980); an argument for this is given by Putnam (1981: chap. 1)).

But this, I think, is not the end of the matter. The considerations just given, and Putnam's argument in support of them, represent just one line of attack on methodological solipsism. But a quite different line of attack, explicitly employed by Evans and Peacocke and suggested by Putnam's remarks about the concept of jealousy (1975), has been far more influential. This is the argument that often, in the psychological explanation of intentional action, one has to refer to thoughts the agent has which are about the particular object to which his action is directed, and which would not be available to be thought at all if that object did not exist. But one can think methodological solipsism incorrect for the reasons already indicated and still wish to resist *this* argument. For if it is accepted it is not merely the methodological solipsist thesis already stated which has to be rejected, but a far more plausible thesis: namely, that whenever an action is directed towards a concrete, contingently existing object, other than its agent, in the sense that it is intentional under a description in which there occurs a term

---

[1] Actually, Putnam's definition of methodological solipsism is ambiguous, as pointed out in Butterfield (this volume, p. 100). But there is no reason to suppose that Putnam was aware of the ambiguity.

denoting that object, then an adequate psychological explanation of it is available under a (possibly distinct) description in which occurs a term denoting that object; and in this explanation the only psychological states of the agent referred to are ones which would also be present in a counterfactual situation in which the object did not exist. It is this thesis that I had in mind at the outset of the paper, when I referred to an important truth mixed in with the errors of methodological solipsism, and I shall devote the remainder of the paper to defending it. I shall henceforth refer to it as thesis R.

Of course, any defender of thesis R must maintain that in any explanation of a successful action there must be two components: a purely psychological component in which the relevant attitudes of the agent are cited; and a second, not purely psychological component, in which the surrounding circumstances which ensure the success of the action are described. (Perhaps this latter component need only make mention of facts sufficient to ensure the truth of those of the agent's beliefs cited in the first component; or perhaps it must mention enough to make it clear that those beliefs are actually instances of knowledge.) If the agent is acting on an object he perceives, for example, then mention of the fact that he actually perceives that object will belong to this second component. This 'two component' view of action explanation is integral to thesis R and must be kept clearly in mind in what follows.

II

The basic argument for thesis R is very straightforward. Suppose I kick a cat, and suppose my action is intentional under a description in which occurs a term denoting that cat. Then there will be a psychological explanation of my action under that description. Suppose now that this action is a counterexample to thesis R. Then there will be no psychological explanation of it under a description in which occurs a term denoting the cat which does not make essential reference to certain of my psychological states which would not exist if the cat did not exist. Imagine now a second situation in which from my point of view everything is the same but in which, in fact, I am hallucinating a cat. Since this is so I presumably lash out at the cat I believe to be within kicking distance in exactly the same way as in the first situation. The difficulty for the opponent of thesis R is now to explain *why* I do so, for if the first situation was a counterexample to thesis R some of the psychological states I was in, reference to which was essential to the explanation of my action in that situation, are not present at all in the second situation. Moreover, there need be nothing about the second situation which requires that I am there in any psychological state which in the first situation

I was not in and which can therefore provide an alternative explanation of my action. So it looks as though, if my action in the first situation was a counterexample to thesis R, my action in the second situation must be psychologically inexplicable. But this is absurd.

In order to resist this argument the opponent of thesis R has just one course. He has to deny that corresponding to any situation in which an agent acts on the basis of veridical perception there is some counterfactual situation in which (a) everything seems the same to the agent and (b) despite the fact that his perception is not veridical, he is in no psychological state which he is not in in the veridical situation. This was precisely the line taken by John McDowell in the discussion at the Thyssen conference where the original version of this paper was read. He argued that in the first situation I have an experience *of* a cat, whereas in the second situation I (merely) have an experience *as of* a cat, so that my psychological state in the second situation *is* different from my psychological state in the first. Now in a sense this is trivially true: in the second situation, but not the first, it is merely that it seems to me that I see a cat. But my psychological state in both situations can be described by omitting the 'merely' and saying that it *seems* to me that I see a cat. An obvious, and standard, explanation of the difference between the two situations, which accounts for the appropriateness of the 'merely' description in the second but not the first, is that I am in the same psychological state in both, but that the cause of this state is different in the two cases, and involves in the first, but not the second, the presence of the cat. Now McDowell can hardly deny that we do allow that the same state can be produced by different causes, so I believe that the burden of proof must be on him to explain why this cannot be so in the present case. (Of course, he cannot just accept the view that – apart from the fact that I have a Russellian thought in the first which I lack in the second – my psychological state *is* the same in the two situations. For then he has an explanatory lacuna: unless this Russellian thought is explanatorily redundant in the first situation there must be *something* occupying its role in the second one.) However, McDowell offered no positive arguments in favour of his view and none are to be found, so far as I am aware, in the relevant literature on this topic. Rather, opponents of thesis R typically concentrate on arguing that in certain cases of action based on veridical perception *only* attitudes to Russellian thoughts about the object to which the action is directed are available to explain the action. The question of what to say about the apparently possible corresponding counterfactual situation in which these attitudes are absent is then simply not addressed. But, of course, this does not mean that these arguments against thesis R can be ignored; on the contrary, no matter how strongly convinced we may be that thesis R *must* be true, unless these arguments can be answered it will remain a complete mystery how it *can* be true.

I turn, then, first to Peacocke's arguments and then to those of Evans.

III

The central claim in Peacocke (1981) is what he terms the Indispensability Thesis: 'No set of attitudes gives a satisfactory psychological explanation of a person's acting on a given object unless the content of those attitudes includes a demonstrative mode of presentation of that object.' (Peacocke is here using 'mode of presentation' in the Fregean way: a demonstrative mode of presentation is something like a Fregean sense expressed, or apt for expression, by a demonstrative singular term.)

At first sight this seems to be a far stronger claim than the mere denial of thesis R. And I think that Peacocke clearly does intend his thesis to imply that Russellian thoughts about particular objects are essential to the psychological explanation of any actions directed to those objects. Whether it does so, however, depends upon the precise nature of demonstrative modes of presentation, that is, upon whether such a mode of presentation can only be employed in thought if it has an object. Peacocke believes that this is so, but we shall consider this view of his later. First let us look at his arguments for his Indispensability Thesis.

Before presenting these Peacocke makes a distinction which provides an important clarification of the Indispensability Thesis. The point of this thesis, he asserts, is *not* that if an action is intentional *under a description* containing a demonstrative mode of presentation its psychological explanation must include some attitude with a demonstrative mode of presentation in its content. For this, he says, will hold *mutatis mutandis* for any type of mode of presentation. The point of the Indispensability Thesis is rather that if an agent acts on an object – say he picks up a container which he believes to contain pills he must take to survive – then no adequate explanation of his acting on *that object* will be possible which does not make reference to an attitude with a demonstrative mode of presentation of the object in its content. In the example of the agent picking up the container, Peacocke says, 'the explanandum is the fact that the former grasped the latter...if we say that the explanandum is the fact that *a* grasped *b* then we must note that the places occupied by '*a*' and '*b*' are transparent. The phrase 'acting on an object' in the Indispensability Thesis is shorthand for any such relational explanandum sentence of the form '*Rab* at *t*''(1981: 206).

This suggests a reformulation of the Indispensability Thesis along the following lines: whenever an action is intentional under a description in which occurs a term denoting a certain object there is no adequate explanation of it under that description, or under any description containing a term denoting that object under which it is intentional, which does not make reference in the psychological component of the explanation to an attitude with a demonstrative mode of presentation of that object in its content. (This reformulation of the Indispensability Thesis makes comparison with thesis R easier. Given the correctness of Peacocke's view that demonstrative modes of presentation of objects are only available for employment in thought given the existence of those objects, the Indispensability Thesis says that what thesis R says is *never* the case is *always* the case. It is thus a very strong claim indeed.)

Let us now look at Peacocke's arguments. The first goes as follows. Suppose someone consumes the contents of the container in front of him. Would it provide a satisfactory explanation of the agent's action merely to refer to his thought: 'The container left by the doctor has the pills I need to live' (supposing that the container left by the doctor is the container in front of him)? Clearly not, for that would not explain his acting on the container in front of him unless he also thought: 'The container left by the doctor is *that* container' where 'that container' picks out an object presented to the subject in a particular way in perception. However many descriptive modes of presentation 'the F' with which we supply the agent for his thoughts 'the F contains the pills I need', we will not supply attitudes sufficient to explain his action on the container in front of him unless the agent has a thought with the same predicate 'contains the pills I need' in which the object is presented demonstratively.

Now there is clearly a large gap in this argument. For an obvious rejoinder is that in the case in question the agent will be able to think of the container not only under the description 'the container left by the doctor', but also under other descriptive modes of presentation: in particular, as the container he can see in front of him, and as the container at a certain distance and direction from him; and reference to these thoughts *will* provide an adequate explanation of his picking up the container.

Peacocke anticipates this rejoinder, and attempts to show that neither type of descriptive thought will in fact by itself provide an adequate explanation of the agent's action. He makes two points about the first kind of descriptive thought ('the container I see contains the pills I need'). First, that it does not seem that someone has to have the concept of seeing or perception for his action on an object to be explicable. This point, I think, is clearly correct. But, by itself, of course, it does nothing to establish the Indispensability Thesis, as understood above. At most it establishes that there *are* cases in which actions directed towards particular objects, which are intentional under descriptions containing terms denoting those objects, are not explicable by reference to descriptive thoughts about those objects, but the Indispensability Thesis requires this to be so in *every* case.

Peacocke's second point about descriptive thoughts of the type 'the container I see contains the pills I need' is that they involve what he calls a *demonstrative-linked* concept: for we say that someone sees those objects of which he is in a position to have (perceptual) demonstrative thoughts. And, he argues, in a case like the one we are concerned with, someone will *be in a position* to have such thoughts only if he actually has them. So, the claim is,[2] if a descriptive thought containing a demonstrative-linked concept is available to explain action on an object, this can only be because a demonstrative thought about the object is available to the agent. Consequently, a full explanation of the action will have to refer to the latter, and so the Indispensability Thesis is established.

Now it does seem that Peacocke is right to call seeing a demonstrative-linked concept. But though this suggests that, in *this* case, a full explanation of the action upon the object will have to refer to the agent's demonstrative thoughts about the latter, or at least refer to the fact that the agent perceives it, which entails the availability to him of such thoughts, nevertheless examination of this one example cannot show that this is true of *all* actions upon objects, as the Indispensability Thesis requires.

Moreover, the example does not in fact even provide an *illustration* of the Indispensability Thesis, as interpreted above. For Peacocke provides no reason to suppose that any such demonstrative thought will have to be referred to in the *psychological* component of the explanation of the agent's action, but this is what the Indispensability Thesis requires. (Indeed, Peacocke gives no argument for supposing that any such demonstrative thought will have to be *referred* to at all, since the most he makes plausible is that in order to explain the success of the action reference will have to be made to *the fact that* the agent perceives the object and so has available to him demonstrative thoughts about it.)

But let us turn now to the second type of descriptive thought Peacocke considers, one containing a descriptive mode of presentation such as 'the object roughly 2 yards away at an 11 o'clock angle to the trunk of my body'. Peacocke's first point about this type of thought is that it will not provide a satisfactory explanation of an agent's action unless he has an adequate knowledge of the relevant units of measurement – unless, for example, he can indicate what a yard is with his hands or by pacing. If he lacks such

---

[2] Or must be. I confess that Peacocke's reasoning at this point is not clear to me. The conclusion he actually draws is merely that 'every descriptive thought which might be alleged as a counter-example to the Indispensability Thesis either makes use of a demonstrative-linked concept or is not sufficient to explain action' – and even this is in fact put forward solely as a conjecture. But Peacocke nowhere indicates that he thinks the Indispensability Thesis too strong, so I think that he must be interpreted as in the text.

knowledge it will still be possible for him to have such a thought, just as I can have a thought about the price of an item in new Israeli shekels, but reference to it will not explain his action.

More often, someone who has a thought with this type of descriptive content will have an adequate knowledge of the relevant unit of measurement, but this, Peacocke says, will be because his thought now contains demonstrative components, demonstrative modes of presentation of distances, directions, angles, measurements and places in his immediate environment, and so this type of case is not a counterexample to the Indispensability Thesis.

Of course, this looks to be just a mistake. For in such a case only the location of the object will be demonstratively presented, not the objective itself. And so, if thoughts with such a content can explain action, does that not in itself refute the Indispensability Thesis?

Peacocke argues that it does not. For, he says, in the example he gives, we have to distinguish between explaining action on the container and explaining action at the location of the container – even if the action is doing something to the container at that location. The explananda '*a* consumes the contents of *b*' and '*a* consumes the contents of whatever container is at location *c*' are distinct even if *b* is the container at location *c*. The point at which we have just arrived in saying that a place is demonstratively presented and that that is sufficient for action commits us only to saying that such demonstrative thoughts about places can explain the second of these explananda, not the first.

But it is hard to see how this reply of Peacocke's can be adequate in view of his earlier insistence that in any relational explanandum sentence '*Rab* at *t*', the places occupied by '*a*' and '*b*' are transparent, and that the Indispensability Thesis is a very different matter from the trivial claim that if an action is intentional *under a description* containing a demonstrative mode of presentation, its psychological explanation must include some attitude with a demonstrative mode of presentation in its content. However, Peacocke goes on to give an argument for the distinctness of the explananda '*a* consumes the contents of *b*' and '*a* consumes the contents of whatever container is at location *c*'; so let us look at his argument.

He imagines a case in which someone hallucinates a container at location *c*, when in fact there is a container there, and argues that in this case, unlike the case in which the agent actually sees the container, his attitudes cannot explain his acting on the object, but only his reaching out to the place. But is Peacocke right about this?

Admittedly, he has a point. In a sense, of course, one can give an explanation of the agent's acting on the container in the hallucinatory situation, but in another sense one cannot. For it is coincidental that the container is where he hallucinates one, and there is a sense in which coincidences have no explanations. In the same way, in a sense one can give an explanation of a meteor's hitting a pond on landing, but in another sense one cannot, since it will be coincidental that the meteor lands where the pond is located. But the question we need to consider is whether the *only* explanation of the fact that the agent's action in the hallucinatory situation is not explicable in the same way as in the veridical situation is that he lacks certain demonstrative thoughts in the former situation which he possesses in the latter.

But this does not seem to be so. Rather, the difference seems to be merely that in the one situation the agent has an accidentally true belief whilst in the other he possesses knowledge; and our unhappiness in saying without qualification that the hallucinator's action on the container is explicable is merely an instance of a general unhappiness we would feel about claiming that accidentally true belief can provide as adequate an explanation of successful action as knowledge. If so, however, since the very same thing can be both known and believed, nothing about the example excludes the possibility that in both the veridical and the hallucinatory situation the agent has demonstrative thoughts about the container, and that the difference between the two situations is merely that in the former but not the latter, he knows these thoughts to be true.

Consequently the example does nothing to support the claim that there is a type of explanation of object-directed action to which it is essential that the objects acted on be thought of demonstratively. That is, it does nothing to suggest a sense of 'explanation of action' under which the Indispensability Thesis is true. I conclude, then, that Peacocke's arguments do not establish his Indispensability Thesis.

But even if they did so they would not necessarily refute thesis R. For, as noted at the beginning of this section, the Indispensability Thesis is incompatible with thesis R only if demonstrative modes of presentation are Russellian, that is, available for employment in thought only if they have an object. Peacocke believes this to be so. But what he says about demonstrative modes of presentation provides no support for this belief.

Demonstrative modes of presentation, he says – more precisely, token demonstrative modes of presentation – are obtained by indexing a type mode of presentation by an object. If Δ is a type mode of presentation Peacocke uses $[\Delta_x]$ to symbolise the token mode of presentation got by indexing the type mode of presentation by the object x. A type mode of presentation, then, can be represented as a function mapping objects onto token modes of presentation. This *may* tempt one, and, I believe, does tempt Peacocke, to think that a token mode of presentation of an object would not be available for employment in thought unless its object existed; however, this conclusion would obviously be unwarranted, for a type mode of presentation can also be represented as a function mapping pairs of thinkers and times onto token modes of presentation. As Peacocke himself writes 'a token mode of presentation is determined by the type Δ together with [thinker] x and [time] t: one could equally write '$[\Delta_{x,t}]$' for a token mode of presentation, so that if $R(x,y,t)$ [i.e. person x is capable of thinking of object y at time t under the type mode of presentation Δ] , then $[\Delta_y] = [\Delta_{x,t}]$' (1981:196). However, in many cases it would evidently be absurd to regard the token mode of presentation $[\Delta_{x,t}]$ as dependent for its existence on the existence of the pair $\langle x,t\rangle$. Indeed, Peacocke himself is clearly aware of this and for this reason explicitly warns us against taking the notion of a token mode of presentation too literally. Yet nothing else he says about demonstrative modes of presentation gives the slightest appearance of providing support for the view that they are Russellian. Consequently, even if his arguments did establish the Indispensability Thesis they would leave thesis R quite untouched. But let us see now whether the same is true of Gareth Evans' arguments.

IV

What has emerged very clearly from the discussion so far, I think, is that the crucial point at issue between opponents and defenders of thesis R must be whether demonstrative modes of presentation are Russellian. For it should now be fairly obvious that cases can be imagined in which an agent's action is directed towards an object which he can identify in no other way – in fact, I shall describe such a case in a moment. And so, if demonstrative modes of presentation are Russellian, this refutes thesis R.

That demonstrative modes of presentation are Russellian is the main concern of chapter 6 of Evans' book (1982). He uses the term 'mode of identification', not 'mode of presentation', because of his views (discussed below) about the connection between thinking about an object and being able to identify it. From now on I shall follow his terminology. I shall argue that, because he ignores the possibility of a mode of identification which is neither descriptive nor Russellian (a possibility which it is plausible to think is illustrated not only by demonstrative, but also by recognition based modes of identification) Evans fails to make out his case.

Before getting involved with details of Evans' arguments, however, I shall, as promised, describe a case in which an agent's action is directed towards an object which he can only identify demonstratively. Suppose, then that one is looking at an array of tightly packed, qualitatively indistinguishable pills (the example is Evans'; I gave a similar one in my 1980). One concentrates on a particular pill, entertains some thought about it and reaches out to grasp it. Clearly one can have no way of identifying it in terms of its appearance, for it looks exactly like all the others. Nor need one be able to identify it by its position in the array – say, as the twenty-ninth pill from the right in the fifteenth row from the top. Nor need one know its distance and direction from oneself sufficiently accurately for it to be possible for one to identify its location as the place at that distance in that direction – which would then enable one to identify it non-circularly as the pill at that location. For as Evans writes: 'in the absence of an object to anchor our dispositions we can make only rather gross discriminations of areas or regions in egocentric space. Try to concentrate upon a pill-sized region in a white wall in front of you: even if you keep looking, do you have any confidence at the end of fifteen seconds, that you are still looking at the same region you began with? The Idea of [i.e. capacity to identify] a point p in egocentric space, precise enough to be adequate to individuate the pill, exists only because there is something at p – the pill – for the subject's perception to latch on to' (1982:172–3).

One might think it is possible to identify the pill using what Peacocke calls a demonstrative-linked concept, but actually in a case of this kind this will not be so. For one perceives not just the pill to which one is attending but also those surrounding it. Of course, *that* one is the only one to which one is *attending*. But there are at least two objections to the idea that this can provide a descriptive mode of identification, available in every case in which there would otherwise be available only a demonstrative mode of identification of an object, and whose availability in any case is adequate to ensure that the case is not a counterexample to thesis R even if demonstrative modes of identification are Russellian. For, first, the concept of attention is surely too sophisticated to be necessarily available to every agent capable of object-directed thoughts. And secondly, even if I *can* also pick out an object I can identify demonstratively as 'the one I am attending to', any action directed to that object will still be a counterexample to thesis R if demonstrative modes of identification are Russellian and I can identify the object in no other way. For I surely cannot think of some object as 'the one I am attending to' without believing that I can identify it in some other way: that is, 'the one I am attending to' is a *parasitic* mode of identification. So while I can *entertain* a thought of the form 'the one I am attending to is so-and-so' without believing anything of the form 'the one I am attending to is X' where 'X' is some other mode of identification, I cannot have any *belief* of the first form without also having a belief of the second form.

So we must take the bull by the horns and seek to understand how demonstrative modes of identification, while non-descriptive, are neverthe-less non-Russellian. It will be easiest to see how this can be so if we first look at what Evans calls 'recognition-based' modes of identification, that is, modes of identification one can employ only because one has a capacity to identify the relevant object when presented with it, which he also claims to be Russellian. Admittedly, this claim poses no immediate threat to thesis R. For it cannot be argued in the case of recognition-based modes of identification, as it can in the case of demonstrative modes of identification, that one sometimes directs one's actions to objects which one can identify in no other non-parasitic way.

But there are two reasons for considering recognition-based modes of identification. First, we can argue that they, like demonstrative modes, are non-Russellian; so they provide an analogy for the demonstrative case.

Secondly, the common-sense idea that attitudes to thoughts involving recognition-based modes of identification can explain action requires such modes to be non-Russellian. For in many cases the attitudes which have to be cited to explain action on an object appear to be ones formed *consequently* upon possession of attitudes containing a recognition-based mode of identification of it.

But if such modes are Russellian this cannot be so. For then when an agent is mistaken in thinking that he has a recognitional capacity targeted on a unique object he will not be able to employ the recognitional mode of identification of that object he supposes to be available to him. Consequently he will not have the attitudes he thinks he has involving that mode of identification. So the attitudes involved in the immediate explanation of his action will *not* be ones formed consequently upon his possession of such attitudes. But such a situation may differ from one in which he has such attitudes only in ways of which he is quite unaware; in particular it need not be one in which he has any other attitudes. So even in the case in which he does have attitudes involving a recognition-based mode of identification of an object it appears that they must be explanatorily redundant if such modes are Russellian. For his having them will not need to be involved either in the immediate explanation of the action itself, or in the explanation of his acquisition of the attitudes which are involved in the immediate explanation of the action.

In chapter 8 of his book, however, Evans argues that recognitional modes of identification are Russellian. He writes:

several philosophers have been prepared to allow that a recognitional capacity can be the basis of an adequate Idea of an object. But, typically, these philosophers have not been sympathetic to a broadly Russellian conception of reference. They seem to think that Ideas of this kind can be treated just like those involving descriptive identification – at least in that someone can possess an Idea of this kind whether or not there is anything of which it is an Idea...But it is not by any means obvious that this is correct. It is difficult to see what could be the content of a thought which purported to rest upon a recognitional capacity, if there was no unique object which the subject was (or at least had been) disposed, in the exercise of the purported capacity, to identify. (1982: 284–5).

But we cannot usefully consider whether Evans is right about this without first looking in more detail at what he thinks recognition-based modes of identification *are*.

In fact two competing accounts are suggested, one in the body of chapter 8 and one in the appendix to that chapter in which John McDowell attempts to reconstruct some of Evans' second thoughts. According to the first a recognition-based mode of identification is wholly non-descriptive and one's ability to employ it in thought depends entirely upon one's possession of a uniquely targeted recognitional capacity. According to the second, a recognition-based mode of identification is one, the capacity to employ which is what Evans calls a 'mixed Idea': it contains the descriptive component 'which I met', which determines the possible targets for the recognitional capacity upon which it rests.

A major difficulty with the first account, as Evans recognises, is that it needs to be backed up by an explanation of how it can be irrelevant to the question whether someone's capacity to recognise a particular individual, as opposed to a kind, is uniquely targeted, whether there is tucked away somewhere in the universe (on a distant Twin Earth, say) an individual he could not distinguish from its unique target. For we certainly do think of ourselves as able to have thoughts about the particular individuals we have met in virtue of our capacity to recognize them; and we do *not* think that our ability to do so is contingent upon the non-existence, anywhere in the universe, of individuals we would confuse with ones we have met.

To deal with this difficulty Evans introduces the idea of the 'relevant area of search'. He illustrates this with the following example. Suppose I am watching some sheep on a hill, and see one of them cough. Then without keeping my eye on that sheep I can have thoughts about it, at least for a short time, in virtue of my capacity to pick it out from all the other sheep *on the hill*. It may be that on the next hill there is a sheep which I could not tell apart from it, but this does not mean that I do not have a recognitional capacity targeted on the unique sheep on my hill which coughed, since I *can* distinguish it from all the other sheep on *my* hill, and sheep on the next hill do not need to be considered – they are outside the relevant area of search. This is the area, Evans tells us, such that I am disposed to identify an object as the relevant sheep, provided it presents a suitable appearance within it. Its extent is a function of my estimate of the probability and speed of movement, and the time that had elapsed since the last sighting, and it will centre upon the estimated position of the last sighting (1982; 279–81).

In outline, then, this is how Evans suggests that we can regard a recognition-based mode of identification as wholly non-descriptive, while doing justice to our intuition that employment of such a mode of identification can enable us to focus our thoughts on a particular individual even if there are, quite unknown to us, perfect duplicates scattered about in distant corners of the universe.

Evans allows that with the introduction of a duplicate into the relevant area of search the recognitional capacity underlying such a non-descriptive wholly recognition-based mode of identification will be rendered ineffective. However, in such circumstances, he says, there will necessarily be a fall-back mode of identification available to the subject – one which is only partly recognition-based and contains as well some such descriptive element as 'which I met'. It is this which it is suggested in the appendix to the chapter is not merely a fall-back, but the usual mode of identification available to a thinking subject when his ability to think about a particular object depends upon his capacity to recognise it.

And, in fact it seems that the view put forward in the appendix should be accepted. The relevant area of search that Evans speaks of is determined by what the subject *believes*: it is, roughly speaking, the smallest area within which he is confident the relevant object can be found provided that he believes that it contains no perfect duplicates. Yet Evans says that in the case of a man one has not seen in a long while one can think of him by employing a wholly recognition-based mode of identification even though the area of search may be very large, perhaps encompassing the entire planet.

But I hope the error in this is obvious. *I* certainly believe that it is immensely likely that somewhere on the Earth there are look-alikes of the people I know whom I would not be able to tell apart from them by sight. Hence in the case of someone I have not seen for many years and who, for all I know, may now be living in America, or Australia or Africa, there is no area which is the smallest within which I am confident he would be found and in which I believe there to be no perfect duplicate. I can, of course, still think about my long-lost acquaintance, but not because I have available any purely recognition-based mode of identification of him. And, I think, the same is true of people with whom I have not lost contact in this kind of way: perhaps there are, in the area in which I live, people who are sufficiently similar to my friends and acquaintances for it to be difficult for me to tell them apart on sight. And so I doubt that I *do* have, in the case of each of my friends and acquaintances, a recognitional capacity uniquely targeted on him – even given that for this to be so I need only to be able to distinguish him from everyone else in the perhaps quite modestly sized area in which I confidently expect he can always be found.

But this does not mean that I am not able to entertain thoughts about my friends and acquaintances, or even that I can only do so, when not in their presence, by employing purely descriptive modes of identification. All it means is that I do not think of them by employing purely recognition-based modes of identification. And, indeed, why should I be expected to do so? Someone about whom it is true only that I would know him again if I saw him is hardly a friend or even an acquaintance. Evans suggests (1982:280 with 283, fn 23) that pieces of domestic equipment and furniture are typically thought of by the exercise of 'mixed Ideas' – capacities to employ modes of identification which are partly recognition-based and partly descriptive. And I do not see why one's friends should be any different in this respect from one's furniture.

This is not to say, of course, that it is impossible to employ a purely recognition-based mode of identification of an object in thought, but only that it is not, as Evans suggests in the body of chapter 8, the general rule. In particular, I see no difficulty with the idea that our modes of identification of places and stationary objects can be wholly recognition-based: the difficulty with people is that they move, so that one can very soon become doubtful whether the minimal region in which one confidently believes they can be found does not also contain look-alikes. Places and stationary objects are, however, the exception to the rule, and even in their case 'mixed Ideas' will be available.

Let us take it then that the usual recognition-based mode of identification of an object is only partly recognition-based. If one thinks of an object by employing such a mode of identification one's thought about it will contain such descriptive components as 'whom I encountered', 'who plays chess', 'who lives in place P', 'who is called "Jones"' – and these descriptive components will be essential to the individuating capacity of the mode of identification into which they enter. Now is such a (partly) recognition-based mode of identification Russellian, as Evans claims?

Well, clearly such a mode of identification is not wholly descriptive, but the same is of course true of *wholly* recognition-based modes of identification and, as McDowell points out in the appendix to chapter 8, it is difficult to see why such a mode of identification must be Russellian merely on that account. As McDowell writes, 'One might say, a recognitional capacity is a disposition to respond in certain ways to an object on the basis of its appearance (the basis being agreed not to be capturable in a description), and surely someone could have such a disposition even if no object capable of presenting the triggering appearance had ever existed – it could still be true that if an object were to present the requisite appearance it *would* activate the disposition' (1982: 301). Equally, it seems, someone's recognitional capacity could cease to be uniquely targeted – by the movement of duplicates into the relevant area of search – without any alteration in his disposition. It thus seems very difficult to see why a wholly recognition-based mode of identification could not be available for employment in thought even if it had never had a unique object, or why such a mode of identification could not remain available for such employment even after it had ceased to have such an object. Of course, these things must be true if wholly recognition-based modes of identification are Russellian, but as McDowell notes, Evans argues only that such modes of identification are not descriptive and this leaves the crucial question begged.

I shall take it then, in line with McDowell's comments in the appendix, that wholly recognition-based modes of identification are non-Russellian. What then of only partly recognition-based modes of identification containing an additional descriptive component? McDowell appears to think that, unlike purely recognition-based modes of identification, these are Russellian; but it is very hard to see why. The descriptive component of such a mode of identification can be thought of as restricting the area of search – to those people I have met, or those who play chess, or those named 'Jones', and the mode of identification will then be a mode of identification of a unique individual if the thinker is disposed to identify that individual alone, of all those in the area of search, as the relevant one. If in fact there never was, or has ceased to be, a unique such individual, the thinker's disposition is unaffected, and, as in the case of wholly recognition-based thoughts, it seems that this is enough to ensure that he can think the very thoughts – containing the partly descriptive mode of identification in question as a constituent – which he could think if his disposition was uniquely targeted.

I conclude, then, that recognition-based modes of identification – whether wholly or only partly so – need not be thought of as Russellian, and thus that the conflict with common-sense envisaged above does not arise.

Now, as I said previously, I have argued this partly because I think it provides an indication of the way in which it can be argued that demonstrative modes of identification need not be Russellian. Just as the recognitional capacity underlying a recognition-based mode of identification of an object can be identified with a disposition which can be possessed whether or not it is targeted on one unique object, so the capacity to employ a particular demonstrative mode of identification of an object can rest upon a disposition which can be possessed whether or not that object exists. Whether I actually see an array of pills or merely hallucinate one, then, I am capable of thinking the very same thoughts, since when my perception is veridical and I concentrate on one of the pills and think some demonstrative thought about it my thought has the *content* it has because of what I am disposed to do – which would be the same if I were hallucinating or not – and it is a thought *about* the particular pill I am attending to because it is that pill on which, in fact, my dispositions are uniquely targeted.

This, then, is the way in which I wish to argue for the non-Russellian character of demonstrative modes of identification. It remains to provide an account of the type of disposition underlying a demonstrative mode of identification of an object which makes it clear how such a disposition can exist whether or not it is uniquely targeted.

An example Evans gives can be elaborated to make it clear what is needed here. Evans argues that it is not a sufficient condition of an object being a possible object of a subject's demonstrative thought that there exist an information link between the subject and the object, that is, that the object be the causal source of information the subject receives (1932: 145f). For, he claims, to think of an object demonstratively one must know what it is for an arbitrary proposition of the form 'that A is identical with B' to be true, where 'that A' is the demonstrative mode of identification one employs and 'B' is a fundamental mode of identification of an object, that is, in the case of spatio-temporal objects, a mode of identification of an object in terms of its location at a time. That is, to think of an object of type A demonstratively one must know what it is for that A to be at a particular place and time. But, he argues, the mere existence of an information link between oneself and an object cannot provide one with this knowledge. For then there would be only one possible account of what it was for one's thought 'that A is identical with B' to be true, namely that B was the object which was causally responsible for the information one was receiving. But to think of an object demonstratively is *not* to think of it as the causal source of one's information, or even to be capable of such a notion. So in this case one would not necessarily know what it would be for 'that $A = B$' to be true; that is, one would not necessarily know what it would be for that A to be at a particular place and time.

To bring home the absurdity of this Evans suggests that we consider the case of a savage confronted for the first time with a radio set. *We* will naturally refer to people we hear on the radio using demonstrative expressions; but, Evans argues, our thoughts about them are nevertheless not demonstrative thoughts, but thoughts about them *as* inputs to the information channel in question. Now Evans supposes that the savage, at first convinced that there is a little man inside the radio, similarly attempts to identify the man he thinks he can hear in the standard demonstrative way. But unlike us, the thought of the relevant information channel is not in the backgound to his thinking and he is totally mystified by the apparatus when it is explained to him and cannot grasp the idea that he might be perceiving someone very distant from him in space (and perhaps in time).

In this case, Evans argues, he cannot be credited with any thoughts at all – demonstrative or otherwise – about the man he is in fact listening to, for he simply has no idea what it could be for someone to be *that man* (the man he hears); but if the mere existence of an information link between a subject and an object were a sufficient condition of the subject's being capable of demonstrative thoughts about the object this would not be so.

All this, I take it, is entirely convincing. But it is an implication of the thesis that demonstrative modes of identification are Russellian that the savage in Evans' example does not merely give expression to no thought *about* the man he in fact hears when he says 'that man is...' but gives expression to no demonstrative thought at all. And this is far less convincing. For it seems very hard to deny that there is *something* in common between this case and the case in which in fact the savage is under no misapprehension, since there *is* a little man in the radio who is causally responsible for the sounds he hears, and hard also to deny that *one* thing in common is that the savage is capable of exactly the same thoughts in both situations. But the latter case is one in which Evans would be happy to allow the savage demonstrative thoughts about the man in the box.

Again it seems hard to deny that these two cases have something in comon with a case in which there is a little man in the box who is, however, unseen and unheard by the savage; and hard also to deny that one thing in common between all these cases is that in each the savage is capable of exactly the same thoughts. But granted that demonstrative thoughts are not descriptive, the only way to argue for this plausible view is to provide an account of the common disposition possessed by the subject in the three cases which underlies his capacity to employ the particular demonstrative mode of identification which is a constituent of the demonstrative thoughts he is plausibly capable of in all of them.

This task is made easier by Evans' discussion of thoughts about egocentrically identified places. In the case of such a thought, Evans argues (1982:155f), the subject's dispositions are crucial both in determining the content of his thought and in determining its object. What makes a thought a thought that 'it is F up there to the left' rather than the thought 'it is F a bit behind me' or 'to my right' or 'down on the left' is that the subject is disposed to a certain type of action if he has a thought of the first type (and desires to direct an action at the place he is thinking of) which he is not disposed to if he has a thought of one of the other types.

One might think that the type of action in question can be characterised as one resulting in one of a certain variety of arrangements of the subject's limbs. But in fact this will not do, as Evans (following Taylor) makes clear. To obey the command 'bring your left arm down' when I am standing with my hands above my head may result in precisely the same arrangement of my limbs as obeying the command 'bring your left arm up' when I am doing a handstand. So we cannot distinguish the thought 'up there it is F' from the thought 'down there it is F' by associating with each a class of action types characterised in the way suggested above, since the classes will then have a common member.

Rather, I think, we need to invoke the idea of the normal posture of the kind of animal the subject is. We can then say that the subject has a thought with the content 'up there it is F' if, given that he desires to direct an action to the place he is thinking of, and his posture is normal, he is disposed to an action resulting in one of a certain variety of arrangements of his limbs, or, if his posture is not normal, he is disposed to an action directed towards a place to which his action *would* be directed if his posture were normal and he were to perform an action of a type he would then be disposed to if he had a thought of the form 'up there it is F'.

Dispositions to action also enter the Evans' account of what makes a place the object of those of a subject's thoughts which involve a particular egocentric mode of identification (1982:161). This is so, he argues, if he is disposed to treat certain perceptions from that place as immediately germane to the evaluation and appreciation of those thoughts and to direct actions towards that place when thoughts involving that mode of identification, together with other circumstances, indicate that this is a good thing to do.

Now Evans emphasises that a subject may entertain a thought about a place under an egocentric mode of identification (or, as he puts it, entertain a thought about a position in egocentric space) even if he is not currently receiving any information from the place (1982:161). For he may still be disposed to treat perceptions from that place as immediately germane to the evaluation of his thought, and to direct actions towards that place when it seems good to him to direct actions towards the place his egocentric mode of identification identifies; and this complex dispositional connection with the place is enough to ensure that his thought is a thought about the place. But this gives rise to the possibility of a situation in which a subject thinks egocentrically about such a place, that is, one from which he is not currently receiving any information, while receiving information from another place which he mistakenly believes to be information from the place he is thinking about. For example, someone might be fitted, unbeknownst to himself, with a pair of earphones, so that the sounds he in fact hears, and which seem to him to be occurring in his vicinity, are in fact being transmitted from some place far distant. But his thought 'It's noisy here' will still be a thought about the place where he is, because it is that place, and not the distant one, with which he maintains the dispositional connection. Again, someone on the mainland may have television pictures of the seabed transmitted to him in such a way that he is deceived into thinking that what he views is happening just a few feet away. His thought 'It's mucky there' will not be a thought about the place on the seabed he is in fact perceiving, but a thought about the place nearby on the mainland, since it will be this place on which his dispositions are targeted. (Actually Evans appears to distinguish the two cases. He says of the former: 'the deluded subject's 'here'-thoughts will be false thoughts about where he is' (1982:188), but of the latter: 'we would not need to say his thought concerned [the place on the mainland]: this is a case of a thought which is not well-grounded' (1982:165). This distinction seems to be unfounded, since the subject's thought is well-grounded in neither case. But what is indisputable is that Evans allows that in both cases the subject has thoughts containing egocentric modes of identification of places, just as he thinks he has, whether or not these are correctly describable as thoughts *about* or *concerning* the place his dispositions are targeted on.)

Now there is an obvious parallel between these two cases and the case I described of the savage listening to the radio and taking the sounds he hears to be produced by a little man inside the set when there is in fact a little man inside the set, who, however, is not producing the sounds. But Evans is committed to treating them as radically unlike. The deluded subject's 'here'-thoughts, he says of the case of the man in the undetected earphones, are false thoughts about the place where he is. But he is committed to saying of the deluded savage not only that he does not have demonstrative thoughts *about* the little man sitting silently inside the radio, but that he has in fact no demonstrative thoughts of the type he takes himself to have at all.

But this, I submit, is unwarranted. The case of the savage is in fact an example of a type of situation Evans envisages at a point in his argument where he is trying to emphasise the similarity between egocentric modes of identification of places and demonstrative modes of identification of material objects. 'Conceivably,' he says, 'one might be so related to a material object that one is disposed to treat information from it as peculiarly relevant to certain sorts of thoughts about it, even though at present one has no information from it' (1982:169). But, he argues, it is not possible in general to *know* that one is dispositionally so related to an object one is not perceiving. 'Places, however, being – how shall we say? – so much thicker on the ground than objects, a subject cannot fail to have a single place as the target of his 'here'-dispositions at an instant' (1982:169). Granted this difference between material objects and places, however, I fail to see how it can justify denying that when one *is* dispositionally so related to an object from which one is receiving no information the existence of this disposition makes it possible for one to have demonstrative thoughts of the type of which one thinks oneself capable, in just the way in which, according to Evans himself, dispositions targeted on a particular location can be the basis of egocentric spatial thoughts.

I think that Evans would reply that it is a consequence of this difference that if one is merely dispositionally related to a material object and is capable of thinking demonstratively about it then *one will not know which object one's demonstrative mode of identification identifies*, since one will not know that it identifies any; whereas this will not be so for egocentric thoughts about places from which one is receiving no information. Now it does seem correct to say that it is a necessary condition of one's having a demonstrative thought about an object or an egocentric thought about a place that one knows which object or place one is thinking of. But unless it is simply assumed that all demonstrative thoughts must be thoughts *about* particular objects, this is irrelevant to the question at issue, which is whether the *mere existence* of a demonstrative thought requires an actual information link – as opposed to a merely dispositional connection – between its thinker and a suitable object.

In fact, reflection on Evans' example of the man taken in by television pictures of the seabed provides support for a negative answer to this question. Let us elaborate the case a little. Suppose that the television screen fills one entire wall in the room the man occupies, and he believes that there is an aquarium on the other side. Coincidentally, there is. He takes the television screen to be a mere plate of plain glass, and so takes himself to be viewing the aquarium. Now Evans will allow that he can think such thoughts as 'there is a large rock over there', in virtue of his dispositional connections with locations in the aquarium, and even that these thoughts can be described as being *about* locations in the aquarium. But he will not allow that he can think such thoughts as 'that rock over there is a large one'. But it seems arbitrary to make such a distinction between the cases.

Of course, it seems wrong to say that the man's thought 'that rock over there is a large one' *concerns* or is *about* a rock in the aquarium if coincidentally there is a rock where there appears to him to be one. But this is irrelevant to the question of the *existence* of the thought. Admittedly we do not need to speak of the coincidence that there is a place in the aquarium where the deceived subject seems to see one, as we have to speak of the coincidence that there is a rock in the aquarium where he seems to see one. But this is merely a consequence of the fact that places *are* so much thicker on the ground than objects. And, so far as I can see, this is simply an irrelevance when what is in question is finding a justification for denying that our subject has the demonstrative thoughts he thinks he has while simultaneously allowing him the egocentric thoughts about places he thinks he has.

I conclude, then, that the distinction Evans wishes to draw is unwarranted and that a suitable dispositional connection with an object can be the ground of demonstrative thoughts even if one is receiving no information from that object. This is not yet to say, of course, that demonstrative thoughts are non-Russellian, but that conclusion now lies very close to hand. For in the case we have been considering it is a mere coincidence that there is in fact a rock where the subject's dispositions are targeted. But whether such a coincidence obtains can hardly make the difference between being capable of a demonstrative thought and being incapable of such a thought.

Demonstrative thoughts, then, are non-Russellian. One is capable of such a thought if there is an object with which one has a suitable dispositional connection, and this may be so whether or not one is currently receiving information from that object. And one may have exactly the same dispositions even if there is no object which is their target. The dispositions, then, cannot be described as dispositions concerning a certain object, to direct actions towards it and to evaluate one's thought in the light of information received from it. Rather, if one's demonstrative thought seems to one to be a thought about a stationary object, they will be dispositions, concerning a certain place, to direct actions to whatever object of a certain type is located there, and to evaluate one's thought in the light of information received from it. These are the two types of disposition the savage confronted with the radio has in all three versions of the story. If one's demonstrative thought seems to one to be a thought about a moving object there will be no *one* place which will be the target of one's dispositions over time, rather a sequence of places; but one's dispositions-at-a-moment will be the same as in the former case.

It is a consequence of this account of the dispositions underlying a demonstrative thought that such a thought, when it has an object, will be as much a thought about a place (or a connected series of places) as about an object, and can be a thought about a place even when it is not a thought about an object. I think that this is an advantage of the account. Consider again the case in which one hallucinates an array of pills and reaches out to grasp one of them. If one's reaching out to the place to which one does reach out, that is, the precise place where it seems to one that the pill one is attending to is located, is psychologically explicable, one must have some thought *about* that place. But one need not be able to identify it by its position in egocentric space or by any description. So unless one's demonstrative thought 'that pill...', though not a thought about any pill, is nevertheless a thought about the place at which it seems to one that there is a pill then one *will* have no thought about the place one in fact reaches out to, and one's action *will* be psychologically inexplicable.[3]

But if a demonstrative thought is always a thought about a place, whether or not it is a thought about an object, what makes it a *demonstrative* thought – a thought containing a demonstrative mode of presentation of an object as a constituent – when there is an object at the place thought about? In other words, what distinguishes thoughts containing demonstrative modes of presentation of objects as constituents from thoughts merely containing egocentric modes of presentation of places at which there happen to be objects? A partial answer is implicit in what has just been said. One need not know with any precision where an object one can identify demonstratively actually is. If so one will lack dispositions to action one would possess if one had a thought containing a precise egocentric mode of identification of the place occupied by the object one is in fact thinking of demonstratively. But this answer is incomplete, for it does not apply to the distinction between a thought of the form 'that thing over there is F' and one of the form 'over there is something F', where 'over there' is a precise egocentric mode of identification.

The real distinction between demonstrative thoughts and egocentric thoughts about places, I think, is that one cannot have a demonstrative thought without one's having information – its seeming to one – that one's thought has an object, while one can have an egocentric thought about a place even though one has no information that there is an object at the place. (Since one need not believe that things are as they seem, that is, one need not accept the deliverances of one's information system, this does not entail that one must believe that one's demonstrative thought has an object and so does not entail that as Evans suggests (1982:352), it is impossible to assent to such a statement as 'That little green man does not exist' construed as the negation of the basic existential statement 'That little green man does exist'.) In other words, unless a subject is in receipt of information that there is an object at a certain place it is not possible for him to stand in the sort of dispositional connection with the place which can ground a demonstrative thought, but a subject can be dispositionally linked to a place in the way required for an egocentric thought about it whether or not he is in receipt of information that there is an object at the place. So demonstrative thoughts are information-based in a way that is not true of egocentric thoughts about places, just as Evans says, but it does not follow from this that they are Russellian.

[3] If this is right, of course, it supports Evans' inclination to describe egocentric thoughts based on merely dispositional links with places as thoughts *about* those places, against his inclination to deny that this is appropriate.

REFERENCES

Butterfield, J., 1986. Content and Context, this volume.

Evans, G., 1982. *The Varieties of Reference*, Oxford: Clarendon Press.

Fodor, J. A., 1980. Methodological Solipsism Considered as a Research Strategy in Cognitive Psychology, *The Behavioural and Brain Sciences 3*:63–73.

Geach, P. T., 1980. Some Remarks on Representations, *The Behavioural and Brain Sciences 3*:80–1.

Noonan, H., 1980. Methodological Solipsism, *Philosophical Studies 40*:269–74.

Peacocke, C., 1981. Demonstrative Thought, *Synthese 49*: 187–217.

Putnam, H., 1975. The Meaning of 'Meaning', in *Mind, Language and Reality*, Cambridge: University Press.

Putnam, H., 1981. *Reason, Truth and History*, Cambridge: University Press.

Content and context*

JEREMY BUTTERFIELD

I. INTRODUCTION

In this paper, I develop a conception of the content of utterances and propositional attitudes that combines some ideas of Perry (1977; 1979), Lewis (1979), Stalnaker (1978; 1981) and Evans (1981; 1982). I confine myself, as do Lewis and Stalnaker, to a coarse-grained conception of content, corresponding roughly to the standard view of a content as a set of possible worlds – viz. the worlds in which the content is true. My main debt to Perry is for his arguments that this standard view of coarse-grained content needs revising to allow for contents with a relativized truth-value. Lewis also accepts the need for revision, and he proposes that for attitudes a content is not a set of worlds, but a set of inhabitants of worlds. My aim is to modify Lewis' proposal so as to meet criticisms made by Stalnaker and Evans.

Stalnaker and Evans both deny the need for contents with a relativized truth-value. Stalnaker argues that for utterances such contents make difficulties in the account of communication. Evans denies an assumption made by Lewis, which I share: that attitudes are narrow. (I believe Perry and Stalnaker implicitly make the assumption.) This denial enables Evans to avoid Perry's arguments for contents with a relativized truth-value. He also proposes a conception of content, urging that it reflects our ability to keep track of objects in time and space.

I shall modify Lewis' proposal so that contents can have relativized truth-values and also meet constraints suggested by Stalnaker's and Evans' criticisms. Thus I will propose that a coarse-grained content is a certain kind of relation among the inhabitants of worlds. This proposal accommodates contents with a relativized truth-value, as Perry demands. It provides a smooth account of communication, as Stalnaker demands. And it accom-

* I am very grateful to the participants at the Thyssen meeting; to audiences at the Universities of Glasgow, Harvard, London, MIT, St Andrews and Stirling; and to Martin Davies, David Lewis, David Lumsden, Hugh Mellor, Harold Noonan, John Perry, Philip Pettit, and Mark Richard.

modates Evans' point about tracking, which turns out to be analogous to Stalnaker's point about communication. Finally, attitudes to these contents can be narrow, which I take to be an advantage.

Thus I provide an account of coarse-grained content that meets several constraints, and that in particular unifies the contents of utterances and of attitudes. I admit that this unity is unlikely to be preserved at the level of fine-grained content. The fine-grained classification of utterances' contents by a grammar will very probably cut across the fine-grained classification of attitudes' contents by a psychological theory (cf. McGinn 1982).

In section 2, I argue, essentially following Perry, that we need contents with relativized truth-values. This prompts a discussion of narrow attitudes, and in section 3 I advocate them; but I also emphasize that attitudes to contents with relativized truth-values do not have to be narrow. Sections 4, 5, 6 and 7 deal successively with Perry's, Lewis', Stalnaker's and Evans' proposals about content. Section 8 presents my proposal.

I should say at the outset that I think present issues are largely independent of how one chooses among the several conceptions of possible worlds on offer. As it happens, I find Lewis' realism (1973:84–91) incredible, so that I have to choose among the other options (cf. Adams 1974; Stalnaker 1976; Kripke 1980: 15–20, 42–50); but I shall not discuss that choice here. This assumption of independence is shared by Lewis; as we shall see in section 5, he agrees that his realism is not necessary to his conception of content as a set of inhabitants of worlds. (Admittedly, Stalnaker doubts this assumption (1981: 144); and Perry and Evans are distrustful of possible worlds, and do not cast their proposals about content in terms of them.)

2. INDEXICAL ATTITUDES

At first sight, it seems that the relativization of truth-values should not prevent us conceiving of contents as sets of possible worlds. Thus consider utterances (or inscriptions) of sentences. Sentences can indeed contain indexicals, that is, expressions whose reference depends on the context in which they are uttered. And these context-dependent referents will induce a context-dependent truth-value; that is, the truth-values of sentence-types containing indexicals will be relative, not absolute: they will depend not just on how the world is, but also on the context of utterance. Nevertheless, each sentence-token being unrepeatable has a unique context of utterance that determines referents for its indexicals; and so it has an absolute truth-value. So why not consider contents as sets of worlds attaching only to sentence-tokens?

The same point can be made for attitudes, though here the type/token distinction is less clear. People do indeed have attitudes that they naturally express with indexicals: 'I'm ill', 'That apple is tasty', 'I want to see that film tomorrow'; and the context-dependent referents of these words, or of the components of thoughts that they express, will induce a context-dependent truth-value, in that one agent might truly believe what she would express by 'I'm ill' while another agent falsely believes what she would express by the same words. Nevertheless, whenever an agent has an attitude, the agent and the time at which she has it supply a context in which the attitude is held; and this context of thought, like a context of utterance, determines referents for the components of thoughts expressed by indexicals. Presumably we can think of attitude-tokens, that are to have a unique context of thought and thus an absolute truth-value. So why not consider contents as sets of worlds attaching only to attitude-tokens?

I believe this defence of all contents having absolute truth-values fails; we also need contents with relative truth-values. Or as I shall say, need relative, as well as absolute, contents. But the argument showing why it fails is rather different in the cases of utterances, and of attitudes. For utterances, the argument is straightforward. Assuming that a sentence-type does have a meaning, or conventional linguistic significance of some kind, then the fact that it has a relative truth-value implies that its meaning cannot be conceived as the set of worlds in which the sentence-type is true. Whatever one's views about meaning, there is no such set. We obviously need an account of this kind of meaning, even if we decide to reserve the word 'content' for something that has an absolute truth-value, and which therefore attaches in general only to tokens. (Later sections will consider such accounts.)

The only way to rebut this argument is by taking an indexical sentence-type to be simply ambiguous, so that there need be no content in common between tokens of it that have different absolute contents. In Fregean terminology, this amounts to taking, for example, 'I'm ill' to be ambiguous, with the occurrences of the indexical 'I' in two tokens expressing different senses (modes of presentation), whenever the referents of the two occurrences are different while the tokens are in the same world; and similarly for the indexical 'now' implicit in the verbal tense. These posited senses will then, by definition, determine a referent relative only to a world; and the contents composed of such senses will be absolute. However, this view is generally agreed to be wrong, both by advocates of relative contents and defenders of absolute contents: indexicals should not be assimilated to ambiguous expressions, since each, despite its varying reference, has a constant linguistic meaning (Perry 1977: 479–81; McGinn 1983: 64–8; Evans 1981: 289–91; Noonan 1984: 209, 214).

For attitudes, the argument for relative contents is less clear-cut, because of controversy about the nature of the attitudes and the way they explain actions. There are two problems. First, the assumption of the above argument that a sentence-type is not rendered ambiguous merely by the presence of indexicals, can be questioned for attitudes. One might hold that even if two agents' utterances of 'I' have the same linguistic meaning, despite their varying reference, they might nevertheless express components of thoughts (in Fregean terminology, senses) that are different, and different not just in virtue of their varying reference. After all, each of us has information about ourselves that no one else does and perhaps this enters the component of thought that we each use 'I' to express – or as one might better say, partially express. Similarly, two agents thinking of two different apples as 'that apple' generally have different information about their respective apples; and perhaps this information enters the component of thought that each might partially express by 'that apple'. This view does not deny that there are features in common between the thoughts of the two agents. But it questions that these features when taken together constitute a common content bearing a truth-value.

I think we should reject this view. We should distinguish between collateral information about an object, and components of thoughts referring to the object; agents can share the latter even while differing on the former. Admittedly this distinction is hard to justify (cf. Fodor, this volume: section 3). But I shall not try to do so, since the distinction is generally accepted both by advocates of relative contents and defenders of absolute contents; and accordingly the view above is rejected (ibid.)

However, unlike the linguistic case, this agreement does not immediately vindicate attitudes directed at relative contents – what I shall call indexical attitudes. For a problem remains about how much work they do in the explanation of actions. Their advocates typically point to the fact that they seem to be just what is needed to explain those similarities in agents' actions that abstract from the identity of the agents and of the objects on which they act; in particular, similarities of body-movements. Thus belief in the relative content, 'that apple is tasty', explains (in conjunction with appropriate desires) two agents reaching forward in the direction of their respective applies; the content is relative, because the agents can be in the same world, one believing truly and the other falsely (Perry 1977: 494; 1979: 17–18; McGinn 1983: 65).

Defenders of attitudes directed at absolute contents – what I shall call non-indexical attitudes – have a reply to this. They typically point out that we usually explain actions described in terms of the specific agent and the objects on which she acts; rather than in terms of body-movements. And in explaining such actions, it is natural to invoke non-indexical attitudes even when the agent would express her attitude with indexicals. Thus for the belief, 'that apple is tasty', to explain (in conjunction with appropriate desires) why the agent picks up a specific apple, we need to construe the belief in some way that picks out the specific apple as against others which the component of thought, 'that apple', can refer to.

Advocates of indexical attitudes reply that they can explain this. Their explanation of an action can simply cite, together with indexical attitudes, the non-psychological fact that the agent's component of thought, 'that apple', refers to the specific apple in question; there is no reason why action-explanation should cite only attitudes, or more generally, only psychological facts (McGinn 1982: 209–10; Barwise and Perry 1983: 236, 242; Perry, this volume: 126f). But defenders of non-indexical attitudes tend to assume that when an action is intentional under a description in which singular terms occur, its explanation must cite attitudes whose contents determine those terms' referents. In the example, this will mean taking the belief to have an absolute content, specified by 'that apple is tasty' together with the context of thought (Evans 1982: 203–4; Noonan 1984: 208–9).

Given this assumption, there are in fact two options: one taken by Evans (and by McDowell 1984), the other by Noonan (this volume). Both take the belief to have an absolute content. And both admit that the content entails the existence of the apple in question, assuming that 'that apple' is a rigid designator; that is, the truth of the content requires the apple's existence. But the first option adds the radical thesis that the attitude, not just its content, determines the apple; that is, believing the content whether truly or falsely (and even just entertaining the content) entails the existence of the apple; one could not think the content in a world not containing the apple. The second option denies this. Thus on the first option, the resources for explaining action on the specific apple lie in the mere fact of belief; on the second they lie in the content of belief being (absolutely) true.

In section 3, I shall reject the first option. That still leaves the options' common assumption about explanation needing attitudes whose contents determine terms' referents. But for my purposes I do not need to deny this. Even if it is correct so that action-explanation often needs non-indexical attitudes, indexical attitudes undoubtedly also have a role. So it is worth asking exactly how we should conceive relative contents (section 4 onwards). We have already noted the role of indexical attitudes in giving a common explanation of similarly moving agents. They also have another, I think more striking, role: they explain why in certain situations the agent acts, while in another similar situation the agent does not. Perry (1979) gives the argument for this, but it will be convenient to spell it out here. (As he acknowledges, it occurs in less pure form in earlier authors, in particular Castañeda and Kaplan.) Though compelling, this argument is admittedly not foolproof: there are alternative explanations of the action/no action contrast. I will consider those offered by Böer and Lycan (1980) and by

Evans (1981); I will reject them, though my rejection of Evans will have to wait till section 3. (Another explanation is suggested by Noonan 1984: 215–16.)

Perry's argument proceeds by examples. Each example contrasts a situation in which an agent performs an action, with another in which an agent (perhaps the same agent as the first) does not. We can focus either on explaining the action or on explaining the fact that an action occurs in the first situation but not the second. In either case, I take it that the explanation we provide must not form an equally good explanation of an action in the second situation. (This assumption, much weaker than Hempel's idea that explanations must provide sufficient conditions, seems uncontroversial: cf. van Fraassen 1980: 146f; Lewis, forthcoming.) So some of the features of the action, or the situation it occurs in, that the explanation cites must either be absent in the second situation, or, if present, unable to explain action there. In each of his examples, Perry urges that the only features satisfying this condition are indexical attitudes of some kind (which are in fact absent in the second situation). In some examples, the attitudes are temporally indexical, that is, their content has a time-relativized truth-value; in others, they are spatially indexical, or personally indexical.

In other words, Perry urges that the non-indexical attitudes that contribute to the explanation of the action are present, and equally able to help explain an action, in the second situation. Similarly for indexical attitudes of a kind other than that the example is urging; and similarly for non-attitudinal features contributing to the explanation, such as the agent's hands being free, or their having some necessary equipment (e.g. a gun for a shooting).

Here is an example in which the attitude is temporally indexical; the other kinds of indexicality are quite parallel.[1] A professor believes she has a departmental meeting at noon and wants to go to it. At noon, after working at her desk all morning, she gets up, walks out of her office and goes down the corridor to the meeting. It doesn't matter whether we take getting up, leaving the office or going down the corridor as the action. Whichever we take, the professor acts at noon but not at, say, 11:30 am. Yet both at noon and 11:30 am the professor believes that she has a departmental meeting at noon, and desires to go to the meeting. And at noon and 11:30 am she believes the meeting is to be held down the corridor, that the way to get there is to get up from the desk and leave the office, etc. So her acting at noon but not 11:30 am cannot be explained just by these attitudes. And it apparently cannot be explained by also citing non-attitudinal features;

[1] In my 1984, I argue that 'this' is parallel to the kinds Perry treats, viz. 'I', 'here' and 'now'.

for these also seem the same at noon and 11:30 am. At both times, she has the means to get up and leave.

The example does not need to require that the professor has at noon and 11:30 am the very same attitudes whose contents are not temporally indexical– which would be implausible. We can, and no doubt should, suppose that she has some different non-indexical attitudes. She may believe at noon but not 11:30 am that dervishes are Sufis, since at noon she reads it. And we can suppose she has some different indexical attitudes: she may desire at noon but not 11:30 am to go to the cinema after the meeting, since at noon she finds out what's on. These new attitudes of hers don't help explain why she acts at noon but not 11:30 am; the reason is, intuitively, that they are irrelevant to the action. Relevance is obscure but however it is clarified, some of an agent's attitudes will be irrelevant to explaining a given action; and we can let the professor have different irrelevant attitudes at noon and 11:30 am, without undermining the argument for a temporally indexical attitude.

Similarly for non-attitudinal features. We can, and obviously must, allow that there are many non-attitudinal differences between the professor and her surroundings, at noon and 11:30 am. But in the example none seems relevant to the explanation.

Assuming that all the relevant attitudes whose contents are not temporally indexical, and all the relevant non-attitudinal features, are the same at noon and 11:30 am, the explanation must cite a temporally indexical attitude: for example, the belief that the meeting is now, or that it is now noon, or the desire to be now down the corridor. And there is of course a straightforward basis for attributing such an attitude – in fact a belief – to the professor at noon but not 11:30 am. It is that the professor, like the rest of us, aims to have true beliefs, while indexicals, with their context-dependent references, induce context-dependent truth-values. So the professor will aim to alter her temporally indexical beliefs systematically as time goes by, believing that the meeting is now, and that it is now noon, at noon rather than 11:30 am.

This is Perry's argument as I understand it. Böer and Lycan (1980) and Evans (1981) offer alternative explanations of the action/no action contrast. Both alternatives deny the assumption that all features relevant to explanation, other than indexical attitudes, are the same in the two situations; in the example at hand, that all relevant features, other than temporally indexical attitudes, are the same at noon and 11:30 am. But the alternatives make this denial in different ways. Böer and Lycan accept that the relevant non-indexical attitudes are the same in the two situations. But they fear that indexical attitudes introduce facts that can be grasped only from certain perspectives (1980: 443–6). And to avoid such mysterious facts, they are willing to postulate that there is some non-attitudinal difference, whose nature we do not know, that explains why there is action in one situation but not another (1980: 450–2). They recognise that postulating this non-attitudinal difference limits the explanatory power of attitudes; but consider this a price worth paying to avoid perspectival facts.

Evans' alternative is very different. He claims that the agent has in the first situation a non-indexical attitude which she lacks in the second. He specifies the attitude; and it turns out that the content he proposes for it could not be believed, nor desired, in the second situation – a result he happily accepts. This attitude is naturally attributed with the same words as Perry's indexical attitudes, although the content has an absolute truth-value. Thus in the example at hand, Evans suggests the professor's belief at noon, whose content we naturally report as 'it is now noon', has in fact a content which has an absolute truth-value, and which cannot be thought at 11:30 am, nor at any time other than noon.

To evaluate these alternatives, we need to distinguish different senses in which a fact can be graspable, or a content thinkable, only from certain perspectives. When we do this, two points emerge. First, indexical attitudes introduce only unmysterious senses. So Boer and Lycan's fear is unjustified; and there is no need to postulate unknown non-attitudinal differences between the two situations. Secondly, Evans is right that there is nothing mysterious about his contents being thinkable only from certain perspectives.

Notice first that accepting indexical attitudes certainly means that some contents can be thought truly only at certain contexts. But there is nothing mysterious in that; it just reflects the relativization of truth-value (cf. Lewis 1979: sect. 7). What about the idea that some contents can be thought, whether truly or falsely, only at certain contexts? *Prima facie*, such limited thinkability certainly seems mysterious. But it will not be if it simply reflects such facts as that only at noon can one think of noon as 'now', and only in London can one think of Cambridge as 'the university town 53 miles north of here'. And this is exactly what happens in Evans' proposal. He thinks we should incorporate context-dependent referents into contents. The content of the professor's belief at noon that it is now noon is a triple, ⟨noon, sense of 'now', sense of 'is noon'⟩,[2] that can only be thought at noon (1981: 297–300). But as Evans emphasizes, this limited thinkability simply reflects the fact that only at noon can one think of noon as 'now'. This lack of mystery does not depend on any substantive view about the sense of 'now';

---

[2] Or instead, allowing 'noon' as well as 'now' to incorporate objects into the content: ⟨noon, sense of 'now', noon, sense of 'is noon'⟩. The point at issue is not affected.

in particular, it is independent of Evans' further views (1981: 281–95; 1982: 87f). It depends only on the sense of 'now' having a context-dependent referent, which is to be incorporated into the content.

I agree that limited thinkability might be mysterious if it arose in some other way than the incorporation of context-dependent referents into contents. I also agree, as does Perry, that such mysterious limited thinkability could account for the examples (1977: 491; 1979: 16). The reason is clear from the exposition above. If the contents of attitudes the professor has at noon can be thought only at noon, these attitudes could not be had at 11:30 am; and so an explanation of why she acted at noon not 11:30 am is liable to cite them.

But though sufficient, such mysterious contents are certainly not necessary to account for the examples – thus calming Böer and Lycan's fear. We can instead join Perry in letting contents be thinkable at all contexts, and appealing to the fact that the professor keeps track of the time; so that although she could have had the temporally indexical belief that it is now noon, or that the meeting is now, at 11:30 am, rather than noon – in which case she would act then – she does not in fact do so.

What then of Evans' claim that we can avoid Perry's argument for indexical attitudes by taking the content of the professor's belief (that we naturally report as 'it is now noon') to have an absolute truth-value, and to be thinkable only at noon? I must agree with this claim. I have already admitted that there is nothing mysterious about the limited thinkability of Evans' proposed contents. And just as Perry allows that contents with a mysterious limited thinkability could account for his examples, I must allow that Evans' contents could do so. In both cases, the fact that an attitude to the content could not be had at 11:30 am means that an explanation is liable to cite it. However, Evans pays a price for his preservation of absolute truth-values; briefly, it is that attitudes to his contents cannot be narrow. As I explain in section 3, I think the price is not worth paying.

3. NARROW ATTITUDES

We should distinguish the general idea of narrowness from a specific idea I need, which I call object-independence. The general idea is that attitudes are narrower, the less they entail about the world external to the agent; and wider, the more they entail. Note that it is the entailments of the attitudes that concern us, not those of their contents. No matter how narrowly we conceive attitudes, and how exactly we conceive contents, contents will generally be about the external world and so will entail much about it. Conversely, an attitude may have entailments that its content lacks. If belief requires participation in a public language, any attitude of belief will entail various claims about such a language, though its content probably will not (for example, if the content is about apples).

It is difficult to make narrowness precise. Attitudes are states, of agents or minds or brains; and states might not be sufficiently proposition-like to have any entailments. Should we then focus on what propositions attributing attitudes entail about the external world? The trouble is that such a proposition, 'A believes that p', may entail a lot about the world because of the agent A. If agents have their parents essentially, it will entail the existence of A's parents. But we don't want on that account to consider the attitude wide. So we have to somehow set aside those of the attribution's entailments that are due to the agent.[3]

Fortunately, this is easily enough done for the specific idea I need: that of object-independence. The idea is that an object-independent attitude entails the existence of no specific object. So an attribution of such an attitude, 'A believes that p', entails the existence of no specific object, other than the agent A and whatever objects are entailed by the existence of the agent (such as, perhaps, the agent's parents). More exactly, allowing for time, and using world-bound quantifiers, strict implication for entailment and 'M' for 'Possibly': 'A at time t believes that p' is object-independent if:

$$(x)[\{(\exists u)(\exists v)(u = A \ \& \ v = t) \dashv 3 \ (\exists z)(z = x)\} \supset$$
$$M(B_{A,t}p \ \& \sim (\exists z)(z = x))].$$

An attitude that is not object-independent, I call object-dependent; in this case, $B_{A,t}p$ entails the existence of some object not entailed by the existence of A and t.

Object-independence is a weak kind of narrowness: object-independent attitudes can entail a lot about the world, though not the existence of a specific object. Object-independence may be what Putnam had in mind when he said that the attribution of a narrow attitude does not entail the existence of any object other than the agent (1975: 220). However, he might also have meant something considerably stronger: that an attribution of a narrow attitude is compatible with the agent's being the only object in the world: that is, allowing for time, $M(B_{A,t}p \ \& \sim (\exists z)(z \neq A \ \& \ z \neq t))$.[4]

---

[3] For a functionalist like me, there are also other entailments to be set aside, since we don't want on their account to consider the attitude wide. They arise from (a) attitudes having causal roles and causation involving regularities; and (b) states occupying causal roles relative to a population. But for my purposes, I do not need to consider exactly how to set them aside.

[4] Putnam says 'presuppose' rather than 'entail'. I take it that if 'p presupposes q' does not mean 'p entails q', it means 'p entails q and not-p entails q'. But if so, Putnam's sense of 'narrow' as not presupposing is not really weaker than I report; for nobody holds that negations of attitude attributions entail the existence of objects other than the agent.

It has recently emerged that attitudes, as conceived in everyday life, are often wide. Indeed Kripke's and Burge's work (1979; 1982) suggest that everyday attributions of attitudes are sometimes wide in the strong sense of object-dependent. They entail the existence of a specific object, mentioned in the that-clause: in their examples, the objects entailed are the city of London and the natural kind water. Thus suppose Pierre visits London and finds it ugly, so that we say that Pierre believes that London is ugly. Could we make the same attribution to him in a world in which London does not exist? It seems not, even if the world is such that Pierre has the same bodily states and qualitative experiences as he actually has, say, because he visits a mock-up of London. So the attribution entails the existence of London. (A similar point can be made about a natural kind like water. However, as Burge points out (1982: 114–16), the case for object-dependence is weaker for natural kinds than for particulars, because of the linguistic division of labour. Presumably, a person in a world without water can believe that water is wet, provided there is enough in the community's experts' talk to credit them with the concept of water.)

Nevertheless, I think there is good reason to conceive attitudes as object-independent. The reason is essentially that we should conceive as an attitude the common mental state of a person and his twin on Twin Earth, when they look at different but similar objects. Thus suppose A points at an apple a and says 'That apple is tasty'; while in another world, B points at a different apple b and says the same. This supposition by itself is not enough to establish that they have a common belief. And if there is a common belief, it might not be object-independent; a and b and sundry other objects might all exist in both worlds, so that the belief might yet entail their existence. But if we suppose that A and B have further similarities (specifiable without reference to their having common attitudes), the more plausible it is that their utterances express a common belief. For example, we can suppose they share their qualitative experiences, their dispositions to action (non-intentionally described) and their physical structure. If we also suppose that the only objects existing in both worlds are those that are entailed both by A's existence and by B's, then this common belief *must* be object-independent. (This means supposing that no object is entailed both by a's existence and by b's; but we can surely choose a and b so that this is so.) And these two suppositions seem compossible. A and B can surely have enough similarities of qualitative experience, dispositions to action (non-intentionally described) and physical structure to give them a common belief, even while their worlds have no objects in common, apart from any that are entailed both by A's existence and by B's.

(Note that it is only object-independence, not the stronger sense of 'narrow' mentioned in connection with Putnam, that is motivated by Twin

Earth thought-experiments. The supposition that A and B have the same qualitative experiences, dispositions to action and physical structure, gives us no reason to think that each of them could have their common belief while being the only object in the world. That needs rather a thought-experiment in which A is the sole inhabitant of his world, yet has a belief in common with B in some other world. Similarly, it is only object-independence that is motivated by a thought-experiment in which there is no apple a. Thus suppose A is hallucinating, but that there are still enough similarities for A and B to have a common belief. In such a case, the belief is not only object-independent; its attribution also cannot entail the existence of an object of a certain kind (an apple presented in such-and-such a way). But that by no means makes the belief compatible with the agent's being the only object in the universe.)

This reason for object-independent attitudes should be distinguished from the reason given in section 2 for indexical attitudes based on the desire to find a common content for the attitudes of similarly moving agents. Both reasons involve a thought-experiment with two similar agents. But the experiments are significantly different. In section 2, the agents must be taken as being in the same world. Accordingly, the fact that some component of the common content, such as 'that apple', has different referents means that the content does not determine referents, even relative to a world; and so it is a relative content.

In fact object-independence and indexicality are independent features: object-independent attitudes can have relative or absolute contents, that is, be indexical or non-indexical; and indexical attitudes can be object-independent or object-dependent. This logical independence arises from the fact that while object-independence is a matter of the *attitude*, that is, its attribution, not entailing the existence of a specific object, indexicality is a matter of the *content* not determining a specific object, even relative to a world.

That an object-independent attitude can have a relative content is suggested by the thought-experiment above: A's object-independent belief, 'that apple is tasty', can presumably be shared, not only with B in another world, but also with C in A's own world; and it can be true for A and false for C. But an object-independent attitude might well have an absolute content, for two reasons. First, we might disregard the everyday conception of attitudes as revealed by Kripke and Burge, and conceive of the belief that London is ugly in 1986 as object-independent.[5] Secondly, even if all attitudes with contents expressed with names or kind terms are object-dependent,

---

[5] A possible motive for this conception would be reconciling object-independence with the assumption mentioned in section 2 that action–explanation needs attitudes whose contents determine terms' referents.

there may be qualitative predicates which when combined with variables, quantifiers, etc. express the absolute contents of some object-independent attitudes.

Conversely, an indexical attitude can be object-independent ('that apple is tasty'), or object-dependent: the belief that London is now ugly might well entail the existence of London and yet have a relative content, on account of the 'now'. This last point is worth emphasizing. It is tempting to infer from the fact that a relative content does not determine all the objects rendering it true or false, that attitudes to these contents are object-independent. But the inference is invalid. Attributions of such attitudes might entail the existence of objects mentioned in the content by non-indexical terms like 'London'; or the existence of other objects quite un-determined by the content. The point can be put another way. Relative contents, since they do not determine all the objects rendering them true or false, are suitable for object-independent attitudes, in the sense that they will not introduce object-dependence as regards indexicals' referents. But this suitability does not mean there are any object-independent attitudes.

This point is reflected in the Twin Earth motivation for object-independent attitudes. Since the relative content, 'that apple is tasty', is about different apples for A and for B, we can suppose that each apple occurs in only one of the two worlds. And so if A and B have a common belief, one way in which it might be object-dependent is ruled out. But this supposition does not establish that they have a common object-independent belief. That requires more: namely, supposing A and B very similar, while their worlds have no objects in common, apart from any that are entailed both by A's existence and by B's.

Advocacy of narrow, and, in particular, object-independent attitudes does not prevent us from explaining actions under 'wide' descriptions, that is, descriptions that entail a lot about the external world. That would be true only if actions had to be explained by attitudes providing sufficient conditions for them – so that the attitude had to entail all that the action-description entailed. But even if we do assume that explanations provide sufficient conditions, the explanans of a widely described action can contain, together with attributions of narrow attitudes, non-psychological premises that entail a lot about the world. Note that these premises can even be indexical without undermining Perry's argument for indexical attitudes. Thus suppose we add to the premises that the professor at noon believes that the meeting is at noon and desires that she be at the meeting (both temporally non-indexical attitudes), the non-psychological premise that it is now noon: all three premises could be true and yet the professor not move.

However, advocacy of object-independent attitudes does conflict with Evans' view. The conflict is obscured by the example of the professor's belief at noon that it is now noon. Evans proposes that the content is ⟨noon, sense of 'now', sense of 'is noon'⟩; and that an attitude to this content entails the existence of noon. But this does not make the attitude object-dependent; that requires entailing the existence of something that is not the agent nor the time of the attitude (nor entailed by them). However, other examples show that Evans proposes object-dependence. The belief that 'that apple is tasty' is to have the content ⟨the apple in question, the sense of 'that apple', the sense of 'is tasty'⟩. And an attitude to this content is to entail the existence of the apple. (Cf. Evans 1982, McDowell 1984; but for criticism, Blackburn 1984: 318–28; Noonan, this volume.)

As we saw in section 2, object-dependence enables Evans to avoid indexical attitudes; though it does not *oblige* him to avoid them, since as emphasized above indexical attitudes can be object-dependent. In any case, my advocacy of object-independence means I reject Evans' view. And accepting indexical attitudes, the question is: how exactly should we conceive their contents?

4. PERRY

Perry suggests that we distinguish two notions, which I call 'character' and 'proposition' (1977: 491–75; 1979: 16–20; as he says, the distinction is originally Kaplan's: 1977: 19–27; 1979: 403f). For my purposes it is convenient to explain these in terms of possible worlds, an explication which Perry avoids. The basic idea is that a character is the meaning of a sentence-type, which in general contains indexicals; and a proposition is the meaning of a sentence-token. A proposition is to be determined by a sentence-type together with a context of utterance (or of thought), the context determining referents for the sentence's indexicals. So we can consider each character as a map from contexts to propositions. The truth-values of propositions are absolute. But the truth-values of characters are relativized: a character is true at a context if the proposition thus determined is true at the world of the context. (Of course, some characters have the same truth-value for all contexts within a world: in particular, those that as maps are constant on the contexts within a world, sending all such contexts into the same proposition.) This account of truth-values is obtained from a natural suggestion about indexicals: namely that their meaning determines a map from contexts to their reference in that context. So the truth-value of a character in a context is got by considering the values of these maps for the context as argument.

The arguments in section 2 for indexical attitudes then amount to arguments for characters corresponding to sentence-types with indexicals. Consider, for example, the professor's action-explanatory belief that the meeting is now. This belief's proposition has an absolute truth-value. What its truth-value is in any world depends of course on the identity or difference of the referents in that world of 'the time of the meeting' and 'now', as said or thought by the professor at noon. But whatever determines these referents, the professor is surely not gathering evidence just before noon that convinces her that the proposition's truth-value is True. That is, whatever determines these referents, it seems the professor could have believed this proposition at 11:30 am. So her believing the proposition does not explain her acting at noon. On the other hand, her believing the character of 'the meeting is now' explains her acting at noon; for, assuming she keeps track of the time, she won't believe it at 11:30 am, when it's false.

Perry combines his advocacy of characters with two further views about indexicals' contributions to fine-grained content. Both are versions of the idea that indexicals refer 'directly'. The first, and for me more important view is that the fine-grained propositions of sentences with indexicals are individuated just by the indexicals' referents. That is the proposition of a sentence with n indexicals (and no other directly referring expressions) is given by a $n+1$-tuple whose first n members are the indexicals' referents, and whose last member is (something like) the relation expressed by the open sentence into which the indexicals are inserted. Thus, like Evans' proposed contents (section 2), the proposition is singular in that it contains objects, viz. indexicals' referents. But while Evans' contents also contain modes of presentation of those objects, viz indexicals' senses, Perry's propositions do not.

Perry's second view is in effect about indexicals' senses. It is that indexicals' contributions to characters not only *determine* maps from contexts to referents; they *are* specifications of such maps. For example, the contribution of 'now' to characters is the specification that each context is mapped to the time of that context.[6]

The first view has two attractive features. First, it fits well with the argument for characters based on the action/no action contrast (although it is not required for it). For, by omitting the modes of presentation that Evans includes, it guarantees that the proposition can be believed in a context other than the context of action. Thus the proposition of the professor's belief that it is now noon is a triple ⟨noon, noon, identity⟩, supposing that 'noon' also refers directly; or a pair ⟨noon, being noon⟩, supposing that 'noon' does not refer directly. In either case, the professor

---

[6] Perry (1977: 485–8) and Kaplan (1977) have convinced me that this is correct for character as the meaning of public utterances, though like others (e.g. Burge 1977: 355–7; Evans 1981: 300–3; 1982) I want to allow for a richer contribution to the contents of attitudes.

Note also that neither of these two views is required for the arguments in section 2 for characters. They require that indexicals have a context-dependent reference, but allow propositions to be non-singular and indexicals to make a rich contribution to character.

could certainly believe the proposition at 11:30 am. Indeed, on some accounts of belief, she certainly would believe the proposition at 11:30 am, provided she then believed the world would exist at noon (so that she believed, truly, that 'noon' has a referent).

Secondly, this view is sufficient, though not necessary, for another view that I (following Perry and Kaplan) find plausible: that indexicals are rigid. This means, for example, that the professor's proposition, my departmental meeting is now, is true in a world w iff the professor and noon exist in w and she has a departmental meeting then. (The compatibility of rigidity with context-dependence reflects the distinction between the language we use to describe a possible world and the language, if any, spoken in it; cf Kripke 1971: 145.)

But there are problems with this view, that have been articulated by Lewis (1979) and Stalnaker (1981).

5. LEWIS

Lewis, in objecting to Perry and proposing his alternative conception of content, writes from the standpoint of his modal realism, and his denial of transworld identity. But as he points out, these doctrines are not necessary to his account; (for the first, cf. Lewis 1979: 148; 1983: ix–x; for the second, cf. Lewis 1979: 140–1; Cresswell and von Stechow 1982: 506–10). A similar point applies to his acceptance of time-slices. I consider it fortunate that the account does not need modal realism and the denial of transworld identity, since I reject these doctrines and yet want to propose a conception of content similar to Lewis'.

Lewis' objection to Perry's singular propositions arises from his advocacy of narrow attitudes. These propositions are apparently not suitable contents for such attitudes, even in the weak sense of object-independence. (Cf. my rejection of Evans' contents in section 3). Of course Perry does not say that propositions are suitable contents for object-independent attitudes. And he might urge that he is under no pressure to make them so, since he has already supplied suitable contents, viz. his fine-grained characters mapping contexts to propositions by each indexical sending the context to its context-dependent reference.

But Lewis sees no role for propositions. He concedes that they seem to give the contents of *de re* attitudes (whose *res* are the objects occurring in the proposition). But, he says, such attitudes are hybrids of a narrow attitude, whose content includes modes of presentation which the proposition does not express; and a non-psychological fact, that the modes of presentation are of the objects in the proposition (1979: 150–6; cf. also Kaplan 1968). And admitting propositions in addition to characters has the disadvantage that it introduces two kinds of content, which is likely to complicate the systematic explanation of action. For the logical relations of the contents of attitudes, which the explanation is bound to exploit, will be more complicated (1979: 134). (This objection does not bite at the coarse-grained level at which propositions are sets of worlds, and characters are maps from contexts to such sets. At this level, Perry can deal wholly in characters, by trading in any set of worlds for the constant map with that set as value. But the objection does bite at the fine-grained level; here, a proposition does not determine a character since it is a value under various characters of various contexts.)

Lewis proposes his own account of what coarse-grained contents are: an account on which they are of a single kind, are suitable for object-independent attitudes, and can have relativized truth-values. The proposal is easier to grasp if we temporarily join Lewis in making two assumptions: denial of transworld identity, so that the inhabitants of each world (animate and inanimate) occur only in that world; and acceptance of time-slices, so that among the inhabitants of each world are all its inhabitants' time-slices. Lewis' proposal is then that a content is a set of inhabitants of worlds.

The set can have members from various worlds; and it can contain some but not others of a world's inhabitants. To believe a content is to ascribe to oneself the property of being a member of the corresponding set; it is to have an opinion about which of all the inhabitants, spread out across the worlds, one is. Similarly, to desire a content is to desire that one be a member of a certain set of inhabitants.

This subsumes the standard view of a content with an absolute truth-value as a set of worlds. For sets of worlds correspond one-to-one with those sets of inhabitants that for any world contain either all or none of that world's inhabitants. Each set of worlds corresponds to the set containing all the inhabitants of those worlds, and no inhabitants from any other worlds. So Lewis proposes to trade in each set of worlds for the set of all those worlds' inhabitants. So to believe a content with an absolute truth-value is to ascribe to oneself the property of being an inhabitant of a world at which the content is true. But Lewis also allows, as the standard view does not, for contents with relativized truth-values. These are represented by the sets of inhabitants that correspond to no set of worlds, that is, the sets of inhabitants that for one or more worlds contain some but not others of that world's inhabitants. Thus the content of 'I am now hot' is the set of all hot time-slices of objects. The content of 'the apple one yard from here is tasty' is the set of all time-slices of objects such that there is a unique apple one yard away from them, and that apple is (then) tasty.

Lewis' proposal is easily modified, if we give up his denial of transworld identity and his acceptance of time-slices. Suppose instead that objects may inhabit more than one world, and may persist through time without having time-slices. It will of course remain true that on Lewis' proposal, not every property we self-ascribe in belief is a necessary property of all its instances, nor is every such property possessed throughout the lifetime of its instances. So we need to capture the idea of a property that an object may have in one world but not another, and at one time but not another. We can do this simply by tagging objects with times and worlds: that is, by taking a property to be a set of triples of an object, a time and a world such that the object exists at the time in the world. Any set of such triples is then a content; and as before, in belief we self-ascribe membership of the set that is the content of our belief.

The relation of Lewis' proposal to Perry's becomes clear when we notice that triples $\langle o,t,w \rangle$ such that o exists at time t in world w, determine referents for indexicals just as contexts do in Perry's scheme. Thus $\langle o,t,w \rangle$ determines the referent of 'now' as t, of 'here' as the place of o at t in w, etc. (Of course, not every triple determines a referent for every indexical; if o at t in w is not pointing at nor thinking about an apple, 'that apple' gets no referent relative to $\langle o, t, w \rangle$ – unless it turns out convenient to assign it an artificial referent of the kind Frege introduced for bearerless terms.) Let us call such a triple a *context*. Then Lewis' contents are simply related to Perry's coarse-grained and fine-grained characters. A context is in Lewis' content of a sentence S iff its image (a set of worlds) under Perry's coarse-grained character of S contains the world of the context; iff its image (a singular proposition) under Perry's fine-grained character of S is (absolutely) true at the world of the context. (A similar relation will of course hold, given Lewis' view that each object is confined to one world and has time-slices: instantaneous objects will act like Perry's contexts.)

6. STALNAKER

Stalnaker's objection to Perry is based on the idea of an utterance's informative content (1981: 147–9): neither Perry's singular propositions, nor his characters, seem to serve as such contents. Admittedly, singular propositions often seem to serve, at least if we waive their omission of a mode of presentation of the objects mentioned. Thus the proposition $\langle$Butterfield, t, being ill$\rangle$, expressed by my doctor's utterance at time t 'You're ill', might be informative. But there is a problem with identity statements. Thus saying 'It is now noon' can be informative; saying it can make someone who has a meeting at noon, but who has lost track of the time, get up to go. But the proposition expressed at noon by this sentence is $\langle$noon, noon, identity$\rangle$: which the person can surely have believed all morning.

So should Perry claim that it is the character (no doubt fine-grained), or the character together with the singular proposition, that gives the informative content of the utterance? *Prima facie*, either claim seems all right. But Stalnaker shows there is a problem if we impose the condition, as he thinks we should, that in communication the informative content is common to speaker and hearer. The problem emerges when we consider an identity statement like 'You are Rudolf Lingens', in which an indexical has different referents for the contexts of speaker and hearer. (Rudolf Lingens occurs in Frege's essay, 'The Thought': 1967.) As in the previous example, such a sentence can be informative, although the singular proposition expressed by it, ⟨Lingens, Lingens, identity⟩, is not: it will be informative if Lingens is an amnesiac who has forgotten who he is. But its common informative content cannot be its character, since the content of the hearer's belief will rather be the character of 'I'm Rudolf Lingens'. (The same problem clearly confronts Evans' contents.)

Stalnaker objects similarly to Lewis' account that it does not provide an informative content common to speaker and hearer: for the speaker, the content of his utterance 'You are Rudolf Lingens' is presumably the set of contexts ⟨o,t,w⟩ such that the object o is at t in w addressing Lingens, while for the hearer it is the set of contexts such that the object is Lingens (1981: 145–7).[7]

Stalnaker makes a proposal about what the common informative contents of utterances are: viz. sets of worlds. Unlike Perry's characters and Lewis' contents, sets of worlds can be common since they incorporate the contribution of context in determining what is talked about. And unlike Perry's propositions, they can be informative. This second claim raises a familiar difficulty: it confronts not only Stalnaker but anyone who believes that indexicals and names are rigid (or sometimes rigid). Rigidity means that the set of worlds corresponding to a token of 'it's now noon' is either the entire set of worlds in which noon exists (in the case where the token is uttered at noon) or empty (in case it is uttered at another time); but in that case how can such tokens be informative as when one tells someone it is noon? Similarly of course for other sentences, with rigid indexicals or names, like 'You are Lingens' and 'Hesperus is Phosphorus'. That is, rigidity makes these sentences similar to mathematical sentences: they are either impossible or necessary (or rather weakly so: true in all worlds in which the common referent exists; cf. Kripke 1971: 137).

The best-known response to this difficulty is simply to let coarse-grained contents like sets of worlds be uninformative, and to posit some kind of fine-graining that gives informative contents (cf. Field 1978: 81–2). But

---

[7] Lewis was in fact careful to propose his account for the contents of attitudes, not utterances. One of his reasons is the contribution of factors outside the agent's head (e.g. experts, in the linguistic division of labour) to determining the contents of utterances (1979: 143). This point about communication is another reason – of which he may well have been aware.

Stalnaker defends the informativeness of sets of worlds by appealing to his (1978) account of assertion. This shows how the convention that a speaker should assert what he believes to be true in the world in which he asserts it allows the hearer to gather information, even if what is asserted is necessarily true. 'Hesperus is Phosphorus', 'You are Lingens' and 'It's now noon' provide parallel examples. Thus suppose I believe I'm in a world in which 'Hesperus' and 'Phosphorus' are used as rigid designators, but have no view about whether they co-refer. Hearing 'Hesperus is Phosphorus' from a speaker I believe reliable and sincere, I conclude that they co-refer, even though what is asserted is in that case necessary (or rather weakly so).

Similarly, suppose I believe I'm in a world in which (i) 'You' and 'Lingens' are used as rigid designators, and (ii) someone I believe reliable and sincere uses 'You' to refer to me – he looks at me and starts an utterance 'You...'; but I have no view about whether they co-refer. When the whole utterance turns out to be 'You are Lingens', I conclude that they co-refer, though what is asserted is weakly necessary (1978: 325–8; cf. also 1976a: 85–91).

I agree with this defence of Stalnaker's: rigidity does not force informative contents to be finer-grained than sets of worlds. But Stalnaker not only proposes sets of worlds as common informative contents. He also suggests that sets of worlds are the only kind of content we need, or at least the only coarse-grained kind (1931: 134f). He seems aware that this means he cannot accommodate Perry's action/no action argument. For he says (1981: 142) he is developing Böer and Lycan's (1980). And as we saw in section 2, they explicitly reject relative contents, while admitting that Perry's examples show that if action-explanation is to be by attitudes, such contents are required. (Admittedly, Stalnaker says it is part of his non-realist view of possible worlds that the set W of all worlds varies from one 'context' to another, so that sets of worlds, giving the contents of utterances and attitudes, get truth-values only relative to the contexts for which they are subsets of W (1981: 135). But this does not give relativized truth-values of Perry's or Lewis' kind, since the notion of context is very different. For Stalnaker a context is not so much a determiner of indexicals' referents, as whatever determines W; in particular, the context of an utterance 'You are Lingens' is the same for speaker and hearer – so that the content can be common: cf. 1978: 321–3; 1973: 450.)

I want contents with a relativized truth-value, so as to accommodate Perry's argument. I also want contents that are suitable for object-independent attitudes, and of a single kind so as to make their logical relations more tractable. These aims I share with Lewis. But Lewis' contents don't satisfy Stalnaker's condition about a common informative content in communication. Nor do they satisfy a condition suggested by Evans.

7. EVANS

I have already discussed Evans' objection to Perry. Evans accounted for Perry's examples with contents that had three features: (i) limited think-ability; (ii) an absolute truth-value; (iii) attitudes to them are object-dependent. I agreed that Evans' account was cogent, but rejected it because of my advocacy of object-independent attitudes (section 3). However, Evans *also* suggests (1981: 291–5) contents of *another* kind, that have features (ii) and (iii) but not (i). He urges that these contents reflect our ability to keep track of objects in time and space. I shall agree with this, and admit that Perry's and Lewis' proposals about content do not reflect this ability. But I shall show in the next section that we can reflect this ability with contents similar to Lewis', which have none of the three features listed.

Consider the sentence 'Today is fine', said on 4 July 1985. Evans suggests this sentence has a content with an absolute truth-value. The content is the same as that of 'Yesterday was fine', said on 5 July; and as that of 'Tomorrow will be fine', said on 3 July; so that the same content can be thought on different days. But the content is different from that of '4 July 1985 is fine'; and from that of 'My birthday in 1985 is fine', supposing 4 July is my birthday. And Evans takes attitudes to this content to be object-dependent (1982: 150f; 192–6).

Thus Evans is urging a notion of content whose individuation is in certain respects intermediate between that of Perry's propositions and that of Perry's characters. It is finer than that of propositions, in that no proposition determines such a content. Together with ⟨4 July 1985, the property of being fine ⟩, we need to be told that 4 July is to be specified by a temporal indexical – by 'today' on 4 July, or 'yesterday' on 5 July, etc. It is coarser than that of characters, in that two sentence-tokens with different characters may have the same content: namely if the differences in the indexicals they contain compensates for their different contexts, so that the same object is referred to by an indexical of the same kind.

Evans thinks this notion of content is a psychologically important one, while Perry's propositions and characters are not. The objection to pro-positions is familiar from section 5: by omitting modes of presentation of objects they are 'psychologically quite uninteresting' (1981: 292). The objection to characters is that with their fine individuation, they suggest an agent could be credited with, say, a belief on 4 July that today is fine, without having any propensity to believe on 5 July that yesterday was fine: the characters involved are after all quite different. And this suggestion seems wrong. However exactly one individuates content, an agent who at a certain time has an attitude with a content expressible with temporal indexicals must surely have a propensity to have at other times attitudes with contents expressible by suitably related indexicals. The advantage, Evans thinks, of this notion is that it explains this point by construing the propensity simply as a propensity to retain one and the same attitude.

Similarly for other kinds of indexical, such as spatial ones. Evans suggests that 'It rains (tenseless) here at time t', said at place p, has the same absolutely truth-valued content as 'It rains (tenseless) five miles north of here at time t', said five miles south of p. And this notion of content has, Evans thinks, the same advantage: it explains a propensity of agents possessing attitudes expressible with spatial indexicals by construing it simply as a propensity to retain their attitudes.

I agree with Evans' point about tracking: an agent possessing attitudes expressible with temporal, or spatial, indexicals must have the propensity, in other times or places, to have attitudes expressible with suitably related indexicals. I also agree that Evans' notion explains this point in a simple and appealing way, while Perry's characters do not. Furthermore, nor do Lewis' contents.

It is tempting to think that Perry and Lewis can explain the point by construing the propensity as a propensity to believe the consequences of what one believes. But this is a mistake. The difficulty can be seen at the coarse-grained level, where the consequence-relation, both for Perry's characters and for Lewis' contents, is the subset relation on sets of contexts. Thus one character implies another iff the set of contexts – triples $\langle o, t, w \rangle$ such that o exists at t in w – at which the one is true is a subset of the set of contexts at which the other is true. Similarly for Lewis, who identifies a content with the set of contexts at which it is true: one Lewis-content implies another iff it is a subset of it.

To see the mistake, consider again 'Today is fine'. The sentence-type, or its character in Perry's scheme, or its Lewis-content, is true at certain contexts $\langle o, t, w \rangle$, viz. those such that in w the weather on the day containing t is fine. (If 'here' is understood in the sentence, the weather need only be fine in the vicinity of o; but for simplicity I ignore this.) 'Yesterday was fine' is not true at all these contexts, and is therefore not a consequence of 'Today is fine'. It is indeed true that for most of these contexts, there are contexts $\langle o', t+1, w \rangle$ for some objects o'; (for the others the world comes to an end in the intervening time). And *these* contexts are exactly the ones at which 'Yesterday was fine' is true. So if an agent at some time believes 'Today is fine' and is still alive the next day, she no doubt should then believe 'Yesterday was fine'; for if the first belief was true at the context it was held at, this second one is also. But this 'should' is not, on Perry's or Lewis' account, a matter of believing the consequences of what one believes; and I see no other way they might explain it. Indeed, this statement of what the agent should believe seems merely to re-express in terms of contexts Evans' point.

8. SYNTHESIS

For Lewis, a content is a set of contexts, triples $\langle o, t, w \rangle$ such that o exists at t in w. Contents can be believed, desired etc. by any agent at any time: there is no limited thinkability. Attitudes to them can be object-independent. And some of them have relativized truth-values (viz. those that for some world contain some but not all of the contexts in that world). We can keep these features while modifying the contents so as to satisfy Stalnaker's demand for a common content in communication, and so as to explain Evans' point about tracking. I shall consider communication first; tracking will turn out to be analogous.

First, a preliminary point. Lewis did not propose his contents for utterances, but for attitudes. And a speaker's utterances can be sincere or insincere while attitudes cannot be; similarly utterances can be accepted or not by the hearer. Thus while Lewis can characterize the content of a belief as the property the agent self-ascribes, we cannot thus characterize the content of an assertoric utterance, even if we allow that there is one content for the speaker and another for the hearer. We need rather the idea of the property that the speaker self-ascribes if they are sincere, that is, the property that they purport to self-ascribe; and correspondingly, the idea of the property that the hearer is enjoined by the utterance to self-ascribe. This shift to properties purported or enjoined to be self-ascribed does not of course undermine Stalnaker's point, that the properties can be different for speaker and hearer, for example, addressing Lingens and being Lingens, thus depriving the utterance of a common content. (Similarly for non-assertoric utterances, such as requests: the speaker purports to desire their content. However, I shall consider only assertoric utterances.)

One might dismiss Stalnaker's demand on the grounds that the idea that an utterance has a determinate content, even a different one for hearer than for speaker, is wrong. This criticism is not directed only at Lewis' contents, but is quite general. It assumes only that the content for a hearer of an utterance is the content of the belief he would acquire by accepting it. And it then points out that for a given utterance, there is a great variety in the beliefs a hearer may acquire. Someone at the optician's says 'I see A, K and L'; the optician concludes that her client is far-sighted; the customer in the next room concludes only that someone sees the letters A, K and L. An example of this is given by Kaplan (adapted from 1977:64): I am looking at a man whose pants are on fire, and who is standing in a hall of mirrors, he points at a reflection of himself and says to me 'His pants are on fire'. I conclude that he does not know it is his own reflection, and is not (yet) in pain. My companion who does not see the man concludes only that some man's pants are on fire. These examples suggest that the idea that an utterance has a single content for its hearers is wrong.

Like many others, I think the idea can be defended, using ideas derived from Grice (1957) and Lewis (1969) about the intentions and conventions involved in utterances. We feel intuitively that the optician's belief and mine go beyond the utterance's content by using collateral information; while the customer and my companion, who cannot identify the referents of the indexicals 'I' and 'his', do not grasp the utterance's content. We also feel intuitively that the customer and my companion do not count as hearers, so much as over-hearers; so that the beliefs they acquire are irrelevant to the specification of content. And there are appealing principles derived from Grice and Lewis that account for these intuitions. The obvious Gricean principles are: a hearer is a person whom the speaker intends to believe something on the basis of recognizing that intention; and the content for the hearer is the content the speaker intends them to believe. To allow for the conventional nature of utterances, emphasized by Lewis, one might suggest instead: a hearer is a person who is party to a linguistic convention with the speaker, and whom the speaker intends to believe something on the basis of hearing the utterance and recognizing the speaker's intention to exploit the convention.

Elaborating this defence would require a theory of assertion; that is, it involves determining the right principles about the roles of intention and convention in assertoric utterances. Fortunately, I can largely avoid the details. My basic strategy for modifying Lewis' contents so as to satisfy Stalnaker's demand needs only two claims, that the defence, if it works at all, can be expected to vindicate. I shall however need a third more contentious claim for a specific proposal that I shall make later.

The two claims are these. First, for any utterance by any speaker, there is a definite set of hearers of the utterance. Second, for any utterance, the linguistic conventions governing it determine a content such that the speaker by the utterance purports to believe the content; and they determine a content (perhaps different from the first) such that the speaker enjoins his hearers to believe it. These claims will surely be vindicated, however the defence explicates 'hearer', 'purport', 'enjoin', etc. in terms of intention and convention.

Given these two claims, I shall use the fact that the conventions governing an utterance determine its speaker-content and its hearer-content, to introduce a single entity that determines both. This will be the common content.

There is a general reason why in modifying Lewis' contents, it is simplest to take as the common content something that determines both speaker-content and hearer-content: that is, on Lewis' account, both the property the speaker purports to self-ascribe and the property the hearer is enjoined to self-ascribe. It arises from the requirement that whatever the common content is, the speaker's and hearer's accepting it should explain how they each act. If we do not require this, we are either letting attitudes fail to explain action, in which case we may as well follow Böer and Lycan and Stalnaker, in rejecting relative contents, or we are implicitly assuming contents of a separate kind, such as Lewis', attitudes to which *do* explain actions. And the simplest way to satisfy this requirement is to make the common content determine the speaker-content and hearer-content. For the speaker's and hearer's acceptance of the common content can then explain all that their belief in these separate contents explains.[8]

I suggest that we take as the common content of an utterance a binary relation among contexts, that is, a set of ordered pairs of contexts. Any binary relation R determines its domain and range: the domain of R is $\{x:$ there is a y such that $\langle x,y \rangle \in R\}$; its range is $\{y$ there is a x such that $\langle x,y \rangle \in R\}$. The common content is to determine the speaker-content and hearer-content (each of them a set of contexts) as its domain and range respectively. Thus by the utterance, the speaker purports to self-ascribe membership of the domain of the relation; and enjoins the hearers to self-ascribe membership of the range. Thus an utterance is like an invitation: the speaker invites each hearer to join him as the first and second members of a pair which is a member of a certain binary relation.

This is my basic strategy for satisfying Stalnaker's demand. It inherits from Lewis the three features given at the start of the section: no limited thinkability; suitability for object-independent attitudes; and relativized truth-values (we take the truth-value at a context of a relation among contexts to be the truth-value of its domain, that is to be True iff the context is in the domain). And by determining Lewis' contents, it explains actions as well as they do. (It also in a sense subsumes Lewis' account, since we can trade in a set of contexts for the identity-relation on it: each determines the other.) However, as stated so far, it is too general. It encompasses various different proposals about what the common content is. All have the features just mentioned; but I shall favour one.

This generality arises in two ways. First, there is considerable latitude, which I have so far been able to ignore, about how much information is included in the speaker-content and hearer-content of an utterance, about

---

[8] Incidentally, this requirement eliminates the suggestion that the common content be simply the disjunction of the speaker-content and the hearer-content (the union of the two sets of contexts). On this suggestion the hearer's accepting the common content of 'You are Lingens' amounts to his believing that either he is addressing Lingens or he is Lingens. And this belief cannot explain actions which belief in the hearer-content can explain.

the fact that an utterance is occurring. Thus consider again 'You are Lingens'. Does the speaker purport to self-ascribe the property of perceiving and attending to Lingens, or the property of perceiving, attending to and addressing Lingens, or even all this and addressing him in English? Similarly for the hearer: is he enjoined to self-ascribe being Lingens, or being Lingens and perceived, attended to and addressed, or even all this and being addressed in English? Thus there is latitude in the domain and range of the relation.

Secondly, given any two sets, there are many relations having the sets as domain and range respectively. So even given a precise choice of domain and range, I have not yet specified the common content; any one of many relations would do the job of determining domain and range.

The latitude in the choice of domain and range is advantageous, because only with a theory of assertion could we say exactly what speakers purport to self-ascribe and enjoin their hearers to self-ascribe. So our account does well to be able to handle various possibilities. On the other hand, the latitude in the choice of a relation is a problem. If for a given speaker-content and hearer-content, *any* relation with them as domain and range would do, we are in effect positing only the speaker-content and hearer-content, and thus not really extending Lewis' original account (considered as an account for utterances not attitudes). All the relation provides is the metaphor that assertion is an invitation to be second member of one of a certain class of pairs. So we need to say more about the relation than just what its domain and range are. There is a trade-off here, between solving this problem, and maintaining the first advantage; the more we say about the relation, the more we are likely to constrain the choice of domain and range.

I prefer to solve the problem of the relation. The proposal I favour takes from the theory of assertion the terms 'speaker' and 'hearer' and uses them to specify the relation completely. The speaker-content and hearer-content that are thereby determined as domain and range turn out to include a lot of information about the fact that an utterance is occurring. But I am willing to accept that result.

Since a sentence-type S can occur in different languages with different meanings, we must specify the relation that is the content of S relative to a language L that S occurs in. A pair of contexts $\langle x, y \rangle$ is in the relation iff x is a true speaker of S as a member of L and y is a hearer of x: that is, iff x is a context $\langle o, t, w \rangle$ such that o utters S as a member of L truly at time t in w, and y is a context $\langle o', t', w' \rangle$ such that o' at t' in w' hears o's utterance. (If the process of assertion must be causal, and causation must be forward in time and intraworld, then t' will in all cases be later than t and w' will be w.) This definition completely specifies the relation. And according to it, the speaker-content and hearer-content are logically strong. The domain of the relation is the set of true speakers of S as a member of L; and the range is the set of hearers of true utterances of S as a member of L. So a speaker purports to self-ascribe being a speaker of a true utterance of his sentence, considered as a member of the language; and enjoins his hearer to self-ascribe being a hearer of such an utterance.

I think these strong contents are a small price to pay for the benefit of specifying the relation. After all, it may turn out to be no price: the theory of assertion may make it part of the content, for speaker and hearer, of an utterance of S in L that a true utterance of S in L is occurring. For example, on the Gricean principle about hearer-content mentioned above, this will be so if the speaker intends the hearer to believe that a true utterance of S in L is occurring – which is plausible enough.[9]

Finally, I turn to tracking. By believing 'Today is fine' on some day, say 4 July, an agent in some sense commits himself to believing 'Yesterday was fine' on 5 July; and similarly for other days before 4 July and after 5 July. In section 7, I agreed with Evans that this motivated the idea that there is a content in common between 'Today is fine' as believed on 4 July, 'Yesterday was fine' as believed on 5 July, and corresponding sentences as believed on other days; and similarly for other sentences and other kinds of indexicals. As we saw, Evans suggests that such a content should have an absolute truth-value; so that the common content of 'Today is fine' as believed on 4 July, and 'Yesterday was fine' as believed on 5 July, is different from the common content of these two sentences, as believed respectively on 4 and 5 December. And Evans also suggests that attitudes to such a content should be object-dependent.

I shall propose two ways of modifying Lewis' contents so as to provide a common content that has a relativized truth-value, and is suitable for object-independent attitudes. The relativized truth-value means that the common contents mentioned above, for July and for December, are one and the same. That is to say, each of my two proposals provides a common content of 'Today is fine' as believed on any given day, 'Yesterday was fine' as believed on the next day, 'Tomorrow will be fine' as believed on the previous day, etc. The main difference between my proposals is that while the first treats the given day and all the others similarly, the second does not: it gives a special role to the given day. I prefer the second proposal;

[9] Furthermore, these strong contents may well be endorsed by Stalnaker's account of presupposition (1973; 1974), which I (and Lewis 1979a) find attractive. Stalnaker allows that the presuppositions that a speaker makes can be conceived as a set W of worlds (viz. all those in which all the presuppositions are true), that is to contain all the worlds in which the speaker's assertion is true (1973: 450, 1974: 199, 1978: 321); so W can be conceived as part of the assertion's content. He also suggests that a speaker presupposes that p iff he is disposed to act as if (i) he assumes that p; and (ii) he assumes that his hearers recognize (i) (1973: 448, 1974: 200–2). It may well be that a speaker of S in L satisfies (i) and (ii) for p = a true utterance of S in L is occurring.

but the first proposal is worth spelling out as it helps one to grasp the second.

I shall describe the two proposals for the case of 'Today is fine', assuming that time is discrete in days. It will be clear how to treat non-discrete time, and how to deal with other kinds of indexical. I shall also focus for the moment on just two successive days: the day the agent believes 'Today is fine', and the next day.

Recall that Stalnaker's demand was for a content in common between utterances whose different indexicals compensated for the differences between speaker's and hearer's contexts, for example, 'You are Lingens' and 'I am Lingens'. So there is an analogy between (a) a speaker's enjoining her hearer (or hearers) to believe that he is (they are) Lingens, by saying 'You are Lingens': and (b) an agent's committing himself to believe on the next day 'Yesterday was fine', by believing 'Today is fine'. This analogy means I can adapt the strategy used above to satisfy Stalnaker's demand.

My first proposal follows this strategy closely. The common content of 'Today is fine' as believed on one day and 'Yesterday was fine' as believed on the next day is to be a binary relation among contexts that determines as its domain and range two properties, that is, sets of contexts, that are contents of the kind Lewis proposes for these two sentences.

In the case of assertion, this strategy had an advantageous latitude in the specification of the domain and range, and a problematic latitude in the specification of the relation. I proposed that we use the communication link between speaker and hearer to solve the problem of the relation, and pay the price of being committed to specific domains and ranges (as it turned out, logically strong ones).

There is a similar predicament here; and my first proposal deals with it in a similar way. The strategy does not completely specify the domain and range, that is, the properties the agent self-ascribes in believing 'Today is fine' and 'Yesterday was fine'. But even given a domain and range, it does not specify the relation; and if any relation with the given domain and range would do, we apparently have not extended Lewis' original account. My first proposal specifies the relation completely using the idea of an object's self-identity through time, just as earlier I used the idea of a communication link between speaker and hearer. And it pays the price of being committed to specific domains and ranges (that are, as before, logically strong).[10]

The proposal is that a pair of contexts $\langle x,y \rangle$ is in the common content of 'Today is fine' as believed on one day, and 'Yesterday was fine' as

[10] Using a memory link rather than self-identity would make for a stronger analogy with communication, though at the cost of stronger contents that incorporate the notion of memory. This may be no cost (Evans 1982: 122–9), but anyway exposition is simpler with self-identity.

believed the next day, iff x is a context $\langle o, t, w \rangle$ such that the weather in w at t is fine and o exists at $t+1$ in w, and y is the context $\langle o, t+1, w \rangle$. The domain of this relation is the content Lewis would propose for 'Today is fine and I will exist tomorrow'; the range is what he would propose for 'Yesterday was fine and I existed yesterday'. The logical strength of these contents shows in the conjuncts about the agent's existence.

How acceptable are these contents? I think that Lewis' self-ascriptive view of belief, according to which in any belief one believes in one's present existence, makes the range acceptable, but not the domain. That is to say, on Lewis' view, to believe 'Today is fine' involves believing in one's present existence. So in the sense in which believing 'Today is fine' commits one to believing on the next day 'Yesterday was fine', it surely also commits one to believing then 'Yesterday was fine and I existed yesterday'. But I don't see how it commits one to believing now 'I will exist tomorrow'.

Fortunately, we can treat the two days asymmetrically so as to capture these intuitions; and this is my second proposal. We take as the common content a relation of variable polyadicity; it is a set containing both ordered pairs and ordered one-tuples of contexts, that is, both pairs and single contexts. (So the polyadicity varies between 1 and 2.) It contains just the ordered pairs that comprised the first proposal's content. It also contains those contexts $\langle o, t, w \rangle$ such that the weather in w at t is fine and o does not exist at $t+1$ in w. That is, it also contains the remainder of the content Lewis would propose for 'Today is fine'. The set of first members of elements of this relation is then just the content Lewis would propose for 'Today is fine'. The set of second members is exactly my first proposal's range, that is, what Lewis would propose for 'Yesterday was fine and I existed yesterday': there is no contribution from the single contexts.

This second proposal may seem artificial; I think that is only because in logic and mathematics we tend to consider relations of fixed polyadicity. In any case, this proposal extends better than the first to the case of more than two days, to which I now turn.

Recall that the basic idea is that believing 'Today is fine' on a given day commits one to believing, n days earlier (or later), 'In n days' time, it will be fine' (or: 'n days ago, it was fine'). So we need a content that determines a sequence of contents of the kind Lewis would propose: a sequence ordered like the integers (positive and negative).

Starting from the first proposal above, the natural suggestion is that someone who believes 'Today is fine' on a given day is committed to believing then that she exists on all the other days that exist in the world. Assuming for simplicity that time is necessarily infinite both ways, the content will be a set of infinite sequences of contexts, each sequence ordered like the integers; it is an infinity-adic relation. A sequence of contexts is in the content iff (1) there is some context in the sequence, $x = \langle o, t, w \rangle$ such that the weather at t in w is fine; call this context x_0; and (2) writing the sequence of contexts as $\langle \ldots x_{-2}, x_{-1}, x_0, x_1, x_2, \ldots \rangle$, $x_n = \langle o, t+n, w \rangle$ for all integers n. That is to say, the content is a set of sequences, each sequence representing the lifespan of an object that lives throughout time and that sometime in its life experiences fine weather.

This content determines contents of the kind Lewis would propose, as follows. First, there is the set, call it X, of all those contexts, in some sequence in the given content, that satisfy the condition in (1). (The sequence for the object o will contain more than one such context if it is fine more than once in o's existence.) This is the content Lewis would propose for 'Today is fine and I exist throughout time'. Similarly, there is the set of all those contexts, in some sequence in the given content, that can be written as $\langle o, t+1, w \rangle$ with $\langle o, t, w \rangle$ in X. This is the content Lewis would propose for 'Yesterday was fine and I exist throughout time'. Similarly, there is the set of all those contexts, in some sequence in the given content, that can be written as $\langle o, t-1, w \rangle$ with $\langle o, t, w \rangle$ in X. This is the content Lewis would propose for 'Tomorrow will be fine and I exist throughout time'. And so on.

The contents of Lewis' kind, that are determined by this proposal, are unacceptably strong. Surely someone who believes 'Today is fine' on a given day is committed only to believing then that if he exists on another day, he is committed to believing the appropriate '$\pm n$ days from now, it is (tenseless) fine'. We can secure this by extending the second proposal above. And with this extension we also avoid having to assume that time is necessarily infinite both ways.

The content is a relation of infinitely variable polyadicity. It is a set of sequences; the sequences can be finite or infinite; and if infinite, ordered like all the integers, or the positive ones, or the negative ones. A sequence of contexts is in the content iff (1) there is some context in the sequence, $x = \langle o, t, w \rangle$ such that the weather at t in w is fine; call this context x_0; and (2) writing the sequence as $\langle \ldots, x_{-2}, x_{-1}, x_0, x_1, x_2, \ldots \rangle$ where each of the entries $\ldots, x_{-2}, x_{-1}, x_1, x_2, \ldots$ may not exist), $x_n = \langle o, t+n, w \rangle$ for all the integers n for which x_n exists. That is to say, the content is a set of sequences, each sequence representing the lifespan of an object that sometime in its life experiences fine weather.

This content determines contents of the kind Lewis would propose in much the same way as before. But the variable polyadicity means that the Lewis-contents allow objects not to exist throughout time. Thus, using the same definition of X as before (viz. the contexts in some sequence in the given content that satisfy condition (1)), we get just what Lewis would propose as the content of 'Today is fine', that is the set of contexts $\langle o, t, w \rangle$ such that the weather at t in w is fine. Similarly, we get what Lewis would propose as the contents of 'Yesterday was fine and I existed yesterday', and 'Tomorrow will be fine and I will exist tomorrow'.

In short, this content is 'centred around' the fine days. We get, as I think we should, logically stronger Lewis-contents away from the fine days: contents that incorporate the agent's existence on the fine days.

REFERENCES

Adams, R., 1974. Theories of actuality, *Nous 8*: 211–31.

Barwise, J. & Perry, J., 1983. Situations and Attitudes, London: MIT Press.

Blackburn, S., 1984. *Spreading the Word*, Oxford: Clarendon Press.

Böer, S. & Lycan, W., 1980. Who? Me?, *Philosophical Review 89*: 427–66.

Burge, T., 1977. Belief *De Re, Journal of Philosophy 74*: 338–62.

Burge, T., 1982. Other bodies, in *Thought And Object*, ed. A. Woodfield, Oxford: Clarendon Press.

Butterfield, J., 1984. Indexicals and Tense, in *Exercises in Analysis*, ed. I. Hacking, Cambridge: University Press.

Cresswell, M. & von Stechow, A., 1982. *De Re* Belief Generalized, *Linguistics and Philosophy 5*: 503–35.

Evans, G., 1981. Understanding demonstratives, in *Meaning and Understanding*, ed. H. Parret & J. Bouveresse, Berlin: De Gruyter.

Evans, G., 1982. *The Varieties of Reference*, Oxford: Clarendon Press.

Field, H., 1978. Mental Representation, *Erkenntnis 13*: 9–61: reprinted in *Readings in Philosophy of Psychology*, vol. II, ed. N. Block, London: Methuen; page references to reprint.

Fodor, J., 1986. Barnish disContent, this volume.

Fraassen, B. van, 1980. *The Scientific Image*, Oxford: Clarendon Press.

Frege, G., 1967. The Thought: a Logical Inquiry, in *Philosophical Logic*, ed. P. Strawson, Oxford: University Press.

Grice, H., 1957. Meaning, *Philosophical Review 66*: 377–88.

Kaplan, D., 1968. Quantifying In, *Synthese 19*: 178–214.

Kaplan, D., 1977. *Demonstratives*, preprint.

Kaplan, D., 1979. The Logic of Demonstratives, in *Contemporary Perspectives in the Philosophy of Language*, ed. P. A. French *et al.*, Minneapolis: University of Minnesota Press.

Kripke, S., 1971. Identity and Necessity, in *Identity and Individuation*, ed. M. K. Munitz, New York: New York University Press.

Kripke, S., 1979. A Puzzle about Belief, in *Meaning and Use*, ed. A. Margalit, Boston: Reidel.

Kripke, S., 1980. *Naming and Necessity*, Oxford: Blackwell.

Lewis, D., 1969. *Convention: A Philosophical Study*, Cambridge, Mass.: Harvard University Press.

Lewis, D., 1973. *Counterfactuals*, Oxford: Blackwell.

Lewis, D., 1979. Attitudes *De Dicto* and *De Se, Philosophical Review 88*: 513–43; reprinted in Lewis 1983; page references to reprint.

Lewis, D., 1979a. Scorekeeping in a Language Game, *Journal of Philosophical Logic* *8*: 339–59; reprinted in Lewis 1983.

Lewis, D., 1983. *Philosophical Papers*, vol. 1, New York: Oxford University Press.

Lewis, D., (forthcoming.) Causal Explanation, in D. Lewis, *Philosophical Papers*, vol. II. Oxford: University Press.

McDowell, J., 1984. *De Re* Senses, *Philosophical Quarterly 34*: 283–94.

McGinn, C., 1982. The Structure of Content, in *Thought and Object*, ed. A. Woodfield, Oxford: Clarendon Press.

McGinn, C., 1983. *The Subjective View*, Oxford: Clarendon Press.

Noonan, H., 1984. Fregean Thoughts, *Philosophical Quarterly 34*: 205–24.

Noonan, H., 1986. Russellian Thoughts and Methodological Solipsism, this volume.

Perry, J., 1977. Frege on Demonstratives, *Philosophical Review 86*: 474–97.

Perry, J., 1979. The Problem of the Essential Indexical, *Nous 13*: 3–21.

Perry, J., 1986. Circumstantial Attitudes and Benevolent Cognition, this volume.

Putnam, H., 1975. The Meaning of 'Meaning', in *Mind, Language and Reality*, Cambridge: University Press.

Stalnaker, R., 1973. Presuppositions, *Journal of Philosophical Logic 2*: 447–57.

Stalnaker, R., 1974. Pragmatic Presuppositions, in *Semantics and Philosophy*, ed. M. Munitz & P. Unger, New York: New York University Press.

Stalnaker, R., 1976. Possible Worlds, *Nous 10*: 65–75.

Stalnaker, R., 1976a. Propositions, in *Issues and the Philosophy of Language*, ed. A. Mackay & D. Merrill, Newhaven: Yale University Press.

Stalnaker, R., 1978. Assertion, in *Syntax and Semantics 9*: ed. P. Cole, New York: Academic Press.

Stalnaker, R., 1981. Indexical Belief, *Synthese 49*: 129–51.

Circumstantial attitudes and benevolent cognition*

JOHN PERRY

An agent's beliefs, desires and other cognitive attitudes depend not only on the agent's mental states and various necessary (or at least universal) facts connecting mental states with the rest of the world, but also on contingent circumstances that vary from individual to individual.

This circumstantial nature of the attitudes is a more or less direct consequence of the circumstantial nature of reference. If the object an idea is about depends on such circumstances as the causal paths leading to its occurrence, the identity of the agent, and the time and place of cognition, then what the agent believes or desires in virtue of the cognitions of which that idea is a component will vary with these contingent facts too.

The circumstantial nature of the attitudes strikes many philosophers as puzzling, inappropriate, or even unacceptable. Sometimes it is thought that there must be a layer of non-circumstantial attitudes underlying the circumstantial ones; this is one thought behind the *de dicto* vs *de re* distinction. Sometimes it is supposed that the whole line of reasoning that leads to the circumstantial nature of the attitudes must be confused.

A central cause of puzzlement is the idea that the circumstantial nature of the attitudes would render inexplicable the regular nomic links between what we believe and desire and what we do. But these nomic links are a central part of common-sense psychology, our conception of how we work.

In this paper, I claim that the circumstantial nature of the attitudes does not threaten, but rather renders intelligible, this insight of common-sense psychology. I do this by showing how an appreciation of the circumstantial nature of the attitudes allows us to state a central principle of the common sense view. The basic idea is that it is a complement to the long-recognized circumstantial nature of action.

* Research on this paper was begun while on sabbatical leave from Stanford University. It was also supported by a grant from the National Science Foundation and a grant to the Center for the Study of Language and Information from the System Development Foundation.

BENEVOLENT COGNITION

Fairly often, what we do helps us get what we need. This fact is the result of two others. First, our beliefs often correspond to the facts fairly well, and our desires often correspond to our needs fairly well. Secondly, the actions that we perform because we have certain desires and beliefs, are often of a sort that will promote the satisfaction of the desires if the beliefs are true. It is this second fact on which I shall focus.

It requires that two aspects of our beliefs and desires be coordinated, their content and their effect. Suppose I believe that the glass in front of me contains water, and I desire to drink. The content of my belief is that a certain glass contains water, and the content of my desire is that I get a drink. Some actions I might perform will satisfy my desire if my belief is true, and others will not. So the contents of my desire and belief determine a certain class of actions: those that are appropriate or reasonable given the contents of the desire and the belief. But the desire and belief themselves are, it seems, mental states. And these mental states are related by laws of nature to certain behaviour. Because I believe and desire as I do, I act in a certain way. I reach out, grab the glass, raise it to my lips, and swallow. This is an appropriate action, one that will lead to the satisfaction of my desire, if my belief is true. So the two aspects of my cognitive state, its doxastic and appetitive contents, on the one hand, and its effects, on the other, are coordinated.

This coordination suggests a certain benevolence on the part of God or Mother Nature. If this belief and desire resulted in my emptying the water on my head, or singing the National Anthem, then attribution of malevolence or a sense of humour might be more appropriate. But the evidence is in favour of benevolence, although perhaps of a rather grudging or parsimonious variety.

The principle that these two aspects of cognition are thus coordinated, I call 'efficient and benevolent cognition'. By 'efficient', I mean to express the idea that we do work in a lawlike way. Other things being equal, others in the same cognitive states that I am in will behave or act as I do.

In this paper I begin by putting before the reader a straight-forward version of the principle, whose conflict with the circumstantial nature of the attitudes will be fairly apparent. I show how appreciation of the circumstantial nature of action raises problems for this version. I then state a second version, which accommodates the circumstantial nature of action and the attitudes, explains it, and defends it against a possible criticism.

Here is the first version:

1. If   (i)   Believing *P* and desiring *Q* cause *A*,
    then (ii) *A* promotes *Q*, given *P*.

The idea is very simple: (i) envisages that there is a certain psychological law, connecting the property of believing *P* and desiring *Q* with the property of performing action *A*. If God or Mother Nature has wired us up in this way, and is benevolent, our environment must meet certain conditions; (ii) gives those conditions.

P and *Q* are propositions.[1] The notion of proposition I have in mind is based on the theory of situations, but the ideas presented here do not require exposition of that theory. It comprehends both objectual and qualitative propositions. That is, propositions may have objects as constituents in some sense, as is natural to suppose given circumstantial theories of reference; for example, 'President Reagan is asleep' expresses a proposition with Reagan himself as a constituent, rather than some properties he uniquely instantiates. But propositions may also have only relations and properties as constituents, as seems natural for 'every President is asleep' and some uses of 'the President is asleep'. For the purposes of this essay, the crucial property of propositions is that they are true or false absolutely, not relative to the circumstances of the agent.

A is an action; I take actions to be properties of a certain sort. As I use the terms an action is a uniformity across acts; that is, if you and I both raise our right hands, the acts are different, but the actions are the same.

I take causing and promoting as primitive. The first is a relation between properties. The latter, in this version, is a relation between a property (performing a certain action) and two propositions. A strong construal of an action promoting *Q* given *P* is that it guarantees *Q* given *P*; a weaker construal is that it merely makes *Q* probable, given *P*. For the purposes of this paper, this difference won't matter.

So the principle tells us that if things are benevolently organized, then a desire and a belief will cause an action, only if the action promotes the satisfaction of the desire given the truth of the belief. That is, if (i) is a psychological law for a class of agents, (ii) should be a principle that governs the environment of the agents.

---

[1] It is a fact of some interest, I think, that we ordinarily take actions or other properties of individuals as the objects of desire, rather than propositions. We are much more likely to say '*x* wants to go to the store' or '*x* desires to be at the store' than '*x* desires that he be at the store'. I think reflection on this point would strengthen the arguments I make here. But for simplicity I take propositions to be the objects of both belief and desire.

Version (1) strikes one, at first, as surely too simple, but headed in the right direction. But if the attitudes are circumstantial, it will not work at all. If what I believe and desire depends, not just on the internal mental states that we can conceive as leading, in lawlike ways, to actions, but also on the external circumstances in which those mental states occur, then the efficient benevolence envisaged by (1) looks impossible. For why should the actions, caused by those mental states, be appropriate to the attitudes one has in virtue of the mental states plus these additional, contingent circumstances, that can vary among cognitively similar individuals? It seems like God or Mother Nature would be faced with the choice of varying the action to suit the circumstantially determined attitudes, and so abandoning efficiency, or letting the actions vary only with the mental states, abandoning benevolence. We must either give up (1), or give up the doctrine of circumstantially determined attitudes.

ACTIONS AND CIRCUMSTANCES

We should give up (1), for it doesn't have things right. It envisages too simple a relation between actions and the propositional contents of belief and desire.

It is a familiar point that there are different ways to individuate actions. Suppose you move your right hand in a certain manner, thus grabbing the glass in front of you and bringing it to your lips, and I move my right hand in the same manner, thus grabbing the glass in front of me and bringing it to my lips. Have we performed the same action or not? It depends on how we individuate actions. Our acts were behaviourally similar, and if we use this as our criterion of individuation, we may be said to have performed the same action: moving in the way one does when one grabs a glass in a certain direction and at a distance in front of one with one's right hand and brings it to one's lips. But we can also individuate actions by their results, by reference to the propositions they make true. Given this criterion of individuation, we did not perform the same action. You made it the case that the glass in front of you was at your lips, but I did not. I could have done so, by moving my arm in a different way, which would have resulted in grabbing the glass in front of you and moving it to your lips. But, had I done that, I would not have performed the same action on the first criterion, for quite different behaviour is required for me to get the glass in front of you to your lips than is required of you to get it there.

When we think of actions as being caused by cognitive states, we must have a behavioural notion of action in mind. We expect agents that are cognitively similar to move their body and limbs in the same way. There is no reason to expect these movements to make the same propositions true, since this will depend not only on the behaviour, but also on the circumstances in which it occurs. Thus *making true* does not have as parameters only behaviourally individuated actions and propositions, but also agents and their circumstances.[2]

Similarly, *promotes* is not simply a relation between behaviourally individuated actions and a pair of propositions but also requires agents and their circumstances as parameters. The movement we are imagining me to make may guarantee or make probable that I get a drink from glass G, given that G contains water, if I perform it when G is exactly 23 inches in front of me in a certain relative direction. The same movement, made by you, with G 23 inches in front of you, will not guarantee or make it probable that I get a drink from G, given that G contains water. Nor would my making that very movement promote my getting a drink from G, in slightly different circumstances, with G, say, 29 inches away instead of 23. In those circumstances the movement would merely make me look silly, as if I thought my arms were longer than they are.

So, given that it is behaviourally individuated actions we need for the psychological principles, the promotion relation (whether it is construed as guaranteeing truth or something weaker), must be made relative to agents and circumstances. Version 1 simply won't work.

AN IMPROVED VERSION

I now put forward and explain an improved version of the principle, which accommodates the circumstantial nature of action, by exploiting the circumstantial nature of the attitudes.

First some preliminaries. The principle will be put forward in the form of a necessary condition for a relation of benevolence holding between three items, a psychology, a projection relation, and an environment. A psychology is a system of psychological states, behaviours and causal principles governing them. In (1) it was assumed that cognitive states can be directly assigned pairs of propositions, which a person in those states believes and

---

[2] Note that to take into account bodily differences, we need to make a further distinction between behaving in the same way and moving in the same way. Extending one's arm fully will not, with individuals of different arm lengths, lead to the same movements, if these are individuated in terms of the number of inches over which the arms move. In an earlier version of this paper, I added another parameter to the promoting relation discussed below, having to do with bodily characteristics, and another parameter to the causing relation. The idea was that a cognitive state caused behaviours depending in psychological type, and where things are benevolent, the psychological type accords with the bodily characteristics. This approach was taken because of a background assumption that perceptual states should be individuated in terms of objectively determined circumstances, and so this should also be true of cognitive states. However, I do not now feel very clear about how things should be handled, and so ignore the issue in this paper.

desires. Now we make the weaker assumption, that they can be assigned such propositions relative to circumstances. We break the circumstances into the context and the wider circumstances. The context includes both the agent and his spatiotemporal location – although here I am ignoring the latter. The wider circumstances are properties, including complex relational properties to other objects that an agent might have. These assignments are made by a projection relation:

Projects (a,C,S,Q,P) iff a desires Q and believes P in virtue of being in state S in circumstances C.

I use 'cognitive states' for those psychological states that have this relation to some agents, circumstances and propositions.

I leave it open just what underlies the projection relation. It might be an additional fact about agents that God or Mother Nature establishes, in addition to the facts of the psychology. Or it might be an artifact of our common-sense theory for dealing with the facts of psychology for the various purposes for which we need to deal with them. Something like the former is, I take it, Searle's view, while the latter I take to be common to various forms of the identity theory and functionalism. I am inclined to favour the latter view, and think that the considerations brought forward in this paper are relevant to arriving at a plausible version of it, but this topic is not further considered here; indeed, couching the project in terms of benevolence – either the real benevolence of God or the metaphorical benevolence of Mother Nature – fits most easily with the first view. If we hold the second view, this benevolence becomes something like a postulate underlying the common-sense theory.

Here then is the improved version:

2   Let Ψ be a psychology, E an environment, and Proj a projection relation. Let a, S and A range over agents, states and actions of Ψ respectively, and C range over circumstances of E. If Ψ is benevolent for E according to Proj, the following must hold:
  Whenever (i) an agent a is in circumstances C such that Proj (a,C,S,Q,P), then
  (ii) a is also in circumstances C' such that some action A caused by S is such that Promotes (a,A,C',Q,P)

In my example, my circumstances included seeing a glass which was in front of me, call it G. In virtue of being in the cognitive state I was in, I believed, of this glass, that it had water in it. Had a different glass, G', been in front of me, I would have then believed that G' had water in it, even though I was in exactly the same cognitive state. The possibility of this sort of relativity to circumstance is built into (ii).

Someone else in the same cognitive state would have desired that they get a drink from G, not that I do so. This involves relativity to context; that is, this difference would remain even if this other person were assumed to be in exactly my circumstances. Thus we need both the agent and the wider circumstances as parameters of the projection relation.

In my example, my being in this cognitive state causes me to move my hand and arms in a certain way, which works effectively to get me a drink. This would only work if I do it, and only in certain circumstances, as we discussed above. So now promoting has become a more complex relation. However, the circumstances that are relevant to my attitudes and those that are relevant to my action are not the same.

In the example, there is a certain glass, G, that I both have a belief and desire about, and act upon. The circumstances that determine that my belief is about G, have to do with the fact that I am looking at it, and it is the cause of certain aspects of my perceptual and cognitive state. The circumstances that determine that my movement intersects with the position of G at about the right point, and thus promotes my drinking rather than spilling water on myself or missing the glass entirely, have to do with the distance and position of the glass relative to me, and also the length of my arms and other such facts.

For this reason, we do not cite the same circumstances in (i) and (ii). Rather, we place a requirement on the environment E, that when an agent is in circumstances that determine, together with his cognitive state, certain attitudes towards an object, he will also be in circumstances that determine, together with the behaviour caused by the cognitive state, actions that are reasonable given the attitudes.

Note that it would be much too stringent to require that every action caused by S stand in the promotion relation. S may cause actions that have parts that are also actions, but which considered in isolation from the larger wholes don't promote anything helpful. And S may cause irrelevant actions, like fidgeting. All of this is compatible with benevolence, so analysed.

The sort of benevolence for which we have evidence is hardly as perfect as this might suggest. Sometimes our beliefs and desires cause behaviour which doesn't promote satisfaction of the desire, even if the belief is true. We might weaken the conditions by saying 'typically when' or even 'sometimes when'. The last alternative might be appropriate for Mother Nature, if her ambition is really just to allow a few agents enough freedom from total frustration that they reproduce. Or, rather than explicitly weakening the conditions, we may think of the analysis as providing us with a constraint that, like most conditionals, holds only relative to certain assumed background conditions.[3]

---

[3] Barwise (1985).

How benevolent are things? Suppose an experimental psychologist puts spectacles on me that make *G* appear closer than it really is, so when I reach for it I miss it and look silly. In this case the environment has not lived up to the demands of unconditional benevolence, given my psychology. So, the presence of experimental psychologists is enough to disprove unconditional benevolence, in this strongest sense. But unless they are allowed to take over the world, a more modest form of benevolence is still a possibility. And, to be fair, various odd circumstances that lead to illusions and clumsy behaviour occurred even before the advent of experimental psychology. Note that the effect of insisting on unconditioned benevolence, would be to insist that all such instances of illusion and ineptitude as instances of false belief. An insistence of this sort, would lead to a criticism of version (2) that I now consider.

(OVER) BURDENING BELIEF

The objection is that (2) is motivated by a misdiagnosis of the problems with (1), and as a result brings in circumstances twice over. The critic[4] would maintain that while action is circumstantial, the attitudes are only contextual. That is, the projection relation should be relative to context, but not to wider circumstance: only the context, the identity of the agent, is needed, to intervene between cognitive state and attitude. And, furthermore, the job of closing the gap between the behaviour a cognitive state causes and the goal it is to promote, should be mainly borne by the proposition believed. That is, the truth of the proposition believed should guarantee that the agent is in those circumstances in which the behaviour caused promotes the goal desired.

On this view, our example is diagnosed as follows. I must have believed not simply that the glass had water in it, but also that it was a certain distance and direction from me – exactly the distance and direction it had to be, for my action to promote my getting a drink.

On this view, we replace projection with a simpler relation:

Projects′ (a,S,Q,P) iff a believes P and desires Q in virtue of being in state S.

On this conception, one can represent cognitive states by pairs of properties of agents. The cognitive state I was in is represented by the pair:

[4] The critics I have in mind are Bob Moore, David Lewis, Roderick Chisholm, and Hector-Neri Castaneda. The first three have independently developed conceptions of the attitudes as relations to properties of the agent, and Castaneda's inclination to suppose that all indexicals and demonstratives can be analysed in terms of 'I' and 'now' makes me think he would also make a criticism of this sort.

being such and such a distance and direction from a glass full of water; drinking a glass full of water from which he is such and such a distance and direction. To get from the stage so represented to the proposition we need only the context.

However, *projects'* can be defined in terms of *projects*:

Projects' (a,S,Q,P) iff for every C, Projects(a,C,S,Q,P)

Not all cognitive states that bear the projecting relation to some agents, circumstances, and pairs of propositions will bear the projecting' relation to agents and pairs of propositions, only those for which the wider circumstances are irrelevant, in that once a is fixed, the content of belief and desire is also fixed. We can call this subclass of contextual but non-circumstantial cognitive states *merely contextual*. There is no need for me to deny the possibility of cognitive states that are merely contextual, and the analysis of benevolence in (2) extends to them. So the possibility of such cognitive states does not count against (2). We can retain (2), and entertain the possibility that all cognitive states are merely contextual as a hypothesis. A psychology with only merely contextual and not circumstantial cognitive states would be benevolent, but a benevolent psychology need not be of this sort. It is just a matter of how much God or Mother Nature wanted to make use of the stabler aspects of our environments.

To see what sorts of issues are relevant to this hypothesis, let us first note how unrealistic it would be to suppose that the content of our beliefs fix all of the circumstances relevant to the success of our action. Consider the force of gravity. If I am in space or on the moon or in some other situation where gravitational forces are much diminished, the movement we envisage me making in the example will not lead to getting a drink; the water would fly out of the glass all over my face – or perhaps I would not even grab the glass, but instead propel myself backwards. If all possible failures are to be accounted for by false beliefs, the corresponding true beliefs must be present when we succeed. So, when I reach for the glass, I must believe that the forces of gravity are just what they need to be, for things to work out right.

But it hardly seems probable that everyone, even those with no knowledge of gravity, believes, when they reach for a glass of water, that the gravitational forces are what they are; such an attribution would drain the word 'belief' of most of its content. Benevolence cetainly does not require such omnidoxasticity, to misbeget a phrase. A more efficient way for Mother Nature to proceed is to fit our psychology to the constant factors in our environment, and give us a capacity of belief for dealing with the rest. She could have been confident that by the time we achieve space travel, and have some need for action-affecting beliefs about gravity, we will have developed the concepts required to do so.

There are countless other circumstances necessary for our action to be successful, that are constant throughout the normal range of man. One might conjecture a general belief, that things are normal, underlies much of our action. But if we distinguish believing that things are normal from not believing that things are abnormal, this conjecture seems groundless.

These reflections do not decide the issue, for the hypothesis in question requires only that all of the non-constant circumstances relevant to action be comprehended by what is believed; the constant factors can be dealt with by admitting our psychology is benevolent only for environments that embody them.

It does, however, suggest where the issue does lie. Let me suggest a crude picture of psychology and projection, that motivates my scepticism about the hypothesis.

Suppose that, although there being a glass 23 inches in front of me is hardly a constant circumstance in my environment, there is a constant relation between a certain perceptual state and this circumstance. And suppose that there is a similar but different perceptual state that is similarly related to there being a glass 29 inches in front of me. Suppose further that these states have the property of referring to the object that plays some prominent role in their causation: in these cases, the glass in question. Finally, suppose that cognitive states are complex, that perceptual states of this sort can be components of them, and that the projective properties of cognitive states are systematically related to the referential properties of their components.

Given this picture, we may expect that different cognitive states, with different components, may project the same beliefs and desires, in slightly different circumstances. In one case I am 23 inches from G. In the other, I am 29 inches from it. My perceptual states are different. But both perceptual states are of the same glass, G, and the cognitive states of which they are components project the same desires and beliefs, that I get a drink from G and that G contains water. Still, given the different components of the different cognitive states, their causal roles may differ, even though their projective properties do not. The first cognitive state gives rise to behaviour suited to the circumstances stably related in the environment to its perceptual component – that is, my arm moves to a spot 25 inches away – and the second gives rise to behaviour suited to the circumstances stably related to it – I extend my arm a bit further.

If this were the way things worked, the hypothesis in question would be incorrect. To understand the relation between cognitive states, the beliefs and desires to which they give rise, and the actions they cause, we would have to recognize circumstances as a significant parameter of the projection relation.

While the picture sketched is crude, it seems the principle it illustrates could survive in more sophisticated accounts. It seems then that version (2) can at least claim the virtue of not ruling out such accounts *a priori*, so that the contextualist hypothesis can be weighed against alternatives.[5]

REFERENCES

Barwise, J., 1985. *The Situation in Logic II: Conditionals and Conditional Information*, CSLI Tech Report 85–21. Stanford: Center for the Study of Language and Information.

Barwise, J. and Perry, J., 1981a. Situations and Attitudes, *Journal of Philosophy 78*: 668–91.

Barwise, J. and Perry, J., 1981b. Semantic Innocence and Uncompromising Situations, *Midwest Studies in Philosophy 6*: 387–404.

Barwise, J. and Perry, J., 1983. *Situations and Attitudes*. Cambridge, Mass: Bradford Books/MIT Press.

Barwise, J. and Perry, J., 1985. Shifting Situations and Shaken Attitudes: An Interview with Barwise and Perry, *Linguistics and Philosophy 8*: 105–61.

Castaneda, H.-N., 1967. Indicators and Quasi-indicators, *American Philosophical Quarterly 4:* 85–100.

Chisholm, R., 1981. *The First Person*, Bright: Harvester Press.

Lewis, D., 1979. Attitudes *De Dicto* and *De Se*, *Philosophical Review 88*: 513–43.

Moore, R., 1985. A Theory of Knowledge and Action in *Formal Theories of the Commonsense World*, ed. J. Hobbs and R. Moore, Norwood, N.J.: Ablex Publishing Corporation.

Perry, J., 1977. Frege on Demonstratives, *Philosophical Review 86*: 474–97.

Perry, J., 1979. The Problem of the Essential Indexical, *Nous, 13*: 3–21.

Perry, J., 1980. Belief and Acceptance, *Midwest Studies in Philosophy 5*: 317–32.

Perry, J., 1980. A Problem About Continued Belief, *Pacific Philosophical Quarterly 61*: 317–32.

[5] This paper owes a great deal to a seminar on planning and practical reasoning at the Center for the Study of Language and Information in the Winter Quarter, 1984. Thinking about Bob Moore's theory of knowlege and action was particularly helpful. While the ideas in this paper are basically in the spirit of Barwise and Perry (1983), the seminar and other discussions with Michael Bratman, Stan Rosenschein, John Etchemendy, Ned Block, David Israel and others led to an increased appreciation of the importance of action in thinking about the attitudes. Both Jon Barwise and I have been thinking a great deal about such matters, and hearing his ideas on the semantics of OLP, a simple programming language based on English commands, was extremely helpful. Other developments in the theory of situations are reported in Barwise and Perry (1985).

This paper can be regarded as part of a series of works, including the book, which attempt to deal with attitudes in the light of issues about context and circumstance. These works, which I list in the bibliography, are not very consistent in terminology, and not perfectly consistent in doctrine, for the insights or mistakes that form their basis have been accumulating with time. But I think a fairly clear point of view emerges from them.

Perry, J., 1983. Castaneda on *He* and *I*, in *Agent, Language and World: Essays Presented to Hector-Neri Castaneda and His Replies*, ed. J. E. Tomberlin, Indianapolis: Hackett Publishing Company.

Perry, J., (forthcoming). Perception, Action and the Structure of Believing, forthcoming in a festschrift for Paul Grice ed. Richard Grandy and Richard Warner, to be published by Oxford University Press.

Replication and functionalism

JANE HEAL

In this paper I want to examine two contrasted models of what we do when we try to get insight into other people's thoughts and behaviour by citing their beliefs, desires, fears, hopes, etc. On one model we are using what I shall call the *functional strategy* and on the other we use what I label the *replicative strategy*. I shall argue that the view that we use the replicative strategy is much more plausible than the view that we use the functionalist strategy. But the two strategies issue in different styles of explanation and call upon different ranges of concepts. So at the end of the paper I shall make some brief remarks about these contrasts.

The core of the functionalist strategy is the assumption that explanation of action or mental state through mention of beliefs, desires, emotions, etc. is causal. The approach is resolutely third personal. The Cartesian introspectionist error – the idea that from some direct confrontation with psychological items in our own case we learn their nature – is repudiated. We are said to view other people as we view stars, clouds or geological formations. People are just complex objects in our environment whose behaviour we wish to anticipate but whose causal innards we cannot perceive. We therefore proceed by observing the intricacies of their external behaviour and formulating some hypotheses about how the insides are structured. The hypotheses are typically of this form: 'The innards are like this. There is some thing or state which is usually caused by so and so in the environment (let us call this state 'X') and another caused by such and such else (let us call this 'Y'); together these cause another, 'Z', which, if so and so is present, probably leads on to...' And so on. It is in some such way as this that terms like 'belief' and 'desire' are introduced. Our views about the causes, interactions and outcomes of inner states are sometimes said to be summed up in 'folk psychology' (Stich 1982a: 153ff). Scientific psychology is in the business of pursuing the same sort of programme as folk psychology but in more detail and with more statistical accuracy. On this view a psychological statement is an existential claim – that something with

135

so-and-so causes and effects is occurring in a person (Lewis 1972). The philosophical advantages, in contrast with dualism and earlier materialisms such as behaviourism and type–type identity theory, are familiar. It is via these contrasts and in virtue of these merits that the theory emerged. See Putnam (1967) for a classic statement.

This is a broad outline. But how is psychological explanation supposed to work in particular instances? What actual concepts are employed and how, in particular, are we to accommodate our pre-theoretical idea that people have immense numbers of different beliefs and desires, whose contents interrelate?

Functionalists would generally agree that there is no hope of defining the idea of a particular psychological state, like believing that it is raining, in isolation from other psychological notions. Such notions come as a package, full understanding of any member of which requires a grip on its role in the system as a whole (Harman 1973). This is true of any interesting functional concepts, even, for example, in explaining functionally something as comparatively simple as a car. If we try to build up some picture of the insides of a car, knowing nothing of mechanics and observing only the effects of pushing various pedals and levers and inserting various liquids, we might well come up with ideas like 'engine', 'fuel store', 'transmission', etc. But explanation of any one of these would clearly require mention of the others. Similarly we cannot say what a desire is except by mentioning that it is the sort of thing which conjoins with beliefs (and other states) to lead to behaviour.

But something more important than this is that the number of different psychological states (and hence their possibilities of interaction) are vastly greater than for the car. There is no clear upper bound on the number of different beliefs or desires that a person may have. And, worse, we cannot lay down in advance that for a given state these and only these others could be relevant to what its originating conditions or outcome are. This 'holism of the mental' (Quine 1960, Davidson 1970) which is here only roughly sketched, will turn out to be of crucial significance and we shall return to it. But for the moment let us ask how the functionalist can accommodate the fact that, finite creatures as we are, we have this immensely flexible and seemingly open-ended competence with psychological understanding and explanation. A model lies to hand here in the notions of axioms and theorems. We have understanding of hitherto unencountered situations because we (in some sense) know some basic principles concerning the ingredients and modes of interaction of the elements from which the new situations are composed.

What can the elements be? Not individual beliefs and desires because, as we have seen, there are too many of them. Hence the view that having an individual belief or desire must be, functionally conceived, a composite state. This is one powerful reason why the idea of the having of beliefs and desires as relations to inner sentences seems attractive (Field 1978: 24–36). The functional psychologist hopes that, with a limited number of elements (inner words), together with principles of construction and principles of interaction (modelled on the syntactic transformations of formalised logic), the complexity of intra-subjective psychological interactions can be encapsulated in a theory of manageable proportions.

But, however elegantly the theory is axiomatised the fact remains that it is going to be enormously complex. Moreover we certainly cannot now formulate it explicitly. There should therefore be some reluctance to credit ourselves with knowing it (even if only implicitly) unless there is no alternative account of how psychological explanation could work. But there is an alternative. It is the replicating strategy to which I now turn.

On the replicating view psychological understanding works like this. I can think about the world. I do so in the interests of taking my own decisions and forming my own opinions. The future is complex and unclear. In order to deal with it I need to and can envisage possible but perhaps non-actual states of affairs. I can imagine how my tastes, aims and opinions might change and work out what would be sensible to do or believe in the circumstances. My ability to do these things makes possible a certain sort of understanding of other people. I can harness all my complex theoretical knowledge about the world and my ability to imagine to yield an insight into other people *without any further elaborate theorising about them*. Only one simple assumption is needed: that they are like me in being thinkers, that they possess the same fundamental cognitive capacities and propensities that I do.

The method works like this. Suppose I am interested in predicting someone's action. (I take this case only as an example, not intending thereby to endorse any close link between understanding and prediction in the psychological case. Similar methods would apply with other aspects of understanding, for example, working out what someone was thinking, feeling or intending in the past.) What I endeavour to do is to replicate or recreate his thinking. I place myself in what I take to be his initial state by imagining the world as it would appear from his point of view and I then deliberate, reason and reflect to see what decision emerges.

Psychological states are not alone in being amenable to this approach. I might try to find out how someone else is reacting or will react to a certain drug by taking a dose of it myself. There is thus a quite general method of finding out what will or did happen to things similar to myself in given circumstances, namely ensuring that I myself am in those circumstances and waiting to see what occurs. To get good results from the method I require only that I have the ability to get myself into the same state as the person I wish to know about and that he and I are in fact relevantly similar.

As so far described the method yields us 'understanding' of another person in the sense of particular judgements about what he or she feels, thinks or does, which may facilitate interaction on particular occasions. We may also get from this method 'understanding' in the sense of some sort of answer to a why-question. If I am capable of describing the initial conditions which I replicated then I can cite them. But the method does not yet yield any hint of theoretical apparatus. No answer is forthcoming to the question 'Certain states are experimentally found to be thus linked – but why? What principles operate here?' We will return in section III to consider what concepts and principles of connection the replication method turns out to presuppose. Could they for example be identical with those the functional strategy calls upon?

But I would first like to discuss in section II three direct lines of attack upon my claim that replication is, at least in its method of delivering particular judgements, a real and conceptually economical alternative to the functional approach, that is, an alternative which avoids the need to credit ourselves with knowledge of complex theories about each other.

II

The first line of attack concentrates on how I am supposed to get myself into the correct replicating state. One might argue as follows; the replication method demands that I be able, on the basis of looking at someone else, to know what psychological state he or she is in, so that I can put myself in the same state; but to do this I must, perhaps at some inexplicit level, be in possession of a theory about the interrelations of psychological states and behaviour; but this will just be the functionalist theory all over again.

Two lines of defence against this attack are available. First, we may object that the attack presupposes that knowledge of another's psychological state must always be inferentially based and rest upon observation of behaviour, conceived of as something neutrally describable. But we need not buy this premiss and may propose instead some more direct model of how we come to knowledge of others' feelings and so forth (McDowell 1982).

Secondly (and this is the more important line of defence) the attack misdescribes the direction of gaze of the replicator. He is not looking at the subject to be understood but at the world around that subject. It is what the world makes the replicator think which is the basis for the beliefs he attributes to the subject. The process, of course, does not work with complete simplicity and directness. The replicator does not attribute to someone else belief in every state of affairs which he can see to obtain in the other's vicinity. A process of recentring the world in imagination is required. And this must involve the operation of some principles about what it is possible to perceive. Visual occlusion is the obvious example. But a theory about what one can know about the world from what viewpoint is not the same thing as a theory about how psychological states interact with each other or about what behaviour they produce.

It is worth remarking here that we need not saddle the replication theory with a commitment to the absurd idea that we are all quite indistinguishable in our psychological reactions – that any two persons with the same history are bound to respond to a given situation in the same way. Replication theory must allow somewhere for the idea of different personalities, for different styles of thinking and for non-rational influences on thinking. It is not clear what shape such additions to the core replication process would take. But there is no reason to suppose that they would take the form of the reimportation of the proposed functionalist-style theory.

Someone might try to press or to reformulate the objection by conceding that looking at the world rather than the subject might be a good heuristic device for suggesting hypotheses about his or her beliefs, but insisting that, nevertheless, we must employ (implicitly or explicitly) some criteria for the correctness of these hypotheses. What shows me that I am thinking of the world in the same way as the person I seek to understand? I must have some theory about what constitutes sameness of psychological state, and this theory, it will be suggested, could well, or indeed must, take a functionalist form.

But why should we accept the foundationalist epistemological presuppositions of this argument? Is it not enough for us to credit ourselves with the concept of 'same psychological state' that we should, first, be able to make generally agreed judgements using the notion and, secondly, that when our expectations are falsified we are usually able to detect some source of error when we cast around for further features of the situation, and hence to restore coherence among our own views and between our views and those of others?

We touch here on large issues in epistemology. But at the weakest we could say this, that there is not in this area any quick knock-down argument in favour of functionalism as against a claimed economical replication view.

Let us turn to a second reason for supposing that replication cannot be more economical than functionalism. Dennett (commenting on something similar to the replication view which he finds hinted at by Stich (1982b)) writes:

How can it (the idea of using myself as an analogue computer) work without being a kind of theorising in the end? For the state I put myself in is not belief but make believe belief. If I make believe I am a suspension bridge and wonder what I will do when the wind blows, what 'comes to me' in my make believe state depends on how sophisticated my knowledge is of the physics and engineering of suspension bridges. Why should my making believe I have your beliefs be any different? In both cases knowledge of the imitated object is needed to drive the make believe 'simulation' and the knowledge must be organised in something rather like a theory.

(Dennett 1982:79)

Of course Dennett is quite right that the psychological case as I have sketched is not one of strict replication, unlike the drug case. It would clearly be absurd to suppose that in order to anticipate what someone else will do I have actually to believe what he or she believes. But Dennett is wrong in thinking that what he calls 'make believe belief' is as alien a state – and hence as demanding of theoretical underpinning – as making believe to be a suspension bridge. Make believe belief is imagining. And we do this already on our own behalf. The sequence of thought connections from imagined state of affairs to imagined decision parallels that from real belief to real decision. If it did not we could not use the technique of contemplating possibilities and seeing what it would be sensible to do if...as part of our own decision making. So to make the replication method work I do not require the theory which Dennett mentions. I require only the ability to distinguish real belief from entertaining a possibility and the ability to attribute to another person as belief what I have actualised in myself as imagining.

The third attempt to show that replication and functionalism coincide takes a bolder line. The replicator supposes that some working out is to be done in order to find out what it would be sensible to do in the situation the other person envisages. Similarly the functionalist also supposes that working out is to be done; it is from a knowledge of particular states together with general principles or laws that a judgement on this case is to be reached. Why should we not suppose that the working out involved in the two cases is, contrary to superficial appearances, the same? The description of the replication method given so far suggests that sequences of thought states occur in me without mediation of any further thought, just as the sequences of reactions to drugs do. But perhaps this is a misleading picture; perhaps transitions from one thought to another occur in virtue of my awareness of some principle or law requiring the occurrence of the one after the other. Doing the actual thinking, which the replicator represents as something *toto caelo* different from functionalist style thinking about thinking, is not in fact fundamentally different. Making up my own mind is just the first-person version of what in third-person cases is functional style causal prediction.

But this will not do at all. For a start an infinite regress threatens. If any transition from thought to thought is to be underpinned by some further thought about links, how are we to explain the occurrence of the relevant thought about links without invoking some third level and so on? But let us waive this objection. More substantial difficulties await.

It is indeed tempting to suppose that whenever I draw a conclusion, that is, base one judgement on another, I must implicitly know or have in mind some general principle which links the two. But whether or not we think it right to yield to this temptation, the only sense in which the claim is plausible is one in which the principle in question is a normative one ('one ought to believe so-and-so if one believes such-and-such') or relatedly a semantic one ('the belief that so-and-so would be true if the belief that such-and-such were true'). In neither case is the principle in question a causal law, such as the supposed axioms of the functionalist theory are to be. The terminology I used above in arguing my opponents case (a 'principle' or 'law' by which the occurrence of one belief 'requires' the occurrence of another) is designed to obscure this vital difference. If we try to restate the proposal being quite explicit that the connections in question are causal we arrive at the most bizarre results. It amounts to supposing that it makes no difference whether a thinker asks himself or herself the question 'What ought I to think next?' or the question 'What will I, as a matter of fact, think next?' On the proposed view, these are just different wordings of the same question.

Suppose then that I do infer that q on the basis that p and that my knowledge that belief that p causes belief that q is integral to the process. We seem to have the following choice. Either we could say that the inference that q is based not just on the premiss that p (as *prima facie* but misleading appearance has it) but also on the (implicit) premiss that belief that p causes belief that q. This amounts to endorsing the principle of inference 'I will be caused to believe that p, therefore p'. Alternatively we could suppose that drawing the inference just is making the prediction. And this amounts to identifying belief that p with belief that one is being made to think that p.

Clearly none of this will do. It makes judgements about the world collapse into or rest upon judgements about me; and moreover they are judgements about me which have quite disparate truth conditions and roles in thought from the judgements about the world they are required to stand in for.

There are certain conditions under which the assimilation would appear less ludicrous. These are that I could isolate causal factors constitutive of my rational thinking from interfering ones; that I am a perfect thinker (that is, I rely on no confused concepts or plausible but unreliable rules of inference) and that I know that I am a perfect thinker. In other words, if I knew that physiologically I embodied a logical system and I knew the meta-theory for my own system, then causal-syntactic knowledge about myself would have semantic equivalents. The discussion of fallibility below will indicate some of the reasons why this is unacceptable.

So far I have been examining attempts to show that the replication strategy cannot be a real alternative to the functionalist one. And I maintain that none of them has undermined the plausibility of the original claim that the two approaches are different and that the former is more economical than the latter.

III

I turn now to a different line of thought, one which concedes the above claim but argues that nevertheless a replicative style of psychological understanding is compatible with a functionalist style. The use of the one does not preclude the other. A functionalist theory could develop out of and dovetail smoothly with use of the replicating strategy. Perhaps it is already doing so; or perhaps it will, when cognitive science is more advanced.

In the case of reaction to drugs something like this is clearly possible. At one stage of the development of knowledge I may be unable to anticipate others' reactions except via the replication method and unable to conceptualise them except through ideas appropriate to that method. For example, I ask of another person 'Why was she sick?' An initial answer might muster all the relevant information I have like this: 'I was sick; she took the same drug as I did and she is like me.' Or we might express it more naturally: 'She is like me and she took the drug which made me sick.' But this is not a stopping point. When I become reflective I shall ask 'In what respects is she relevantly similar to me?' and 'What feature of the drug connects with this feature of us to make us sick?' There is no reason in this case why the answers should not be ones the finding of which precisely does amount to my finding a causal theory which will emancipate me, wholly or partially, from the need to replicate. The key feature here is that the relevant similarity will probably turn out to be something about body chemistry. When I have these physiological concepts to hand I can specify directly what sort of creatures will be affected by some drug without mention of myself as a standard of similarity. And I can describe directly what the drug does to them instead of pointing to myself and saying 'It makes you like this.'

Now why should this not also be the case with psychological replication? Perhaps replication is a method by which primates unreflectively facilitate their social interactions. But we, it might be said, are in the process of emancipating ourselves from this primitive approach. (This is a view suggested to me by some remarks of Andrew Woodfield (1982: 281–2).) So when one unreflectively attributes a thought to another creature one may replicate that thought, and at the first attempts one may be unable to characterise the state in question in any other way than by pointing to oneself and saying 'Well, it is like what I am doing now.' And one will be unable to anticipate others except by recreating and attempting to rethink their thoughts because one has no access to the nature of the thought as it is in itself or the respects in which the other subject and oneself are relevantly similar. Nevertheless reflection shows us that there is such a thing as the nature of the thought in itself, some intrinsic character that it has, and some non-demonstrative specification of relevant similarity. So when we use psychological terminology reflectively it is to these things that we intend to refer. And cognitive science is about to fill in the actual detail of what they are.

But I want now to argue that this will not do. When we reflect on the notion of 'relevant similarity', as it needs to be used in psychological explanation, we discover an insuperable bar to imagining it being superseded by the sort of physiological or structural description which functionalism requires. And relatedly we find that we cannot get at the nature of the thought as it is in itself but continue to have access to it only in an indirect and demonstrative fashion.

The difference between psychological explanation and explanation in the natural sciences is that in giving a psychological explanation we render the thought or behaviour of the other intelligible, we exhibit them as having some point, some reasons to be cited in their defence. Another way of putting this truism is to say that we see them as exercises of cognitive competence or rationality. (I intend these terms to be interchangeable and to be under-stood very broadly to mean what is exercised in the formation of intention and desire as well as belief.)

This is a feature of psychological explanation which the replication method puts at the centre of the stage. When I start reflecting upon the replication method and trying to put the particular judgements and connections it indicates in a theoretical context, it is the notion of cognitive competence, of the subject struggling to get things right, which must present itself as the respect in which I and the other are relevantly similar.

But what further account can we give of rationality? Could it be discovered to be identical with and replaceable by something which would suit the functionalist programme? Initial thoughts about rationality or cognitive competence suggest that it surely has something to do with the ability to achieve success in judgement (that is truth for belief and whatever the analogous property or properties are for desires, intentions, etc.) But the nature of the link is difficult to capture. Is rationality something which guarantees the actual success of judgement in particular cases? Arguably not, since the question 'But have I got this right?' can always be raised. We must recognise ourselves to be thoroughly fallible. This is one important implication of the extreme complexity of interaction of psychological states which our earlier discussion did not bring out. In our earlier remarks about functionalism the complexity served merely as a spur to thinking of psychological states as molecular rather than atomic. That move was needed because we could not specify in advance what beliefs might be relevant to any other – as premisses or conclusions. Thus given enough background of the right sort any belief could bear upon the truth of any other. It is this which prevents the individuation of beliefs as atomic units by their placement in some specifiable pattern of a limited number of other psychological states. But a further implication of this (as Quine constantly stresses) is that we cannot pick upon any belief or beliefs as immune to any possible influence from future information.

So cognitive competence is not the claim that for at least some sorts of judgement success is guaranteed. Could it be defined, then, in terms of inference rules relied on or judgement-forming procedures, for example, by mention of specific rules like *modus tollens* or inductive generalisation or, more non-committally, via the idea of inference rules which are generally reliable? This again will not do and its failure is crucial to the incompatibility between replication and functionalism. I can fail to follow simple and reliable inference rules and can adopt some most unreliable ones, and recognise later that this was what I was doing, quite compatibly with continued trust in my then and present cognitive competence. The only constraint is that I should be able to make intelligible to myself why I failed to notice so-and-so or seemed to assume such-and-such. And, as with the case of individual judgements, enough scene setting can do the trick. This is not to say that I can make sense of my past self – or of someone else – even where I can find no overlap at all between my present judgements and inference procedures and those of the other. Rather my claim is that we cannot arrange inference procedures (or judgements) in some clear hierarchy and identify some as basic or constitutive of rationality.

We may have models or partial views of what constitutes rationality (in logic, decision theory and so forth) but thinking in accordance with the rules or standards there specified cannot be definitive of or exhaust the notion of rationality. This is not only because our current views on these matters may be wrong but for another reason also. If rationality were thus definable then the claim that I myself am rational would acquire some specific empirical content, would become just one proposition among all the others which form my view of the world. It would thus be potentially up for grabs as something falsifiable by enough evidence of the right character. But, notoriously, any attempted demonstration to me by myself that I am a non-thinker must be absurd because self-undermining. Hence any account of what it is to be a thinker which seems to make such a demonstration possible must be at fault.

How does all this bear upon the idea that as we gain more knowledge and conceptual sophistication some primitive replication method could gracefully give way to a more scientific functional understanding? It is relevant because this idea does require exactly the assumption that rationality can be given a complete formal definition in terms of syntactically specifiable inference rules. It is only if this is the case that the replicating assumption of relevant similarity – 'they are like me in being cognitively competent' – can be replaced by the functional assumption – 'they are like me in being systems with inner states structured and interacting according to so-and-so principles'.

I have used as a premiss a strong version of fallibilism which some may find implausible. Surely, one might protest, some propositions (that I exist, that this is a desk, that here is a hand) are in some sense unassailable, as are also some rules of inference. Am I seriously suggesting that the law of non-contradiction or universal instantiation might be overthrown?

Suppose we concede the force of these remarks; does it then become defensible again to maintain that functionalism will turn out to be compatible with the replication approach and will ultimately replace it? It does not. As long as we admit that there are any parts of our implicit inferential practices which may be muddled – that is, as long as we admit (as we surely must) that the world has some funny surprises in store for us as a result of which we shall recognise our earlier thinking patterns as muddled and inadequate, then we must also admit that our formal grip on rationality is not complete.

It is position within the network defined by the supposed formal account of rationality which is to provide the functionalist account of what a thought is in itself. Thoughts are, for functionalists, identified and individuated by causal–explanatory role. So a corollary of the non-existence of a formal account of rationality is the non-availability of that mode of characterising thoughts which functionalism counts on – a mode imagined to be independent of our entertaining or rethinking those thoughts.

IV

I turn finally to some sketchy and programmatic remarks about the concepts and modes of explanation which will be called on under the two strategies – replicating and functionalist.

Recent writings in the functionalist school have produced powerful arguments to show that upon their approach the semantic properties of psychological states, that is, their referential relations to particular objects or sorts of stuff in the world, are not directly relevant to their explanatory roles. We think of psychological states (they say) both as things which are true or false in virtue of semantic connections with the world and also as things which are explanatory of behaviour. But these two ways of thinking about them are in some sense independent. So that-clauses are systematically ambiguous; sometimes we use them to ascribe truth conditions and sometimes to ascribe causal–explanatory role (Fodor 1980, McGinn 1982, Field 1978).

I shall not fully rehearse the arguments for this view here. The nub of the matter is just this, that admission of the referential as explanatory in the functionalists' causal framework would amount to admitting a very mysterious action at a distance which goes against all our causal assumptions. Distant objects exert their causal influence over us via chains of intermediate events, where these events could occur from other causes even if the distant object did not exist. The functionalist views as explanatory a state which could exist even if the supposed referent did not; and thus he claims to unite economically, in one form of account, actions guided by true beliefs (i.e. ones which are referentially well grounded) and also actions which are based on illusion. The functionalist claims that we have a concept of what is common to referentially well-based cognition and illusory cognition, a concept which is specifiable without mention of referential success; and that referential success is thus a conjunctive notion (cf. McDowell 1982).

But what is this something else, this non-referential content which we sometimes use that-clauses to ascribe? One thing which is clear is that in attributing non-referential content to someone's thought I do not commit myself to the existence of any particular thing (or natural kind) outside him. I merely characterise him as he is intrinsically.

But obscurities remain. One of these has been noted (Bach 1982). Non-referential content could be something thought of merely syntactically – that is, to be labelled 'content' only in an exceedingly stretched sense. On the other hand the notion of non-referential content could be recognisably a notion of meaning in some sense. In reporting it we report the subject's 'mode of representing the world' – but without commitment to the existence of anything outside him.

But within the latter option there is also an important further obscurity. Is non-referential content strongly conceptually independent of reference and truth, in that someone could have the former idea without the others so much as having crossed his mind? Or are they only weakly conceptually independent in that ascription of non-referential content does not commit one to an actual referent or truth conditions but does commit one to some disposition concerning reference and truth? On the second view, in thinking of something as having non-referential content we are thinking of it precisely as something which in a certain context or under certain other conditions would have such-and-such referent and truth conditions.

There are thus three options. Non-referential content is

(a)   a merely syntactic notion
(b)   a notion of meaning strongly independent of truth and reference
(c)   a notion of meaning only weakly independent of truth and reference.

Which of these do the functionalists propose?

It is claimed that classification of beliefs as explanatory and classification of them as truth bearers are 'independent' because such classifications can cross cut (e.g. in the case of indexicals or Twin Earth situations: cf. Fodor 1980: 66–8, McGinn 1982: 208–10). And in the discussion of why we are interested in reference at all, it seems to be assumed that this 'cross-cutting classification' argument has established (a) or (b) – that is, has established 'independence' in a strong sense of complete conceptual detachment. These discussions proceed on the assumption that grip on the non-referential notion of content has provided no foothold at all for truth and our interest in it has to be motivated totally *ab initio* (Field 1978: 44–9, McGinn 1982:225–8). But in fact the cross-cutting classification point does not establish this. Consider 'fragile' and 'broken': these classifications cross cut. But this would hardly show that we could understand 'fragile' without understanding 'breaks' or that our interest in breakage needed to be motivated independently of our interest in fragility.

On the other hand the notion of non-referential content is sometimes elucidated in terms of notions like subjective probability, inference, Fregean sense, or Kaplanesque 'character' (Field 1977, McGinn 1982). And these notions are ones which *prima facie* have conceptual links with reference and truth. Thus Kaplan's notion of the character of an indexical utterance or belief is precisely the notion of something which, placed in a certain context, determines a referent and hence a truth value.

Whichever of these options the functionalist takes there will be difficulties. On (a) and (b) it turns out that a view which I earlier offered as a truism, namely that in psychological explanation we exhibit the explanandum having a point or being at least in part justified, is false. The explanatory notions postulated in (a) and (b) are ones which provide no foothold for talk of justification or point. So, if presented as a view about everyday psychological talk and explanation, this philosophical theory has the problem of explaining where the semantic and related justificatory aspects of the practices fit in and why they seem to loom so large for us. I do not say that this cannot be done, only that attempts so far have not been convincing.[1] On the other hand, if the theory is presented not as an account

---

[1] Field suggests (1978: 44–9) that we attribute reference and truth conditions to the inner states of others because we find it useful to 'calibrate' them; we can then use facts about their inner states, in conjunction with some reliability theory, to gain information about the world for ourselves. McGinn (1982: 225–6) objects to this that it makes assignment of reference to others' beliefs and utterances too contingent. On Field's account we would not

of notions we now employ but as a blueprint for a future, highly abstract version of neurophysiology, then it is not faced with that problem but its relevance for philosophical accounts of current practice is non-existent.

If the functionalist adopts (c) as his account of non-referential content then his problems are different. This content notion is one in which two elements are linked – namely the idea of a 'a mode of representing the world' and the idea of a 'causal–explanatory role'; moreover they are linked in such a way that the one 'is constitutive of' the other (McGinn 1982: 210). The mode of representing notion now invoked has enough link with truth for notions like justification and seeing the point to get a grip. So it would not be absurd to offer this as an account of part of what we are ordinarily doing with psychological statements. But, if the arguments centring on fallibilism in the earlier part of the paper were persuasive, the difficulty will be to show convincingly how there *can* be a notion which dovetails this 'mode of representing' idea with the 'causal–explanatory role' idea. Grip on a causal explanatory role is grip on some pattern, thought of as fixed and where the *relata* are known. But grip on a justificatory content is confidence in my power to see the point, to understand arguments and justifications involving this notion when I am called upon to do so, without supposing that I *now* know what those other related thoughts are. That such a functionalist notion, that is, one in which the two elements are dovetailed, is called for by a plausible version of functionalism is not an argument for its coherence, unless functionalism itself is unassailable.

In summary, then, in this section I have been arguing that much work needs to be done to clarify the notion of non-referential content which

bother to do it if we thought the other person, through limitations of his knowledge or his unreliability, had nothing to teach us. Yet surely we might assign reference even in these circumstances. So McGinn proposes (1982: 226–8) that we need the notion of reference in characterising the practice of communication. 'A hearer understands a speech act as an assertion just if he interprets it as performed with a certain point or intention – viz. to convey information about the world.' But this, on McGinn's own earlier showing, will hardly do. The phrase 'about the world' is itself subject to the bifurcation of role which McGinn claims to find in all that-clauses or content ascribers. When I ascribe to another an intention to 'convey information about the world' on McGinn's account I may understand this attribution of content to his or her intention in either of two ways – first as ascribing an inner explanatory state, grasp of the nature of which requires no semantic concepts, or secondly as ascribing an inner state with semantic relations. And only the former is needed for psychological explanation and understanding of communicative behaviour. So, failing some further account of 'characterising the activity of communication' (an account which shows it to be other than psychological explanation of it), we are no further forward.

What is odd about both these accounts, Field's in particular, is that they take for granted that we want true beliefs for ourselves. But once this is acknowledged the attempt to anchor the notion of truth and our interest in it by pointing to some complex of causal facts and correlations observable in third person cases seems strange. The interest in truth is already anchored as soon as a person comes to express reflectively his or her own beliefs and to ask 'But is that right?'

functionalists ought to espouse and to demonstrate that such a notion is coherent.

What will be the theoretical apparatus and modes of explanation which the replication account calls for? In stressing that one is only in position to understand another psychologically by rethinking his or her thoughts, I am putting the idea of 'doing the same thing oneself' in a prominent place. And it may thus seem that Cartesian introspectionism is reappearing on the scene. But this is not so. And the crucial difference is that, on the view I maintain, one has no more access to the intrinsic nature of one's own thoughts than one does to the intrinsic nature of others'. Thinking about my own thoughts is not, on my model, direct and intimate confrontation with something about whose nature I cannot be deceived. It is, in my own case as for others, to replicate – that is, putting on a certain sort of performance, rather than being in possession of a certain kind of knowledge. Psychological ascriptions – the use of that-clauses – might better be called re-expression than description. I do not by saying this mean to outlaw the phrases 'psychological knowledge' or 'psychological description' but rather to put us on our guard against a certain way of conceiving of such knowledge or descriptions. We may agree that a person knows of himself or herself what he or she is thinking more easily than he or she knows this of others. In one's own case one does not have the complexities of recentring to deal with, so replication comes very easily. But the technique for doing it, namely looking at the world, and the outcome, namely placing oneself in a position to put on a certain sort of performance, are just the same whether one thinks of oneself or another. And the emphasis on fallibilism shows that my easy replication of my own thought gives me no privileged position *vis à vis* claims to understand it, see what follows from it or the like.

I have argued that the notion of rationality or cognitive competence is central on the replication account. But equally I have argued that no substantive definition of it can be given. It is not that rationality has no conceptual connections with other notions. The idea of cognitive competence must have something to do with the idea of attaining success in cognition, that is, truth for beliefs and whatever the analogous properties are for other intentional states. Hence the idea that semantic notions such as truth have no importance in psychological explanation will clearly be mistaken on the replication view. Rationality cannot be understood without a grip on the semantic notions which define success or failure in cognition.

But one might still wonder about the point or usefulness of deploying the notion of rationality. If I affirm of myself that I am rational what point can my action have if I am not offering something with a testable content, a description of the world? I conjecture that we have here one of those items at the limits of our conceptual scheme which present themselves sometimes as statements but at other times rather as programmes of action or announcements of a stance. One thing that I might be doing in affirming myself to be rational is acknowledging the necessity of taking success as the norm in my cognitive enterprises, that is, taking success as what is to be expected unless evidence of mistake appears. I suspect that pursuit of this clue might lead to a more illuminating picture of what psychological explanation is than attempts to elaborate a functionalist account. But that is a topic for another paper.

REFERENCES

Bach, K., 1982. *De re* Belief and Methodological Solipsism, in *Thought and Object*, ed. A. Woodfield, Oxford: Clarendon Press.

Davidson, D., 1970. Mental Events, in *Experience and Theory*, ed. L. Foster and J. W. Swanson, Cambridge, Mass.: University of Massachusetts Press.

Dennett, D. C., 1982. Making Sense of Ourselves, in *Mind, Brain and Function*, ed. J. I. Biro and R. W. Shahan, Brighton: Harvester Press.

Field, H., 1977. Logic, Meaning and Conceptual Role, *The Journal of Philosophy 74*: 379–409.

Field, H., 1978. Mental Representation, *Erkenntnis 13*: 9–61.

Fodor, J. A., 1980. Methodological Solipsism Considered as a Research Strategy in Cognitive Psychology, *The Behavioral and Brain Sciences 3*: 63–73.

Harman, G., 1973. *Thought*, Princeton, N. J.: Princeton University Press.

Lewis, D., 1972. Psychological and Theoretical Identifications, *Australasian Journal of Philosophy 50*: 249–58.

McDowell, J., 1982. *Criteria, Defeasibility and Knowledge, Proceedings of the British Academy 68*: 455–79.

McGinn, C., 1982. The Structure of Content, in *Thought and Object*, ed. A. Woodfield Oxford: Clarendon Press.

Putnam, H., 1967. The Nature of Mental States, First published as Psychological Predicates in *Art, Mind and Religion* ed. Capitan and Merrill. Pittsburgh: University of Pittsburgh Press; reprinted in H. Putnam, *Mind, Language and Reality: Philosophical Papers*, vol. II, Cambridge: Cambridge University Press, 1975.

Quine, W. V. O., 1960. *Word and Object*, Cambridge, Mass: MIT Press.

Stich, S., 1982a. On the Ascription of Content, in *Thought and Object*, ed. A. Woodfield, Oxford: Clarendon Press.

Stich, S., 1982b. Dennett on Intentional Systems, in *Mind, Brain and Function*, ed. J. I. Biro and R. W. Shahan, Brighton: Harvester Press.

Woodfield, A., 1982. On Specifying the Contents of Thoughts, in *Thought and Object*, ed. A. Woodfield, Oxford: Clarendon Press.

Anti-realism: cognitive role and semantic content*

JOHN SKORUPSKI

I shall argue two main points. The first is that naturalism – according to which 'minds are no more than a part of nature' – cannot be reconciled with realism, understood in the particular sense which Dummett has made familiar. Realism in this sense is a conception of what it is to understand a sentence. Understanding is grasping truth conditions; and – this is an essential qualification – the concept of a truth condition is given in terms of a correspondence notion of truth.

The claim may seem paradoxical. Is not naturalism, on the contrary, incompatible with the *rejection* of realism? Can naturalism and realism ultimately be distinguished at all? Is not 'anti-realism' nothing but a new form of idealism? I claim that naturalism and realism are distinct, that naturalism is consistent with the rejection of realism and indeed requires it. But for this to be plausible, the implications of the realist conception must be carefully traced, and what is, and what is not being rejected in it identified.

If one can indeed endorse naturalism while rejecting realism, rejection of realism cannot preclude a distinction between evidence warranting the assertion of a statement, and that statement being true. For it must be an implication of the naturalistic view of the mind that any information I have or conclusion I draw is always defeasible. And this connexion between naturalism in metaphysics and fallibilism in epistemology leads to my second main claim. I shall argue that anti-realism can accommodate defeasibility only if it is possible to distinguish two notions or aspects of meaning: 'cognitive role' and 'semantic content'. And in section v I shall make some very tentative remarks about the notion of cognitive role.

I ON 'ANTI-REALISM'

'Anti-realism' I take, again in Dummett's sense, as the idea that to understand a sentence is to grasp its assertion conditions. This can be

* I am grateful to David A. Bell and Jeremy Butterfield for detailed criticisms of earlier drafts.

developed in a wide variety of ways; but the essential thought is constant: understanding a sentence is nothing other than a recognitional ability – the ability to recognise data, against a background context of belief, as licensing assertoric utterance of the sentence understood.

Now if this is what is meant by anti-realism, the claim that realism and anti-realism are jointly exhaustive requires some defence. 'Anti-realism' in this sense is a positive doctrine. It gives an epistemic account of what language mastery consists in. Understanding is constituted by a grasp of the evidential situations which warrant assertions in the language; it does not consist in a grasp of something *else*, something which enables one to recognise evidence as evidence only when combined with an intrinsically separate mastery of inductive rules.

Given my earlier definition of realism, on the other hand, rejecting realism must mean rejecting either the claim that understanding is constituted by grasp of truth conditions, or the claim that truth is to be understood in terms of correspondence, or both. So far it seems to imply no positive doctrine. A question therefore arises about how 'anti-realism' – the positive thesis – hangs together with the rejection of realism. Does rejecting realism commit one to 'anti-realism'?

A person who rejects realism may simply mean to reject the correspondence notion of truth. He may not mean to reject the claim that meaning is determined by truth conditions. What he denies is the intelligibility of the correspondence notion, as this is intended by the realist: that is, as a substantial philosophical thesis and not simply an incontrovertible and innocuous truism. Whether he should go on to offer an account of truth in terms of assertibility, or of meaning in terms of assertion conditions – these seem to be separate questions.

As far as truth goes, he has two crucially different options. He may reject the correspondence notion in favour of an epistemic conception of truth couched in terms of some notion of *assertibility* (truth as assertibility, as assertibility in the long run..., in an optimal theoretical framework..., by rational inquirers in an ideal speech situation...). He can then still agree that to understand a sentence is to grasp its truth conditions. But he will equate truth conditions with assertion conditions of some kind. He thus endorses both an epistemic conception of understanding and an epistemic conception of truth.

But it should not be assumed that rejection of the correspondence notion must lead to identification of truth with assertibility of some kind or other. One may reject the correspondence notion because one rejects *any* substantive philosophical conception of truth. (The redundancy 'theory' should be seen as a rejection of all such philosophical 'theories' of truth; it is however in no way inconsistent with the project of providing truth definitions for particular languages.) This is the second option. A person who takes it rejects the correspondence notion of truth, but does not affirm any other philosophical conception of truth in its stead – not, in particular, an epistemic conception.

This *second option* may in turn, at first sight, seem to contain a further pair of alternatives. The first rejects the correspondence 'theory' of truth along with any other 'theory'. But it still clings to the dictum that understanding is constituted by a grasp of truth conditions, seeing it as something which yields fundamental philosophical insight into the nature of language mastery. The second rejects correspondence – and accepts 'anti-realism' characterised in the positive way: as the view that understanding is constituted by a grasp of assertion conditions. On this latter approach, one affirms an epistemic conception of understanding, but without putting forward an epistemic conception – or any other substantial philosophical conception – of truth.

Many philosophers, I suspect, take it for granted that the first alternative within the second option is viable, and for that reason do not take 'anti-realism' (i.e. as characterised in the positive way) seriously. They consider that they can reject the correspondence account of truth, along with any other philosophical definition of truth, yet still force a philosophical insight into the nature of language mastery out of the dictum that to understand a sentence is to grasp its truth conditions.

It is hard to give a clear account of what is intended by the 'correspondence theory', and hard, therefore, to get any grip on what is involved in rejecting it. The success of anyone who rejects it will be measured by the extent to which he finally appears to be rejecting nothing of substance – and thus (it may seem) asserting nothing of substance either. That is a familiar situation in philosophy. It does not mean that exorcising the correspondence conception is easy or unimportant. On the contrary, we have here an entrenched philosophical pre-conception which shapes our thinking in ways which are both pervasive and hard to bring into reflective view.

What then is rejected when correspondence is rejected? Not, as I have already said, the view that understanding a sentence involves knowing its truth conditions, if that is understood as expressing no more than the unilluminating truism, that someone who understands a sentence, and grasps the use of the truth predicate in the appropriate language, thereby understands a sentence which can be used to state the truth condition of that sentence.[1] What is rejected, rather, is nothing other than the picture

---

[1] I mean that the truism is unilluminating considered as an answer to philosophical questions about what it is to understand a language. I do not mean to deny that a semantic account of the language should be cast in terms of truth conditions. This will emerge more fully in what follows.

in which grasp of a sentence's truth conditions *appears as something determined independently of a mastery of rules of evidence.* That is to say, rejection of correspondence simply comes down to affirmation of an epistemic conception of understanding. They are, despite initial appearances, nothing but aspects of one position. For what the correspondence theorist intends is precisely a model of truth in which I first grasp what it is for a sentence to be true and only then move on to the further question of what rules of evidence, if any, could in principle bear on it.

The 'first alternative' within the second option represents, then, no genuine possibility. It is not possible to reject realism while refusing to affirm anti-realism; realism and anti-realism are indeed jointly exhaustive.

Still that leaves a vital difference between the first and the second option. The second option gives us an epistemic conception of understanding but it does *not* propose an epistemic definition of truth. It holds that my grasp of the truth conditions of sentences in a language draws essentially on my mastery of rules of evidence, but it does not concede that truth can be defined in terms of warranted assertibility, under whatever conditions.

It is an important question whether this second option is viable: just how important becomes plain only when one examines the roots of anti-realism. In the next two sections I shall argue that the basic source for anti-realism is naturalism. Naturalism begins with the elementary or primitive notion that we are simply and straightforwardly a part of the world we know. It becomes a reflective position when its philosophical consequences are taken seriously. 'Minds are no more than a part of nature' – perception, cognition, motivation, action and so on are purely empirical, causal processes. They are an integral part of a larger causal order, and no more than that. Let us consider more closely how it is that anti-realism springs up naturally on this ground.

II THE ARGUMENTS FROM NATURALISM TO ANTI-REALISM

As I use the terms, then, idealism in its various forms should be opposed to 'naturalism', not to 'realism'. The distinction between realism and anti-realism cuts across that between naturalism and idealism, producing a table of four positions. In practice, 19th-century idealism and 20th-century anti-realism can be seen as competing responses to certain unavoidable difficulties which are thrown up by the combination of naturalism and realism.

Given naturalism, two lines of thought converge in support of an anti-realist view of understanding. The first I shall call the 'direct argument'; it simply analyses, within a firmly naturalistic framework, what it is or could be to understand an expression or a sentence. I shall consider it in section

III. The second argument is indirect. It urges that the combination of naturalism and realism entails an absurdity, and reacts by discharging the realist premise.

It is a venerable thought that naturalism is incompatible with the possibility of knowledge. The argument goes back to Kant's reading of Hume, and his 'Copernican revolution'. If man is straightforwardly a part of nature, there can be no *a priori* limits to the empirical study of man; in particular, to the study of man's cognitive relations with the world – no transcendentally limiting characteristics of experience, consciousness, or cognition, which constrain natural explanations and cannot themselves be naturally explained.

According to 'critical philosophy' in the post-Kantian sense, the possibility of knowledge presupposes that there are such limits. For someone in this tradition, naturalism is 'pre-critical' in that it fails to see (1) that if knowledge is to be possible, there must be *a priori* elements, not purely verbal or in any intelligibly rigorous sense 'analytic', in our thinking about the world; and (2) that there can be such *a priori* elements in our thinking only if the mind is more than just a causal process within a larger causal order.

It is at just this point that the indirect argument relies on the possibility of making a distinction between naturalism and realism. Naturalism can be squared with the possibility of knowledge when it is combined with an anti-realist conception of meaning. When combined with realism, it collapses into self-defeating scepticism. But when combined with anti-realism, the same considerations establish only a kind of fallibilism which there was every reason to accept anyway. One might say that on this approach (1) is accepted (though to say only that is rather misleading, because the significance of the claim is so thoroughly transformed), whereas (2) is rejected.

The naturalistic picture of perception and thought views them as causal processes within a larger causal order. On that picture our information about the environment is necessarily perspectival and corrigible: causally mediated by the fallible sensory modes in which the world of which we are a part is presented to us. If scientific inquiry transcends this perspectival predicament, it does so only by inferences to the best explanation which take us beyond the perspectivally given. Let these methods of reasoning succumb to sceptical attack, and naturalism is itself undermined: we have no grounds for the claim that our sensory data are products of causal interaction with an encompassing natural world.

When naturalism is combined with realism it becomes impossible to defend inference to the best explanation as a method of attaining truth. There can be no answer to the sceptic's question: Why should we think that the theory which is predictively adequate, and which we find simplest, most intelligible, etc, is *true*? A theory's being predictively adequate, simpler than its competitors and so on, does not entail its truth. The respective truth conditions of the two statements are distinct. Given realism, there can be no reason to infer one from the other. For if you combine, with a naturalistic view of cognition, a conception of meaning according to which the meaning of a sentence is given, in a manner which predetermines no rules of evidence, by the state of affairs which it pictures, you make it quite impossible to see how a state of information could warrant assertion of a statement in a manner which was simultaneously defeasible and *a priori*.

For the anti-realist, the rules of evidence which, as a matter of natural fact, we reflectively agree on, enter constitutively into our understanding of the language we use. To understand a sentence is to be able to recognise data as contextually warranting its assertion. But such an ability – recognising kinds of data, in appropriate contexts of background information, as warranting assertions – can only take the form of a grasp of rules of evidence. The 'rules' of inductive inference (the distinctive, and perhaps impossible to spell out, principles which determine what we agree on as 'the best explanation') are fundamental rules of this kind. To say that T is predictively adequate, simpler, etc., just is to give a reason for asserting T – for asserting that T is *true*. It is a defeasible reason, because we can never rule out the possibility of a simpler, etc. alternative. Consequently it cannot entail that T is true. But it warrants the assertion that T is true nonetheless.

This, in outline, is the indirect argument. The direct argument remains to be considered. There is a subtle interaction between them: each eases the path of the other, each is hard to set out in a compact or immediately persuasive way. But, of course, both arguments are effective only if anti-realism is not itself a form of idealism. Otherwise they would simply amount to yet another *reductio* of naturalism.

Here the tenability of the second option becomes decisive. Since the first option defines *truth* in epistemic terms, it belongs within the idealist tradition. On the naturalist view all evidence – collected in however long a run, assessed by human inquirers who can be as rational as you like (though of course they can only have the powers of *human* inquirers) – is defeasible. Just because we are part of the natural world into which we inquire, it cannot follow from the fact that the evidence warrants the assertion that P, that P. So to identify truth with assertibility is to embrace some form of idealism – according to which the knowing subject is *not* simply part of the world he knows.

Thus if naturalism forces an anti-realism of the first kind then it implies its own negation. But such *reductios* of naturalism have never carried conviction for long. Partly, no doubt, because there seems to be nothing intelligible at the end of the idealist line. But this factor is inextricably woven into a larger historical fact, which one must bear in mind in order to understand the present philosophical situation. The naturalistic frame of mind emerged – and continues to send down even deeper roots – for reasons largely external to philosophy in any narrow sense. Its relations are with broader currents of thought: gestured at in such phrases as Max Weber's 'disenchantment of the world'. Of course, even if the sources of naturalism are largely external to philosophy, the question of its consequences and coherence are matters for philosophical discussion. It is no exaggeration to say that two centuries after the Enlightenment those consequences are still sinking in.

If my account of the dialectical position, and of the place of naturalism in our thinking is correct, there is immense pressure to find some way of vindicating the second option. But can one endorse an anti-realist view of understanding without committing oneself to an idealist definition of truth? Only, I shall conclude, by making some sort of distinction between *semantic content* and *cognitive role*.

But before we examine the implications of defeasibility for anti-realism further, let us consider the direct argument.

III THE DIRECT ARGUMENT

The centrepiece of the direct argument is that there can be nothing more to the truth or falsity of statements which attribute understanding of a language to a speaker, than is contained in facts about how experiences dispose him to behaviour, including utterances.

Distinguish two conceptual levels at which an agent can be described: call them the 'naturalistic' and the 'hermeneutic' level. At the naturalistic level, we see behaviour and internal states, and dispositions to, or causal connexions between, them. Physicalism is not the issue here. The internal states can be a stream of experiences, as well as a stream of physical processes. Whether, as the physicalist holds, they can all be described physically does not matter. Experiences are such things as: a perceptual or bodily sensation; a sudden sinking feeling or a feeling of elation; a tune, or the sounds 'Got it!' or 'Bingo!' running through one's head; the sudden image of a peculiar expression on a friend's face; and so on.

The hermeneutic level adds to this the full resources of our language of desire, emotion, reasoning, inference, deliberation, choice. Statements which attribute understanding of a language to a person obviously belong at this level.

Naturalism affirms the primacy of the naturalistic level. Whatever facts there are about an agent either directly are, or are in some sense constituted by, facts characterisable at the naturalistic level: behaviour, inner states, physical or experiential, dispositions to and causal connexions between these.

Belief, understanding, meaning are not directly given as episodes or processes at this level. They are not experiences. The same could be said for emotions and desires; nor are choices or inferences mental events. But neither do these phenomena add a distinct and new class of facts to what is already on the naturalistic scene. We get to them by *interpreting* what is given. So it seems that when we describe an agent at the hermeneutic level the facts which make what we say true or false must either be in some way *constituted* by facts visible at the naturalistic level – or we are not engaged in a genuinely fact-stating kind of discourse at all.

The premise of the direct argument is simply a special case of this general claim: there can be nothing to mastery of a language beyond a system of causal uniformities among processes given at the naturalistic level.

Notice that this is a constitutive, not an epistemological thesis. It is a claim about what there could possibly be to understanding, not about how we know that a person understands. The point is worth stressing. It is obscured if the anti-realist issues his 'challenge' by pressing questions about how the mastery of a language is 'manifested'. Then it seems that the argument might simply run as follows. The assertion conditions of any statement that ascribes understanding to a speaker must take the form of facts about his dispositions to linguistic behaviour in observable circumstances. Hence a statement of the form

(1) N understands S.

will have the same assertion conditions as some statement of the form

(2) N is disposed to utter S…in (publicly observable) circumstances C.

If we conclude from this that the two statements have the same content, we have the basis of a general anti-realism about what it is to understand a sentence.

Waive all difficulties about producing any such *statement* of the assertion conditions for (1) (and thus also the question of whether they are relevant). The argument still looks question-begging: we are assuming an anti-realist view of statements of form (1), and pointing out that a general anti-realism, about what it is to understand any statement at all, follows. But what gives us the right to make the assumption? On this approach it looks as if the anti-realist case rests from the start on some form of epistemological positivism applied to the case of other minds.

But when the claim is understood as constitutive, it issues in a powerful and non-question-begging argument for anti-realism. To understand a term or a sentence is to grasp rules, and to be able to apply them correctly. What then is it to *know* a rule, to *see* its implication, to act *on* that implication?[2]

A tempting reply is that it consists in being aware of something – something abstract, or something mental. Awareness is taken relationally, as the quasi-perception of an entity: a picture, representation, proposition. Let us call this the 'relational' model of understanding. The relational model is a kind of 'realism', in one good sense of the word, about rules, or meanings. That is to say, it treats them as a class of self-interpreting objects to which we have cognitive access. The rejection of *this* kind of realism about understanding and inference is what leads to the rejection of 'realism' in the sense of this paper.

Whether one thinks of these self-interpreting objects, or 'pure meanings' in psychologistic or platonistic terms the same objection immediately applies. How *could* any object require or impose a way of going on? Imagine the 'pure meaning' as a concrete physical object or process (e.g. a physical inscription, or a sequence of noises). How could this object or process *require* or *impose* an interpretation? Then how does making it mental or abstract help? (This might be called 'Wittgenstein's patent antidote'.) In short, the moment a rule is conceived as an *object* of awareness, it necessarily requires, and necessarily resists, interpretation.

At this point one might immediately conclude that since what makes rule-following ascriptions, and thus ascriptions of understanding, true cannot be any kind of episode of grasping a self-interpreting entity, it must be nothing but a pattern of dispositions. The anti-realist conception – that understanding a sentence consists in nothing more than a disposition to respond appropriately to data – would immediately follow. But this is too brisk. 'Dispositionalism' presents a closely related difficulty.

Rule-following as against merely regular behaviour can be said to be correct or mistaken. Descriptions of N at the rule-following level – in general, at the hermeneutic level – can entail that N acted correctly or incorrectly, rationally or irrationally. In contrast, descriptions of N at the purely dispositional level cannot do so. Thus it seems that the former level cannot be reduced to the latter. Statements at the hermeneutic level cannot have truth conditions couched in purely dispositional (or causal-connexions-between-internal-states) terms. Consider:

---

[2] It was Wittgenstein, of course, who stated the question in this specific and illuminating way. But it is also a vexed question, what the strategy or upshot of Wittgenstein's discussion of rule-following is supposed to be. See the discussions in Kripke (1982); Wright (1980); Baker and Hacker (1984); McDowell (1984); Budd (1984). On 'semantic externalism' – the epistemological as against the constitutive argument – see Craig (1982). What I set out here seems to me a sound argument, the materials for which are in Wittgenstein. But I shall not argue the latter point.

(i) N has endorsed the rule (formed the general intention) 'Whenever P, do A', and he observes that P.

(ii) Whenever N observes that P he does A (or: that causes him to do A), and he observes that P.

(i) entails a normative statement: he should, in consistency ought to, do A. (ii) does not: it simply entails a prediction. Moreover, if N does in fact do A, and we say that N has applied the rule, then we are claiming that he has seen, recognised, that he ought, given the rule, to do A, and done it for that reason.

The full breadth of the issue involved here is worth bringing out. The concept of a rule and the concept of generality are closely connected. Asking what it is to grasp and follow a rule is closely akin to asking what it is to form and carry out a general intention, and that in turn to asking what it is to form, and reason in accordance with, a general belief. The issue is a global one: about understanding, inference, generality-involving attitudes, and ultimately perhaps, about intentionality as such. (It will stretch as far as that, if one holds that intentional states cannot be ascribed to a creature which cannot be said to have generality-involving attitudes or to infer.)

Descriptions of an agent at the hermeneutic level have this normativity because, when we describe an agent at this level, we credit him with rational autonomy: the ability to recognise rational requirements. To say that N does A *because* he has endorsed the rule is to say that he has recognised that in current circumstances *the rule requires him to do A*. To say that he has *inferred* that Ga is to say not merely that he has been caused to believe that Ga because he believes, say, that $(x)(Fx \rightarrow Gx)$ and has come to believe that Fa, but that this is true in virtue of his having recognised that Fa together with $(x)(Fx \rightarrow Gx)$ entail Ga.

We are tempted to think of the recognition of a rational requirement as an episode or act which figures essentially in the antecedents of a rule-application. But it appears that the supposed episode is just what the naturalistic level cannot yield. No experience or behaviour will do. Nor will any causal connexion between experiences, or between experiences and behaviour. The relational model of what it is to grasp a rule was exploded precisely because no object of awareness could have the property of 'pure meaning' – could instruct me on its own application. Yet a rule is internally related to its own application. So a rule is not an object of awareness. If the naturalistic level is fundamental, we are threatened with the conclusion that rational autonomy, the central category of the hermeneutic perspective, is unintelligible.[3]

---

[3] Compare Stroud (1979), and his discussion of Lewis Carroll's story of Achilles and the tortoise. One cannot make recognition of the implication into an extra episode, *in* the causal nexus. (A similar point lies at the back of the idea that agent causality is presupposed in autonomous choice.)

This is what Kripke (1982) calls the 'sceptical problem'. A 'sceptical solution' would somehow balance three apparently irreconcilable elements: recognising the primacy of the naturalistic level, it would nevertheless show how descriptions at the hermeneutic level can simultaneously be in some sense acceptable *and* irreducible. On Kripke's interpretation of Wittgenstein, Wittgenstein's view is of this kind: the hermeneutic perspective is 'all right', and irreducible, yet in some sense not fundamental; its status must be philosophically grasped in the naturalistic perspective.

Of course a *sceptical* solution is redundant if the hermeneutic perspective is not after all irreducible. It is important here not to underrate the resources of functionalism.[4] But this is not the place to pursue delicate questions about the notion of a function. The essential point, as far as the argument for anti-realism is concerned, is the primacy of the naturalistic level. Once that is accepted, anti-realism follows, whatever may be the most satisfactory view to take of the reducibility issue. For on any such view, it will remain the case that statements ascribing understanding of language to someone will be right or wrong only in virtue of facts given at the naturalistic level. And that is enough for the constitutive argument.[5]

The core of that argument is rejection of the picture of rational autonomy as transcendental activity in, or in relation to, a non-natural realm. In our interpretative understanding of ourselves we are subject to a kind of transcendental illusion. We rightly think the essence of understanding, inference and general belief is rule-guidedness. But we think of being guided by a rule as relatedness to some self-interpreting entity, and we think of the dispositions that a person who understands acquires, as *results* of that relation, as accident rather than essence. This may be built into the very concepts, and projected onto a person we interpret, so that no purely naturalistic analysis of the concepts of thought, deliberation, inference and choice can succeed. Or it may be a detachable philosophical misconception. Or it may be that these alternatives already impose an over-sharp distinction. In any case, the force of the direct argument is that content is exhausted by role. When it comes to language mastery, the only fact of the matter is functional appropriateness of response.

[4] That is to say, a functionalist view, by characterising psychological states in *functional* terms, and not directly in terms of their causal role, has the makings of normativity built in. To say that X functions in S to produce Y is to say more than that in standard circumstances it causes Y. In cases where, standard circumstances applying, it fails to cause Y, one can say that a malfunction or breakdown has taken place. (This is not to deny that the concept of function may in turn be analysable in causal terms. See Wright 1973.)

[5] McDowell (1984) interestingly argues that Wittgenstein offered no 'sceptical solution' – nor is there one. Instead, Wittgenstein argued backwards from the unavoidability of the sceptical problem given naturalism, to rejection of the primacy of the naturalistic level. I do not find this a plausible reading, but I cannot argue this here.

IV DEFEASIBILITY

Having surveyed the anti-realist case, we can turn to its difficulties. They stem from the strangely protean character of the concept of meaning, and the difficulty of reconciling the roles it plays in different contexts.

The first context is the naturalistic perspective on action and cognition. Here meaning is correlative with understanding, and understanding a matter of systematic appropriateness of response. This is meaning as *cognitive role*.

The second context is that of logical theory; the theory of which sentences can be correctly inferred from which. Here the meaning of a sentence is that which determines its logical powers: its role in sound inferences, as premise or conclusion, and its contribution to determining the logical powers of sentences in which it appears as a constituent. Equally, the meaning of a term is the contribution it makes to determining the logical powers of sentences in which it appears. Thus a requirement on meaning in this sense is that it should be compositional: the meaning of a complex expression is wholly determined by the meaning of its constituent expressions.

Here we have the connexion with truth: to say that an argument is deductively sound is to say that certification of the premises as *true* indefeasibly warrants acceptance of the conclusion as *true*. So the meaning of a sentence will determine the role it can play in inferences – and its contribution to the role a complex sentence in which it is a constituent plays in inferences – precisely inasmuch as meaning determines truth conditions. Meaning in this sense – *semantic content* – will equate at the sentential level with truth conditions.

Are cognitive role and semantic content simply two aspects of a unitary concept, or do they come apart?[6] Perhaps there is a class of essentially first-personal and indefeasible statements reporting the speaker's current experience. But apart from any such class, all statements are defeasible.[7] That is to say, it is always possible that a state of evidence which warrants the assertion of a statement may be enlarged in such a way as to produce a new state of evidence which no longer warrants its assertion. This defeasibility is radical: no sense can be attached to the idea of enlarging a

---

[6] Questions about proper names, indexicals, and the concept of a 'mode of presentation' may come to the reader's mind here. I ignore these issues in what follows.

[7] The reader may wonder how these remarks square with my previous characterisation of deductive inference as indefeasible. Two notions of indefeasibility should be distinguished. (1) If a conclusion is a deductive consequence of certain premises, the addition of further premises cannot defeat the proof; (2) logical principles are not revisable. In characterising deductive inference as indefeasible, I meant sense (1) rather than sense (2). I think naturalism also entails rejection of (2) – though no doubt even someone who thinks logic revisable has to make *some* sense of the at least 'local' sense (2) indefeasibility of deductive inference.

state of information to the point where it indefeasibly warrants an assertion. That, as I have pointed out, follows from the naturalistic view of mind as such. There is no unimprovable state of information. (As an information state is enlarged, its assertion-licensing powers, while being reduced in some respects, may also of course be extended in others – so that statements which were previously neither assertible nor deniable may become so. I shall use 'defeasibility' as shorthand to cover both these aspects.)

But where the assertion conditions of a statement, S, are defeasible, 'S is true' cannot be interderivable with 'The assertion of S is warranted', and in general the logical powers of such pairs of statements will not be the same. Truth cannot be identified with assertibility. This being so, one cannot identify the notion of a truth condition – the state of affairs which 'makes a sentence true' – with the notion of an assertion condition – the state of affairs knowledge of which justifies one in asserting the sentence.

The consequence, in turn, is that one must either give up anti-realism, or else make some sort of distinction between cognitive role and semantic content – treating semantic content as a notion which is in some way to be explained or motivated in terms of the basic notions: the network of sentences with which we confront the world, and their assertion conditions and cognitive roles.

Consider: (a) It is true that P; (b) The assertion that P is warranted. They have the same assertion conditions. (They are asserted and withdrawn under the same conditions.) But their semantic content is different: as witness their different contribution to complex assertions in which they occur unasserted, for example, 'It was the case that...', 'It is not the case that...'.

Filling the blanks with (a) and (b) gives pairs of semantically complex sentences, where the members of each pair do *not* have the same assertion conditions. But, given compositionality, if a constituent of a sentence is replaced by another expression with identical semantic content, the sentence which results must have the same semantic content as the original. It follows that we cannot define *semantic content* in terms of assertion conditions. But the only account we can give of understanding – and correlatively, of *cognitive role* – is in terms of assertion conditions.[8]

---

[8] The essential argument here is foreshadowed in Dummett (1973). See especially pp. 449–51: 'One reason why [the realist conception] appears so plausible is that the notion of truth is born...from the necessity to distinguish between it and the epistemic notion of justifiability: and this necessity is in turn imposed by the requirements for understanding certain kinds of compound sentence (p. 451). Cp. Brandom (1976), where the point is clearly brought out.

V BEARINGS AND CONSEQUENCES

If the arguments for anti-realism, and the difficulties for it, are balanced in this way, it is hard to see how to go on. What follows is no more than tentative suggestions.

How do semantic content and cognitive role interrelate? Can there be a systematic account of cognitive role? To say that S is complex in respect of cognitive role is to say that understanding of S flows from an understanding of its constituents, together with grasp of their mode of composition – of the function which takes their cognitive roles into the cognitive role of S. So where a sentence is complex in respect of cognitive role, it ought to be possible to give a compositional account of that role. And does not the possibility of understanding new sentences containing sentential constituents establish that there is such complexity, so that the anti-realist has an obligation to give a systematic compositional 'theory' for the cognitive role of sentential operators?

This is a popular argument which richly deserves critical attention. But instead of facing it head-on I shall restrict myself to some remarks on negation. The anti-realist might approach negation in various ways; the way I want to consider is modelled on the intuitionistic idea of taking the negation of a sentence to be justified just when an 'absurdity' is derivable from that sentence. To apply this to the general case we distinguish theoretical and observational sentences. The negation of a theoretical sentence will be justified just if it has a falsifiable consequence at the observational level.

To follow the idea through one would have to elucidate and defend two main claims, concerning negation and implication respectively. First, the concept of a falsification presupposes that the notion of a negated observation sentence is given. So we must envisage a base level of observation sentences which are in a certain sense decidable. Let us, as a first step, ignore the fact that the assertibility of observation sentences can be defeated by theoretical considerations. The cognitive role of an observation sentence's negation can then be understood as a function of the cognitive role of that sentence itself. We initially learn the assertion conditions of observational negations as functions of the assertion conditions of their constituents.

The second claim is about implication. The assertion that 'P implies Q' is licensed if there is reason to think that Q could be derived from P – in accordance with rules of reasoning currently entrenched in our thinking. Only within an accepted theoretical framework does one have reason to think that Q is derivable from P. But that does not mean that the assertion 'P implies Q' contains an implicit reference to that framework. If we are warranted in holding a theory in our current state of information, we are warranted in asserting it to be true, *tout court*, and thus in detaching its consequences.

Even in this brief sketch two points are clear. First, an account of the assertion conditions of 'not-*S*' along these lines cannot be regarded as a definition of 'not-*S*'. It may be recognisably true that '*S*' has falsifiable consequences in the total fabric of sentences *T*, but *T* is itself defeasible in an enlarged information state. To say this is only to reiterate the fact of defeasibility, and its consequence: that the anti-realist's account of negation comes at the level of cognitive role, not at the level of semantic content.

Secondly, such an account of the assertion conditions of 'not-*S*' does not determine them as a function of the assertion conditions of '*S*'. For substitution of 'It is assertible that *S*' for '*S*' in 'not-*S*' will produce a sentence with different assertion conditions. Rather, in grasping the assertion conditions of 'not-*S*', where '*S*' is a theoretical sentence, I am guided by a picture of what it is for '*S*' to be *true*. Imagination, the use of analogical representation, thus enters into our grasp of assertion conditions for theoretical sentences.

But at this point the realist's rejoinder is plain. He will object that in admitting that the picture of the truth condition of a theoretical sentence enters into our theoretical inferences, we have conceded the case. We have accepted that it is in virtue of his grasp of its truth condition that a person grasps the assertion conditions of a theoretical sentence, in all their indefinitely ramifying complexity across varying theoretical contexts. How does this differ from realism?

Scientific models explain the truth conditions of theoretical sentences by analogical extensions of observable situations. Compare the role of analogy with one's own case in understanding the mental states of others. In each case the picture we form regulates our assertion and inference. But there is no reason why the anti-realist should not recognise the legitimate role played by analogy in reasoning about the world. On the contrary, anti-realism precisely need *not* be a finitistic or inductivist stance. The anti-realist can accept that imagination enters into our construction of a scientific world-picture. (Indeed one might go further: to reject models and analogies as mere 'manners of speaking', betrays an adherence to the realist conception of meaning. For it is that conception, together with familiar epistemological constraints, that leads one to a reductionist or instrumentalist view of science, of other minds, and so on.)

What matters is whether analogy-based explanations equip one with an ability to grasp how a given theoretical sentence could interlock with a theoretical context in which it would have assertion conditions. If they do, they earn their keep. It remains the case that there is no more to grasp of a theoretical sentence than ability to recognise its assertibility in a given information state: a recognitional capacity which we obtain against the background of reasoning propensities which we share. The picture of the sentence's truth condition comes in just inasmuch as it contributes to that.

Realism offers the idea that grasp of meaning *is* possession of a picture or representation of the truth condition. What is wrong with this is not the idea that pictures can play an indispensable role. It is treating any such picture as a 'pure meaning', something which lays down its own application. We concluded in section III that the reverse holds. It is not a self-validating significance which the picture has that determines its application, but its application that determines its significance. Consequently – this is the essential point in which anti-realism differs from the realist conception – the fact that a given state of information warrants the assertion of the sentence is in a certain sense *a priori* – because our reasoning propensities enter constitutively into our understanding of what we say.

To return to the case of negation. In a language game of simple observation, the cognitive role of denials can be grasped as a function of the cognitive role of the sentences denied. But of course the moment observation sentences are put into their theoretical context, sufficiently weighty theoretical considerations *can* defeat their assertibility. Once the language game has been enlarged by theory, theory spills back into observation: the negation of an observation sentence may be justified on holistic theoretical grounds. Nevertheless the simple language game does not simply disappear without trace, any more than the distinction between observation and theory does. Observation sentences remain 'relatively' or 'contextually' indefeasible – there is a guiding but not absolute rule that they should not be overturned. It is a vital point that grasp of this rule enters into full mastery of the language game, and of the cognitive role of negation.

Thus the semantic representation of negation as an operator which uniformly takes the truth conditions of a constituent sentence into truth conditions for a complex negated sentence, is a construction at the semantic level; a construction out of data which are untidy and multifarious, in this kind of way, at the cognitive level. The construction is possible because of the particular rules of reasoning (inductive and deductive) which are entrenched in our thinking. The anti-realist who accepts my second option need not be a revisionist about these rules of reasoning. In particular, he has no reason, *qua* anti-realist, to reject classical logic and truth-theoretic semantics.[9] All that he rejects is a metaphysical picture of meaning that tends to go with them.

---

[9] Certainly for an anti-realist stance the point of a principle such as bivalence, in its application to theoretical levels of inquiry, calls for elucidation: Cp. Quine (1981). Equally though, the combination of naturalism and realism ought to issue in an empiricist view of logic like Mill's: cp. Putnam (1978: 140, n. 10, last paragraph.) For a succinct statement of Dummett's view, that classical logic can be accepted by the anti-realist only at the expense of an untenable holism, see his (1980).

REFERENCES

Baker, G. P. and Hacker, P. M S., 1984. *Scepticism, Rules and Language*, Oxford: Blackwell.
Brandom, R., 1976. Truth and Assertibility, *Journal of Philosophy 73*: 137–49.
Budd, M., 1984. Wittgenstein on Meaning, Interpretation and Rules, *Synthese 58*: 303–23.
Craig, E. J.,1982. Meaning, Use and Privacy, *Mind 91*: 541–64.
Dummett, M., 1973. *Frege: Philosophy of Language*, London: Duckworth.
Dummett, M., 1980. L. E. J. Brouwer, *Collected Works*, *Mind 89*: 605–16.
Kripke, S., 1982. *Wittgenstein on Rules and Private Language*, Oxford: Blackwell.
McDowell, J., 1984. Wittgenstein on Following a Rule, *Synthese 58*: 325–63.
Putnam, H., 1978. *Meaning and the Moral Sciences*, London: Routledge and Kegan Paul.
Quine, W. V. O., 1981. What Price Bivalence, *Journal of Philosophy 78*: 90–4.
Stroud, B., 1979. Inference, Belief and Understanding, *Mind 88*: 279–86.
Wright, C.,1980. *Wittgenstein on the Foundation of Mathematics*, London: Duckworth; Cambridge, Mass.: Harvard University Press.
Wright, L., 1973. Functions, *Philosophical Review 82*: 139–68.

Privacy and rule-following

EDWARD CRAIG

This paper is a sequel to an earlier one. My intention is that its argument should be comprehensible without the need for knowledge of the earlier paper, but it would be too much to hope that its point will be clear without such knowledge. It is part of the investigation of a central topic in the theory of meaning, more specifically of epistemic privacy and its relation to language. So a little stage-setting is called for.

The earlier paper (Craig 1982) is largely a discussion of arguments put forward by Michael Dummett at the beginning of 'The Philosophical Basis of Intuitionistic Logic' (Dummett 1978) in favour of a certain stance in the theory of meaning, a stance which in his view is one of the principal supports for constructivist and anti-realist doctrines. In the earlier paper I did not address the question of these alleged consequences, nor shall I do so in this one; my interest is confined for the present to the semantic thesis itself. I shall label it 'semantic externalism'. It states that no item which is epistemically private to a speaker – which no one other than he can know the nature of – can be essential to the meaning of any symbol, word or phrase he uses:

> The meaning of a statement cannot be, or contain as an ingredient, anything which is not manifest in the use made of it, lying solely in the mind of the individual who apprehends that meaning. (Dummett 1978:216)

In 'Meaning, Use and Privacy' I argued that the grounds Dummett gives for this view are fallacious, unless one is prepared to adopt unargued and controversial premisses. But I also asked whether there might be some other route to Dummett's conclusion not mentioned in his paper. And in the light of remarks about privacy and meaning recently made by, *inter alia*, Kripke (1982), it naturally came to mind that there might be an approach via Wittgenstein's treatment of rule-following. For reasons of length, that had to go into another paper – this one.

I

I start with a proposition I take to play a central role in Wittgenstein's famous argument of *Philosophical Investigations* §258 that there can be no such thing as a private language: the idea that the speaker applies his word *S* to the same sort of item on various occasions is spurious, that is

(A) In the case of epistemically private items (understood by reference to the traditional picture) there is something radically wrong with the notion of recurrence or sameness of kind.[1]

From this, given that meaningfulness calls for the consistent use of symbols, so that whatever plays an essential part in their meaning must play it consistently, we arrive at the notorious conclusion that a private language, one which allows a speaker to make reference to items epistemically private to him, is impossible. But my main interest isn't for the moment in that conclusion; rather I am interested in the possibility of deriving Dummett's position, the necessity of semantic externalism, from those premises.

In a bracket, so to speak: it might appear that if we can derive Dummett's conclusion, the anti-private-language thesis will follow as a simple corollary. This isn't because the references of the terms of a private language are epistemically private – the reference of a term isn't essential to its having the meaning it has, unless it is a purely referential term, and we might well want to think of the symbols of a private language as having descriptive content. But they will still have to be given a sense which fits the items they refer to, and there only the speaker can know what the choice is, since only he knows what the items are like. So something knowable only by the speaker will be essential to the semantics of the language, and if Dummett is right there can be no such semantics: nothing epistemically private, nothing 'lying solely in the mind of the individual', can be essential to meaning.

Though plausible, this is not straightforwardly true. If Dummett's semantic externalism is to be established in the way he proposes in 'The Philosophical Basis of Intuitionistic Logic', then it would emerge as a thesis about the public language only. The arguments he gives there work with considerations about what one individual could communicate to *another*, what one person could teach to or learn from someone *else*; their fulcrum is the point that neither could know enough about the other's private scene

---

[1] I emphasise 'understood by reference to the traditional picture' so as not to seem to deny that there is a way of understanding (A) which would make it in Wittgenstein's eyes plainly false. Are not pains, for instance, private, and don't we successfully talk of having a pain similar to the one we had yesterday? For Wittgenstein, however, this is a remark about the 'grammar' of 'pain', and is completely misrepresented by the traditional picture of private objects of consciousness.

for any of this to be possible. Nothing would follow about the semantics allowable in a private language, where all the speaker/hearer needs to know is the nature of his *own* states. If he can't even do that, then of course there can be no such language, but that line calls for supportive argument of a completely different kind.

Perhaps there is some completely different argument in the offing. Suppose that Wittgenstein's thoughts about rule-following enable us to establish (A). Since (A) says something about private items, not just about others' knowledge of them, there would rapidly follow both the impossibility of a private language and Dummett's semantic externalism.

To repeat: Dummett isn't talking about a private language, in which one individual supposedly makes reference to his own inner states; he is talking about conditions which the public language has to satisfy no matter what is being referred to. But (A) doesn't become any the less relevant because of that. If we accept that meaning requires consistent behaviour, then we have to accept that any item which plays an essential semantic role must play it consistently. So if there is no proper sense to 'the same', nor hence to 'consistency' in the case of private items, no such item can be essential to the meaning of any expression.

In the previous paper, I considered various ways of establishing Dummett's favoured position, and found them unsatisfactory. Now I want to see whether one can establish it by first establishing (A). I shall not question that Dummett's stance is a consequence of (A); I shall just ask whether (A) can be proved, in particular whether it can be proved, as some philosophers seem to think, by starting from the business of following a rule.

II

Can the rule-following considerations be made to yield a proof of (A)? If so it must, I take it, be by some such argument as this: suppose that a particular use of a given word on a certain occasion is consistent with its use on earlier occasions, that is, the speaker uses it in the same way as he has used it previously. Then there must be some fact in virtue of which his procedure is essentially of the same kind as on the earlier occasions, some fact in virtue of which he uses the word now with the same meaning as before. What could it be? It cannot (I just state the lemma and leave the reasons for it aside) be either a fact about his publicly observable behaviour or about his inner mental state. So if it is a fact at all it must be one which in some way involves the behaviour of other speakers of his linguistic community, namely that they would go on just as he does in those circumstances, or approve of his going on in that way. But when these 'circumstances', or 'the way he goes on', essentially involve some item of which only he can have knowledge there is no such thing as a communal pattern of behaviour. Therefore there is no such thing as 'sameness' or 'consistency' to be had here.

Two stages of this argument call for scrutiny. First, why should it be thought that no fact about the individual by himself can decide the issue of whether he is now 'going on in the same way'? And secondly, suppose we do reach the stage of saying that the notion of going on in the same way only has sense against a background of communally agreed practice. Must we conclude that no private item can figure in the description of the way one is going on? Can there be no such thing as communal practice in regard to such items?

In this paper I address myself to the second point only, thus thankfully ducking the hardest question: what exactly do the rule-following considerations show? My strategy is provisionally to allow that they do take us as far as the first stage, the requirement that there be communal linguistic behaviour, and then to ask whether the argument to (A) can proceed any further. My justification for the strategy is that it gives (A), hence also Dummett's semantic externalism and the anti-private-language thesis, the best possible chance: if they don't follow from this they are unlikely to follow from anything that emerges out of the rule-following material.

There is a gain in decisiveness from considering the second stage of the argument rather than the first: it avoids controversy about the exact form of the first premiss. What is it exactly that requires consensus? Is it that there is no such thing as sameness without a background consensus? Or that there is no such thing as a speaker meaning anything by an utterance? Or something else again? To make and justify a choice would be very difficult, to try to take account of all possibilities would be messy and inconclusive. But all of that can be avoided should the second premiss, that there can be no consensus with regard to epistemically private items, turn out to be defective. Then, whatever it was which the first premiss declared to need consensus, there would be no question of passing to any conclusion like (A).

So, can there be communal linguistic practice relating to items, knowledge of which is confined to one person? We shouldn't rush to say 'No' – *prima facie* there are at least two lines of thought which look as if they might lead to the affirmative answer. For one thing, might there not be a *hypothetical* consensus in usage? Might it not be the case, for a private item of one individual's experience, that virtually all the members of his linguistic community would describe it as he does, if they had experienced it? And for another, might there not be an *actual* consensus, that is, might not several members of the community actually describe the inner state of the subject in the same way as he does himself? They wouldn't, since it is an inner state of another individual, *know* that they were describing it correctly, but they might firmly believe that they were, and if their belief is in fact correct, why shouldn't that be enough?

Beginning with the first of these, we should notice that at any rate there is nothing wrong with hypotheticality as such. After all, in the case of very many public objects the notion of a consensus about their correct description is hypothetical: we are talking about the way in which the great majority of language users *would* describe those objects *if* they ever got round to doing so. Otherwise we find that if some pot-holer was the only person ever to see a certain stalactite, he cannot possibly have misdescribed it. But there is a problem about the first alternative, even though it is not the fact that it employs hypotheticals. It also employs the idea of others experiencing the same inner state as the original subject, and there may be reasons for finding this inadmissible.

One is by now depressingly familiar. It consists in disqualifying the clause 'if they experienced the same inner states' on the grounds that the corresponding indicative is unverifiable. That would make the defence rest on the verification principle, and indeed on the particularly implausible form of it which I remarked on in the previous paper. I shall say no more about this line – since the previous paper suggested that the verification principle is unsupported, my aim is precisely to find a reason for (A) which does *not* depend on it.

The proponent of the inference to (A) is faced with the suggestion that there is consensus, hypothetical consensus, since if others had qualitatively similar inner states they would say the same things about them. Instead of adverting to verificationism he might point out that this conditional uses the very notion under suspicion, qualitative similarity, so that one can't have recourse to it in this context without question-begging.

How should we assess the force of this response? Interest centres on the conditional:

> (C)   If others experienced the same inner states they would use the same words in connection with them.[2]

One thing at any rate is clear: if we agree that *being the same* has sense only against the background of consensus in usage, then the use of that concept in (C) is allowable only if the concept of a consensus with regard to inner states is allowable. But that seems very close to, if not identical with, the question whether (C) is in order. Whether (C) makes good sense depends on whether 'the same inner states' makes good sense; but whether 'the same inner states' makes good sense depends (on our present assumption) on

---

[2] The phrase 'in connection with' is used here to blanket such more precise concepts as 'to refer to them', 'to describe them', 'to express them'. Nothing in the argument hangs on this.

whether (C) makes good sense. Whoever has the burden of proof, loses; but batting the burden of proof backwards and forwards is a device for reaching a decision, not for getting at the truth. From our perspective the proper view of the matter is this: the proponent wants to disallow (C) in order to clear the passage from the need for consensus to (A). But rejection of the concept of 'the same inner states', unless backed by some independent reasoning, is just the bare assertion of (A), and so completely inadmissible in the context. And if there were some independent reason for rejecting 'the same inner states', it would be an independent argument for (A), whereupon the argument from the need for consensus could go into early retirement.

Still to be examined was a second alternative which does not go via the conditional (C). Perhaps there is a consensus, not a hypothetical but an actual consensus, about the description of the inner states of the original speaker; perhaps his fellows have, on a number of occasions, described his inner states as he has himself described them. After taking a look at the patient, we might confidently confirm his complaint that he feels sick; or seeing an angler eagerly getting out his tackle we might judge (what he shortly afterwards tells us himself) that he believes that this is a likely spot for catching fish.

It has become standard to reply that in this case, first appearances notwithstanding, the others are not describing inner states of the patient and the fisherman after all.[3] What reasons can be given for this? One is that if they are inner states others wouldn't know about them; they wouldn't know what sort of states they were or when they were occurring or even whether there were any, so how can they be describing them? But that isn't enough. Reasons will have to be given, not just why they can't know of these states, but why they can't hold correct beliefs about them. Either that, or it has to be argued that only a consensus based on knowledge is capable of grounding the notions of sameness and consistency, and that one based on true belief isn't. That, so far as I can see, would call for a completely fresh start.

Incidentally: it may not be all that easy to keep the two – knowledge and true belief – apart. If we hold a causal theory of knowledge, and analyse it as true belief arrived at by a reliable causal route – one which usually leads to true beliefs – very many of our beliefs about the inner states of others will, if true, be knowledge. And then the premiss from which the above argument starts will be false, as well as being insufficient for the conclusion.

So why might it be thought that others can't even hold true beliefs about the inner states of the subject? One attempt would be: how do they come to be right, except occasionally by sheer luck, given that they are inner states

---

[3] Not, that is to say, inner states as the traditional theory would have us see them.

of another individual? But there is at least a *prima facie* answer to that question. It lies in an idea that was prominent in the previous paper, where it was called the hypothesis of the assumption of uniformity. Note that it need only be a hypothesis – so long as it remains unrefuted its mere possibility is enough to open a disastrous gap in many of the arguments to be found in this area, among them the one we are now considering.

The hypothesis is this: human beings naturally assume that other members of their species experience inner (that is to say, epistemically private) states which are pretty much like the ones they experience themselves, and that they experience them when the outward circumstances are, broadly speaking, similar. 'The outward circumstances' is to be understood widely here. Nothing which is accessible to me is excluded as in principle incapable of helping to generate a belief about your inner states. It may be some aspect of your behaviour, where 'behaviour' again has to be interpreted widely, including typically your movements, facial expression, bodily posture, tone of voice and so on. But it may also be an aspect of your environment: if I see you standing on the beach on a summer's day facing out to sea I shall assume, so the hypothesis goes, that you see the blue of the sky, hear the ripple of the waves, smell the salt in the air much like I do. And 'like I do' means: your sensations are very like mine; could I be transposed into your consciousness I wouldn't find things (at any rate in these respects) much different.

The hypothesis bears a certain resemblance to the old argument from analogy, which used to figure in the thought of those who held to the traditional dichotomies between inner and outer, private and public, and still wanted to resist scepticism about other minds. That argument very properly came under heavy fire from two directions. First, the inference it proposed to make was exceedingly weak, involving as it did an enormous generalisation founded on a single case. Secondly, it was very doubtful whether anyone could justly claim the required knowledge of the correlations between types of inner state and their outward manifestations. We don't, it was said, spend that much time observing ourselves.

It is quite clear that the hypothesis avoids any trouble from the first direction. It speaks of an *assumption*, not an argument, and presents the beliefs about other minds as caused, not reasoned. So objections about the logical strength of the inference are beside the point. But it might still be thought that the second line of criticism has some force. How can such things as my posture and facial expression play even a causal role in generating any belief of mine if I am not aware of them?

We have to remember, though, that if all we want is the possibility of a causal explanation the awareness needed is of a pretty low order. It doesn't have to be the outcome of self-observation in any contentful sense, and it doesn't have to be conscious. Only if we knew that our brains had no way of registering these facts about ourselves could we know that the causal link required by the hypothesis was fictional. But we can do better psychology than this, if we must, without straying far from the armchair. From the remarkable ability of children to mimic movements and gestures we can safely conclude that the brain has some means of correlating the posture of its own body with that of others. Once that is admitted, only very sophisticated experimental work could show that the hypothesised causal link doesn't exist.

As I have remarked, the hypothesis of the assumption of uniformity doesn't have to be shown to be true in order to cause a lot of trouble in the area of privacy and meaning. It is enough for it to remain an unrefuted possibility. We had been discussing the suggestion that there might be an actual consensus of linguistic behaviour with respect to the description of inner states, a consensus which could satisfy the rule-following requirements and so block the inference to (A). This faced the objection that since the states in question were epistemically private there could be no such consensus, as no one but their owner could even hold true beliefs about what they were like or when they were occurring. But that cannot be said, so long as it remains a possibility that the assumption of uniformity is made and is frequently correct in particular cases. In a similar way we saw in the previous paper that, so long as these possibilities remain intact, certain arguments purporting to show that epistemically private items can't be semantically essential to any learnable public language are short of a crucial premiss.

The hypothesis of the assumption of uniformity is not one of those things which, like Descartes' demon, remain eternal possibilities without having any tendency to engage our belief. On the contrary, the hypothesis is in fact quite plausible – I would almost go so far as to say that everyone who has thought of it believes it, with the exception of a number of modern philosophers, who don't believe it because they think that strong arguments have been given against it. Yet it begins to look as if those very arguments derive their strength from a hidden assumption that the hypothesis is false.

Before I go on to apply that remark to the current state of our discussion about establishing (A), two more points about the hypothesis itself. Firstly, it does not say that the assumption is made by every human being about every other, and in its full generality. It isn't. If no incentives can persuade me to distinguish blue things from green things correctly you will soon stop assuming that I see them as you do. Physiological, or even marked racial and cultural differences may reduce one's confidence. So may developmental differences – not many of us would put a lot of faith in their idea of what it is like to be a three-month-old baby, for instance. Secondly, the hypothesis isn't supposed to suggest that the assumption stops dead for us at the boundaries of our own species. On the contrary, it extends in some measure to our picture of the mental life of the higher animals. And it has been suggested to me that, in view of the animistic beliefs encountered in many primitive peoples and most human children, it could even be thought that there was an inbuilt tendency to assume that practically everything has an inner mental life like our own, and that what is due to education is not the development of this belief but its *restriction*.

Now back to (A). The tactical position is this: the proponent of the inference to (A) needs to deny that there can be any consensus with regard to the description of inner states. He therefore has to explain why the assumption of uniformity would not allow there to be such a consensus, and that means arguing either that there is no such assumption made, or that if it is made it is false. The latter is a virtual non-starter. Any argument to the effect that the assumption was false would provide traditional scepticism about other minds with an even better equipped playground than the attempt to argue that it is true has done. So it must be the former if it is to be anything: one will have to claim that there is something spurious about the whole idea of such an assumption. This is of course just the position we found ourselves in in the previous paper. We saw then that it could be done by adopting an unargued and implausible version of the verification principle, and it was in trying to find a method with fewer disadvantages that we began looking at the issue of following rules, and in particular at the argument stated above (pp. 171–2). Does it establish (A)? If so, it establishes the fraudulence of the supposed assumption of uniformity (since the assumption uses the idea of sameness with respect to epistemically private items), and also, at one remove, the truth of Dummett's view about meaning, which was our original interest. But now it seems that in order to show that it establishes (A) the proponent must *first* show the bogusness of the assumption of uniformity, since it otherwise threatens to undermine his crucial premiss that there can be no such thing as a consensus in the description of inner states. So the hypothesis that there is such an assumption can't be nullified by an argument going via (A) – not unless (A) itself is asserted on some grounds quite different from the ones we have been looking at.

Another response would be to admit the hypothesis, but deny that it made for the communicability of inner states. It might go along the following lines: the hypothesis has an effect on the communicability of those states of a person, and those only, which stand in regular correlation with some observable state of his body, behaviour or environment. For consider the situation when the relevant parts of the language are being acquired. If the learner is to come to associate a given mental content with some expression, then the teacher must decide when that content is prominent in the learner's consciousness, and this and many other similar decisions must be right most of the time. How could this possibly happen unless there was some regular concomitance between the mental content in question and some state of the learner observable by the teacher? But, so the argument goes on, when we speak of *inner* states in this connection we are really talking about *private* states, and by private states we mean such as do not match up in this way with any publicly observable facts about the subject.

Two points need to be made here, one in clarification, one in reply. First, this response, which bypasses (A) altogether and makes essential use of the situation in which two persons are involved, can have nothing to do with the impossibility of a private language and relates only to Dummett's view of the semantics of the public language. Secondly, it is very weak – in effect it evacuates the position it was supposed to be defending. For if it is held to be only *private* inner states, in the sense indicated, and not inner states *tout court*, which are shown to be inessential to meaning, then for the moment nothing has been excluded. Any inner state of speaker or hearer may play an essential role, until it has been shown that there is nothing publicly observable about a person sufficiently reliable to give the teacher the clue he needs. Nowhere does one find a serious attempt to do any such thing, and this is scarcely surprising when one reflects on what would be involved. Surely no *a priori* considerations are going to set limits to how good we can be at forming true beliefs about the inner states of others, except those that purport to show that we can't do it at all?

The weakened version of (A) – the one which understands 'inner state' or 'epistemically private item' only in the very restricted sense of what has no outer correlates at all – is quite useless as a step towards Dummett's conclusion: indeed I doubt whether it yields anything substantial in the theory of meaning. And the stronger version of (A) can't be derived so long as it remains undecided whether there can be consensus about inner states.

III

We might instead go back one step. What blocked Dummett's argument in the previous paper was the hypothesis of the assumption of uniformity, which seemed to permit interpersonal language learning even if inner states of speakers and hearers are (sometimes) essential to meaning. Is it possible either to refute the hypothesis, or to show that it can't do this job, without first having to establish (A)? (A), we recall, was supposed to be a consequence of the rule-following lemma:

(L)   Being of the same kind (whatever sort of item is in question) consists in being the object of a consensus in classificatory practice.

Getting from (L) to (A) turned out to be none too easy. But can one mount an attack on the hypothesis based directly on (L), forgetting altogether the question of whether (A) follows from it? It would not, admittedly, have quite the same effect as a proof of (A). If (A) were proved, Dummett's conclusion would follow; if the hypothesis of the assumption of uniformity were destroyed, all that would follow is that one counter-argument to Dummett would have to be abandoned. But 'all that would follow', though strictly correct, could give the wrong impression – without this counter-argument Dummett's line of thought would in fact become very much harder to resist.

(L) doesn't appear to discredit the hypothesis itself. The hypothesis, after all, simply says: we assume that others experience states like ours under similar circumstances. (L) wouldn't imply that there is anything wrong with that; it would just mean that we make an assumption about what sort of consensus there is or would be. What seems more likely is that (L) should obstruct the route by which the assumption of uniformity is supposed to permit language learning. It would do so if, at some point on that route, the learner had to operate a notion of sameness that related only to his practices, and did not involve the community. Is this the case?

Here is an argument for thinking so: the learner has to recognise the various states that he is in when he hears the word W as being in some respect the *same sort* of state; only then can that sort of state come to play, for him, an essential role in the semantics of W. But his recognition that they are the same sort of state can't possibly be the recognition that others would describe them in the same way. After all, he is still trying to form a *hypothesis* about the teacher's behaviour, and we can't speak of his having to recognise such facts about that behaviour simply in order to form the hypothesis.

Put in that way, the argument makes the whole process sound far too conscious and calculating. There is no need (rather, it is a definite distortion) to talk of any *recognition* on the part of the learner. What happens is that the teacher uses W on a number of occasions when the learner's state is in some respect the same, and this in due course causes him to use W in connection with states of that kind. All of which, unless we decide that no consensus is ever possible with regard to inner states, can be translated into consensus terms. There need be no conflict with (L).

But if it is so translated, something begins to sound suspicious: how is the similarity of the states of the learner which were concomitant with the teacher's utterances of W supposed to bring about learning? Given (L), this similarity consists in the existence of a certain consensus, and the learner's brain must have some kind of access to this fact if it is to affect him. And not only to this fact; there is also the fact that the teacher has offered the *same word* on a number of occasions; that fact consists, on the view defined by (L), in the existence of a 'second-order' consensus about the right description of the teacher's utterances. We can very well imagine that such consensus exists, but how is the fact of its existence supposed to have impinged upon the learner? He may have had only one teacher, and if he has had many teachers he may never have heard any 'meta-' uses, uses of language to describe utterances.

Without investigating the merits and demerits of this line, we can say one thing straight away: the supporter of the consensus theory had better not use it. On his view any fact about similarity is really a fact about linguistic consensus; but *that* fact, since it consists in similarity between different individuals' linguistic behaviour, is itself a fact about a further consensus, and so on. Does all this consensus exist? Quite likely it does, if we allow hypothetical existence in the form that if certain questions were asked, certain answers would be given, and then accept that the whole infinite series is true. But if we are allowed to argue that this makes language learning impossible, since the learner's brain needs access to all these facts right at the beginning of the process, that will mean that on the consensus theory language, the public language, can't be learnt. So the supporter of (L) had better steer clear of this argument; either there is a flaw in it, or it is a *reductio* of his own position.

A likely reaction (especially from those who have been reading Kripke's account of the matter) is that this could indeed be a *reductio* of (L), but that they never supposed it to be (L) which the rule-following arguments prove. (L) sounds too much like a statement of the *truth-conditions* of claims about similarity, and that isn't what we want here. Wittgenstein's idea is precisely that we should get away from thinking in terms of truth-conditions and ask about the *point* of utterances; and the whole business of describing people as classifying, or using concepts, or meaning something specific, or 'going on in the same way' only has a point within a community whose members agree, on the whole, in their linguistic practice. So instead of (L) we ought to have something more like:

> (L') That two things are of the same kind is only assertible against the background of a consensus.

Shifting from (L) to (L') wouldn't alter the first two sections of this paper significantly, that is, it wouldn't improve our chances of deriving (A). What prevented the derivation of (A) was that the relevant consensus may exist, even if epistemically private items are involved, and this point is equally effective whether our premiss is (L) or (L'). But with regard to the argument of the present section things may not be quite so clear. The trouble with (L) was that it seemed to be too strong, so that if it blocked the road to language learning suggested by the hypothesis then it blocked all language learning. Might (L') achieve the former without blundering into the latter?

I spoke of 'something like (L')' because it is not altogether clear what (L') as formulated means, or what we should take its consequences to be. In particular: does it imply that a judgement of sameness of kind (or perhaps any classification) requires that the person making the judgement know of the consensus, or that his brain have causal 'access' to the fact of the consensus, or is it only important that there *be* a consensus?

If I have the right feel for the 'assertibility-conditions' view, what we should say is this: if teaching is to be successful the learner must react to it in a certain way, but this reaction can only be regarded as exhibiting mastery of a concept if he is a member of a community whose members behave similarly. There is no need for him to be aware that they do so, still less to assert it (implicitly) every time he uses a word. Nor is there any need for him to be causally affected by the fact that they do so – the desired modification of his behaviour can come about in any case, it is just that unless the consensus exists that sort of behaviour is not properly called mastery of a concept, or 'going on in the same way' or whatever.

But that being so, (L') poses no threat; it has no tendency to block the route to a non-Dummettian language (to the semantics of which the nature of epistemically private items is sometimes essential). The only question is: does the relevant consensus exist to make it right to call the learner's newly acquired behaviour 'concept-application'? That, of course, is just the question we have been dealing with in section II. The result: there is no reason to deny that it does exist. And so any threat from (L') evaporates.

One further point may be worth mentioning. Suppose we had decided (rather against the spirit of the underlying theory, I feel) that in accordance with (L') the learner would have to be aware of the consensus. If that means *know* of the consensus then a quite gentle scepticism will be enough to show that no language learning whatever would be possible. If, on the other hand, it means *truly believe*, then it will not follow that any kind of language is unlearnable. The burden of much of this paper has been that, for all that has been shown to the contrary, there may well be the required consensus; so the belief, if it exists, may be true. And why shouldn't it exist? Only a slight broadening of the hypothesis of the assumption of uniformity is needed to make it include the idea that a human being will, if struck by the similarity between two items, confidently expect all other human beings to react in the same way, that is, he will believe that there is (at least potentially) agreement in practice.

IV

Kripke's extended paper 'Wittgenstein on Rules and Private Language' is a notable attempt to clarify this whole area, and demands special attention. Most of it consists of a penetrating account of the rule-following considerations, which he takes as an argument to the effect that an individual can only be regarded as employing concepts if he is seen as a member of a community that exhibits agreement in linguistic practice. My strategy is provisionally to accept all this and look closely at the next step, the application of it to the case of language for 'inner processes'. I shall suggest that nothing comes of it beyond what we have seen already.

Having expounded Wittgenstein's thought about rules, Kripke goes on to offer arguments for two corollaries. The first is the impossibility of a private language, the second is the Wittgensteinian view of the semantics of the mental vocabulary of the public language, often summarised as 'an inner process stands in need of outward criteria'. Both turn out to have their problems, and they turn out to be problems which we have met before.

First, the impossibility of a private language. The waters here are muddied by the adoption of the definition of a private language as one which only its speaker can understand – as we saw in the earlier paper (Craig 1982:560–1), to assume that a language in which a speaker refers to his inner states (always understood as in the traditional picture) would have that property is to beg too many central questions. For if, perhaps because of something like an assumption of uniformity, others hold true beliefs about the speaker's inner states, they may in principle be able to understand a language in which he refers to them. It is better, therefore, to get straight down to the real business, and define a private language directly in terms of reference to the speaker's epistemically private states; but then the argument that Kripke proposes seems to fail. It follows from the nature of rules, he says, that an individual *considered in isolation* cannot be said to follow them (Kripke 1982:110). But does the speaker of a private language, as such, necessarily have to be 'considered in isolation'? If we define a private language as one which no one else *could understand* then perhaps he does, but if we define it as one in which he refers to his (traditional) inner states then it isn't at all clear. Might he not do this and still form part of a consensus? The whole tendency of this paper has been that we know no good reason to deny it.

Secondly, the matter of outward criteria for inner processes. Having got as far as the need for agreement between speakers, Kripke says:

How does agreement emerge in the case of a term for a sensation, say 'pain'? It is not as simple as the case of 'table'. When will adults attribute to a child mastery of the avowal 'I am in pain'? The child, if he learns the avowal correctly, will utter it when he feels pain and not otherwise. By analogy with the case of 'table', it would appear that the adult should endorse this utterance if he, the adult, feels (his own? the child's?) pain. Of course we know that this is not the case. Rather the adult will endorse the child's avowal if the child's behavior (crying, agitated motion, etc.) and, perhaps, the external circumstances surrounding the child, indicate that he is in pain. If a child generally avows pain under such appropriate behavioral and external circumstances and generally does not do so otherwise, the adult will say of him that he has mastered the avowal 'I am in pain'.   (Kripke 1982: 99–100)

This ought to do two things. One is to show that 'I am in pain' cannot relate to the pain as 'That's a table' relates to the table – its semantics must have a different structure, in which the outward manifestations play the leading role. The other is to show something about this role, namely that it relates the outward manifestations to the proposition asserted in the particularly close way that is indicated by calling them 'criteria'. Though the passage does give the impression of doing this (although Kripke does not commit himself to it *qua* argument, he does present it in a very seductive form) it in fact achieves neither.

How is the trick worked? The case of the table, with which the disanalogy is to be shown, has been described thus:

A child who says 'table' or 'That's a table' when adults see a table in the area (and does not do so otherwise) is said to have mastered the term 'table': he says 'That's a table' based on his observation, in agreement with the usage of adults, based on their observation. That is, they say, 'That's a table' under like circumstances, and confirm the correctness of the child's utterances.   (Kripke 1982:99)

Note the way the reader's attention is directed towards *observation*. ('When the adults see a table', 'the usage of adults based on their observation' etc.) This is misleading. What is essential is that the adults should believe that there is a table there.[4] How they come by this belief is not important, though no doubt seeing a table is the most common way. Making it sound as if perception were the crucial thing makes all the difference when we come to the next paragraph. Recall:

By analogy with the case of 'table', it would appear that the adult should endorse this utterance if he, the adult, feels (his own? the child's?) pain. Of course we know that this is not the case.   (Kripke 1982: 99)

Why should it be? The adult will endorse the child's utterance if he *believes*

---

[4] We should really be more accurate than this with our armchair psychology. If we are thinking of an infant's one word utterance 'table' then the truth is that the parents will endorse it if they believe that the child is *thinking of a table*. They won't need to see a table – indeed, their reason for believing that the child is thinking of tables could be precisely that it is pointing to a place where there usually is a table but now isn't.

that the child is in pain. Feeling the child's pain, even if it were possible, would be unnecessary, and feeling his own is irrelevant. And if it be asked how he can even believe that the child is in pain, if pain is a private state of the sufferer, then there enters the hypothesis of the assumption of uniformity, playing the now familiar tune.

Once we have seen this, it becomes apparent that the argument doesn't achieve the second goal either. The only addition required to the traditional view is one which, assuming the step from rule-following to the need for agreement, we have already adopted, namely: that an inner state can be an object of language only if there are outer circumstances which, *de facto*, allow others to hold true beliefs about its nature and occurrences. But it will not establish that they must be 'criteria', if that means that there is some *logical* connection between them and the ascription of the inner state to the subject, or that it is a necessary truth that they are good evidence for the ascription, or even that they are *evidence* for it at all.

Interestingly, there is a sentence which suggests that Kripke himself may not think that anything more than this has been shown:

Roughly speaking, outward criteria for an inner process are circumstances, observable in the behavior of an individual, which, when present, would lead others to agree with his avowals. (Kripke 1982:100)

If 'lead' ('roughly speaking') can be read as 'cause', then from the point of view of this and the previous paper there is nothing unacceptable about that – it just needs to be pointed out that neither is there anything incompatible with a thoroughly traditional picture of the nature of mental states and the content of beliefs about them.[5]

But even in saying this much we risk giving the impression of something more than we have reason to claim. It might sound as if we had found some *a priori* reason for asserting it – what Kripke calls a 'deduction akin to Kant's' (1982:100). We haven't. We have made an *a posteriori* (if widely accepted) assumption: that there is nothing like regular telepathy between human beings, and hence that any reliable method of forming beliefs about another person's inner states must depend on the existence of observable states of him and his environment which do in fact correlate with them[6] – unless what we are doing is arbitrarily extending the title of 'observation' to any reliable method of forming such beliefs, and the epithet 'outer' to anything which can be so 'observed'.

The argument Kripke presents makes its effect by speaking of observation and experience when it should be speaking of belief. It is interesting to recall

[5] Though I don't myself believe that such a reading would be in the spirit of the Wittgensteinian concept of a criterion.
[6] As Kripke in fact knows perfectly well – see his footnote (1982:100–1).

that Schlick's argument for the verification principle, which was discussed at the beginning of Craig (1982), traded on the same conflation. We have come very nearly full circle. It may be that not all argument in this area is verificationist, in the sense of using the verification principle as a premiss; but it does seem that verificationism is only just around the corner.

v

Taking the results of this paper together with those of its predecessor, what balance ought we to draw? There are certain widespread doctrines about privacy and language, broadly to the effect that nothing epistemically private can be an object of language (the impossibility of a private language), or in any way essential to the semantics of a language (Dummett's 'semantic externalism'). It is also widely believed that there are arguments which give these views a cogent foundation.

The moral is that all this is very doubtful. There may be such arguments – nothing in either paper rules that out – but it is becoming increasingly unclear what they could be. It seems unlikely that the rule-following material will do the work, since the present paper argues that even on an optimistic estimate of its force it does not provide a sufficiently powerful premiss. Verificationism does provide such a premiss, but, as emerges from the first paper, one there is no particular reason to believe. And – another outcome of the first paper – Dummett's argument from incommunicability faces very serious difficulties: either to refute the hypothesis of the assumption of uniformity or show that there is some (non-arbitrary) requirement which cannot be met even if it is true.

If the hypothesis of the assumption of uniformity lies at the centre of this whole area, as I believe it does, then that is where inquiry ought to be concentrated. Good reason has yet to be shown why, if there can be beliefs about the inner states of others, the nature of those states should not be essential to the semantics of a language that is used successfully for interpersonal communication. Thus the investigation focusses on the possibility or otherwise of such beliefs; the central issue lies primarily in the philosophy of mind and not – where current tendencies locate it – in the theory of meaning. It is true that particular views in the philosophy of mind, those that make language essential to thought or certain areas of thought, may return it to the philosophy of language. But in the present state of things we are at liberty to regard that as little more than speculation.

EDWARD CRAIG

REFERENCES

Craig, E. J., 1982. Meaning, Use and Privacy, *Mind 91*: 541–64.
Dummett, M., 1978. The Philosophical Basis of Intuitionistic Logic, in *Truth and Other Enigmas*, London: Duckworth.
Kripke, S., 1982. *Wittgenstein on Rules and Private Language*, Oxford: Blackwell.

Inventing logical necessity*

CRISPIN WRIGHT

I INTRODUCTION

1. The topic of this paper is the *objectivity* of logic; specifically, the objectivity of the relation of logical consequence and of the notion of logical proof. Both, as ordinarily conceived, implicitly involve the idea of logical *necessity*: if B is a logical consequence of $\{A_1...A_n\}$, then – according to our ordinary conception – if the latter are all true, B *must* be true; likewise, if a structure constitutes a valid logical proof, then its starting point and its successive operations are such that what eventually results *must* result if exactly those operations are correctly carried out on exactly that starting point. The latter consideration is what, according to our ordinary thinking, essentially distinguishes a proof from an experiment (and even if a similar-sounding claim can be made of certain very well-established experimental routines, we think of the 'must' involved as being quite different).

The notion of logical necessity is not in good standing among many contemporary philosophers, but the perception does not seem to be widespread that, for such simple reasons, our intuitive conceptions of logical consequence and of logical proof must fall with it. Perhaps some appropriate refashioning of those notions is possible. But in this paper I shall work within the framework of the intuitive conceptual connections outlined. The strategy will be to make a case for a certain sort of doubt about the objectivity of necessity, and then to let that doubt transfer, via those connections, to the subject matter of logic. If the doubt is sustained, we shall find in favour of those philosophers – most notably, the latter Wittgenstein – who have urged that proof in logic ought not to be viewed as a medium of discovery of a special category of fact, and that logical relations do not stand independent of our cognition of them in the manner of, say, spatial relations among material objects. Wittgenstein's own distrust of the opposing belief in the objectivity of logic is closely connected to that cluster of

* I am grateful for comments and criticisms received both at the Lyme Regis Thyssen conference and at the Universities of Belfast, Manchester, Pennsylvania and Harvard at which versions of this material were presented.

challenges, against certain intuitive preconceptions about meaning and understanding, to which in (1980) I gave the rather pedestrian title of the 'Rule Following Considerations'. The critique which I shall outline here also has Wittgensteinian roots; but is succeeds or fails, I believe, independently of the ideas on rule following.

2. Let me begin with some brief remarks by way of elaboration of the conception of logic which is at stake. Eventually we shall require a more refined account of what a believer in the 'objectivity' of logic is committed to, but the following rough characterisation of a familiar syndrome of ideas will serve for now. The believer will likely accept each of the following.

(A) There is a special category of truths which could not be conveyed in any language from which was absent (the means for defining) a unary sentential operator equivalent to 'it is logically necessary that...'. That is, some statements just are logically necessary truths; a language which failed to contain the means for affirming their necessity would, in consequence, fail to contain the means for saying everything true that can be said. The task of formal logic is, as far as possible, to codify algebraically this type of truth.

(B) The 'spectator conception' of proof; if, for example, we are applying a decision procedure to some formula of monadic predicate calculus, then the idea would be that we have only a *passive* part to play (cf. Dummett 1959); that what constitutes correct implementation of the procedure at every stage, and its eventual outcome, are predetermined – not causally but conceptually – by the character of the procedure and the identity of the tested formula. There is a similar predetermination even in cases where no effective decision procedure is to hand: of any well-formed formula of predicate calculus with identity, for example, it is, so to speak, stored up in the specification of the system whether an admissible proof of that formula can be constructed within it. What is *possible* in logic is laid down from the outset; and laid down, to repeat, purely conceptually, independently of any neurological or cybernetic considerations. The task of the logician is to unpack the store, and to make an inventory of its contents.

(C) Less figuratively, the logician is a *scientist*, his task one of discovery. His project is to chart the extensions of *logical necessity, logical consequence* and *cogent argument* (valid proof). These notions have determinate extension, fixed independently of his investigations, every bit as much as the concept, 'mountain exceeding 20,000 feet in height' has an extension fixed independently of the investigations of the terrestrial geographer. The difference is only that the extensions of the concepts in which the logician is interested could not have been otherwise than as they are.

There cannot be many students of logic who have never felt the tug of these ideas. Nevertheless they should be resisted if the drift of section III of this paper is correct. First, however, an account is owing of why an attack is still in point: why, in particular, the objectivist syndrome was not routed a third of a century ago by Quine.

II TWO DOGMAS OF EMPIRICISM

3. Quine's famous paper, it will be recalled, mounts a two-stage attack on the notion of an *analytic* statement – a statement whose truth is settled purely by the meanings of its constituent expressions and the way in which they are put together. The first two-thirds of the paper are devoted to arguing that the concept of analyticity eludes satisfactory explanation and so is not, presumably, fully intelligible. Then in the last third of the paper, where the famous holistic picture of language is presented, it is contended that, to the extent that the intention of proponents of the notion of analyticity *is* clear, there are actually no analytic (or synthetic) statements.

Now, the formulations above involved the notion of necessity rather than that of analyticity. For Quine himself there is nothing at stake in the contrast (1961: 29–30). But, should any reader scruple over the switch, it is easy enough to see that the intuitive notions of logical proof and logical consequence depend upon the notion of analyticity in a manner very similar to the dependence upon necessity noted above. For B's being a logical consequence of $\{A_1 \ldots A_n\}$ is standardly taken to involve the analyticity of the conditional: if A_1, then if A_2, ... then if A_n, then B. Likewise the status of the structure as a formal proof would standardly be taken to require the analyticity of the *corresponding descriptive conditional*: that conditional, that is, whose antecedent hypothesises correct implementation of a series of specified procedures on a certain initial basis and whose consequent specifies a certain outcome.[1] Accordingly Quine's attack upon analyticity, whether or not it is *eo ipso* an attack upon the notion of logical necessity, threatens similarly destructive consequences for the intuitive set of beliefs in the objectivity of logic. How may the logician be conceived as a scientist aiming to map the domain of a special category of truths if the notions of logical consequence, and of proof, enter into contaminating relations with the very notion which Quine sought to discredit? Quine himself originally seemed to see no threat to logic from his attack, believing that both logic and mathematics would secure an appropriate dignity by placement at the deeply entrenched core of the totality of empirical science. But the threat is there; and I shall try to indicate briefly below why Quine's holistic empiricism is no satisfactory response.

4. How strong, though, is Quine's attack? Let it be true, for example, that

---

[1] Cf. Wright 1980: 454. We shall consider a simple example below.

analyticity, syntheticity, meaning, and other cognate concepts interlock in a circle, no one member of which is explicitly definable without recourse to the others. Still, no conclusion seems to be warranted about their intelligibility unless we have reason to suppose that the situation prevents the construction of any coherent model of how an understanding of (any one of) those concepts might be acquired. Yet that supposition will be justified only if we have reason to suppose that the route into each of these concepts has to be by explicit definition. Do we have any reason to suppose so? At least part of the role of the notion of meaning, for example, is as a theoretical concept in the explanation of linguistic behaviour – and no one since Carnap has expected that it should generally be possible to explain theoretical concepts by explicit definition in terms of concepts of a somehow less problematic status. Besides, if the challenge is merely to indicate how the notion of analyticity can possibly be explained, what is wrong with the obvious answer, appropriate to most of our concepts: by example, and by immersion in linguistic practices in which the concept is in play?

Quine, like Socrates, seems to have supposed that the absence of any clear, non-circular definition of a concept somehow calls its propriety into question. The proper response is that it does nothing of the sort, provided there is independent evidence that the concept is teachable and is generally well understood. A sceptic about the intelligibility of a concept does not have to be answered by a rigorous explanation of it; it is enough to supply unmistakable evidence that the concept *is* well understood. And what better evidence could there be than that there is manifest in the community at large a disposition towards non-collusive assent in the application of these concepts – crucially, in our application of them to previously unconsidered cases? (cf. Grice and Strawson 1956.)

Strategically Quine ought, it seems, to have denied that there is any such manifest disposition. But the nearest he came to such a denial was to dwell on the unclear status, in point of analyticity, of certain examples like 'everything green is extended' (1961: 32). This consideration is not to the purpose. It is quite consistent with our possessing a genuine concept that in certain cases we hesitate over its application or contradict one another. Quine requires that such cases be typical. But they do not seem to be so. What is evident is that if there is indeed among speakers of English, who have had a certain sort of standard training in logic and philosophy, a disposition towards non-collusive assent in the application of 'analytic', 'logically necessary', and their kin, then it is folly to deny that we have *some sort* of concept of analyticity, *et al.*, and that any argument which, if allowed, establishes that we do not must therefore contain error.

5. We noted, however, that Quine stops short of suggesting that we have no genuine concept of analyticity at all. The central thrust of the last third

of 'Two Dogmas' is rather that such concept as we have has no instances. For Quine, belief in analyticity is thus rather like belief in witchcraft: the central concept is poorly explained, and the practices which are based on the belief that it applies to anything are based on a mistake.

Quine writes, in a famous passage,

> It becomes folly to seek a boundary between synthetic statements which hold contingently on experience, and analytic statements, which hold come what may. Any statement can be held true come what may, if we make drastic enough adjustments elsewhere in the system. Even a statement very close to the periphery can be held true in the face of recalcitrant experience by pleading hallucination or by amending certain statements of the kind called logical laws. Conversely, by the same token, no statement is immune to revision. Revision even of the logical law of excluded middle has been proposed as a means of simplifying quantum mechanics; and what difference is there in principle between such a shift and the shift whereby Kepler superseded Ptolemy, or Einstein Newton, or Darwin Aristotle? (1961: 43)

What exactly is the argument here? Analytic statements, Quine evidently supposes, whatever other properties they may have, ought to be immune to revision. Whereas, he urges, our total corpus of belief has a kind of holistic elasticity which involves that no statements are immune to revision. But it is hard to see why a defender of analyticity should wish to resist the suggestion that logic, or other disciplines conceived to involve analytic statements, are revisable. What a defender fundamentally wishes to maintain is that the truth of some statements is generated purely by the semantic machinery of the language. He has no legitimate interest in maintaining that we cannot be *in error* in judging a statement to have that status. He can therefore give Quine the claim – however implausible it may seem in certain cases – that any particular statement which we accept as analytic could, in certain circumstances, reasonably be discarded. For to grant the claim need be to grant no more than that our assessment of any particular statement as analytic may always in principle turn out to have been mistaken. Quine, like so many writers on the topic,[2] has slipped into thinking of analyticity as involving indefeasible certainty. To claim that a statement is analytic, however, is only to make a claim about the *kind* of truth it has – there is no immediate reason why the claimant has to agree that, when statements are analytic, their truth may be known with special sureness.

That we have the practice, then, of very occasionally effecting revision among beliefs formerly regarded as analytic is no argument for Quine's view of the matter. Indeed it is quite irrelevant to Quine's claim, properly understood, whether we ever carry out such revisions or not. The crucial question is rather what latitude is left to a rational subject by his experience

[2] Including the later Wittgenstein in off-guard moments. But contrast, for example (1969: §651).

when he endeavours to mould a system of beliefs adequate for explaining and predicting that experience. A defender of the traditional distinction between analytic and synthetic statements will hold that there are certain beliefs – the analytic ones – which, no matter what the course of the subject's experience, he cannot rationally be constrained to discard; and others – the synthetic ones – which, should his experience take a certain course, he must, rationally, discard.

Quine's claim – a generalisation, just as he says (1961: 41), of what Duhem held concerning scientific hypotheses – is that, such is the mode of functioning of our system of beliefs, experience *cannot* bear on the acceptability of single beliefs in the manner which the defender of the traditional distinction endorses. Only in the context of a theory, with its underlying logic, can experience confirm or disconfirm a particular belief; and, in principle, it is possible that the most fruitful response to a range of experiences may be to modify the underlying logic rather than the non-logical part of the theory.

Philosophy is still, I think, some distance from the stage at which it could be claimed that we have adequately taken the measure of the holism which Quine expressed in his classic paper. Unquestionably there are the most profound implications for the theory of meaning and for our view of the nature of truth if Quine is right. At present, however, my only concern is whether this holism, whatever other insights it may prove to contain, can be made to yield a satisfactory philosophy of logic. I want to suggest that it cannot. The reason is one which I have tried to express elsewhere (1980: 327–30).[3]

Schematically, Quine's picture is somewhat as follows. Let θ be a theory, and L its underlying logic. Suppose that from θ we can derive, via L, a conditional, $I \rightarrow P$, whose antecedent describes certain initial conditions and whose consequent formulates a prediction relative to those conditions. Now suppose that we suffer a barrage of experience, E, which is *recalcitrant*: that is, I suppose, it inclines us to assent both to I and to the negation of P. Now, since there are no synthetic statements, it cannot be the case that E forces our denial of P; likewise, since there are no analytic statements, it cannot be the case that we are rationally prevented from pointing the arrow of suspicion, as it were, at L. Thus the theory, plus its underlying logic, plus our 'observational' responses to E confront the recalcitrant experience *en bloc*; and how it is best to respond is to be determined by pragmatic criteria, applied to the belief-systems which respectively result from the variety of responses open to us.

It wants remarking, to begin with, that this schematic picture is

[3] I hope that I have improved, in this paper, upon a presentation which succeeded only in being suggestive of what I believe, properly formulated, is a conclusive objection.

incomplete. Experience E is recalcitrant for θ-with-L only if it is presupposed that $\theta \vdash_L I \rightarrow P$. This statement – call it W – will have been established by constructing a derivation of $I \rightarrow P$ from θ using L; and would ordinarily be conceived as, if true, analytic. Clearly, however, the acceptability of W need in no way depend on the acceptability of L; ratifying the proof of W simply consists in checking that $I \rightarrow P$ does indeed follow from θ by a series of L-accredited steps – no endorsement of the principles of L need be involved in so working with the notion of an L-accredited step. So the very description of E as recalcitrant for θ-with-L presupposes acceptance of a statement which is established by proof, which is analytic if any statements are, and which is independent of L.

The reader may now be expecting to be presented with an argument to the effect that the notion of analyticity is implicit in the very idea of recalcitrance. But, supposing that is true, it would not be a very destructive conclusion against the Quine who holds not that the notion of analyticity is unintelligible but that it requires holistic reconstrual. There is nevertheless a serious difficulty close by. For Quine, presumably, judgments about recalcitrance are in the same boat as the rest: even after the proper description of a particular sequence of experience has been granted, its recalcitrance for a particular theory-with-a-logic will have to be regarded as a *hypothesis*. And if we now ask: under what circumstances is it reasonable, on the Quinean view, to hold such a hypothesis?, it is clear what answer Quine officially must give. He must affirm that among the responses available to us in the original schematic situation is indeed the option of denying that E *is* recalcitrant for θ-with-L, by way of rejection of W; and that, as in the case of other available responses, pragmatic considerations should be allowed to determine whether this is a good move. But determine it how? The decisive consideration ought to be, presumably, the degree of further recalcitrance with which the various alternative courses tend to be beset. But once the recalcitrance of experience becomes, in the way noted, a hypothetical matter, the question is transformed into: how often are the various alternative courses beset by sequences of experience which, *according to the best hypothesis*, are recalcitrant? And now, in order to decide whether recalcitrance *is* the best in hypothesis, we have to consider how it tends to fare in pragmatic competition with the alternatives – and the beckoning regress is evident. So the official Quinean answer to the question, when is it reasonable to believe a statement like W, is no answer. The moral is that it cannot be a correct account of the basis of our confidence in statements like W that belief-systems in which they figure enjoy relative success; if that were the right account of the matter, there could be no explaining the requisite notion of 'success'.

In summary, the Quinean methodology is, crudely: where experience is recalcitrant, make whatever adjustments suffice both to eliminate the recalcitrance and to minimise subsequent recalcitrance. But if the latter part of the injunction amounts to: make whatever adjustments suffice to minimise the occurrence of situations whose recalcitrance is the *best hypothesis*, it is hopelessly impredicative – nothing has been said concerning by what methodology such a 'hypothesis' should be judged 'best'. So the reasonableness, or otherwise, of judgments of recalcitrance must be exempted from appraisal via the Quinean methodology. And that must go for the ingredients in such judgments, including statements like W. The Quinean, as noted, might well have been prepared to regard such statements as candidates for analyticity anyway – in his laundered sense of the term. But now it transpires that that is not enough. If we are supremely certain of the truth of at least some such statements, the source of this certainty simply cannot be accounted for by Quine's generalised holistic model. The very coherence of the model requires an account of a different sort.

The right account is, I believe, the obvious one: such statements, or at least an important sub-class of them, admit of totally convincing *proof*. We must, I suggest, take seriously the idea of proof as a theoretically uncontaminated source of rational belief. One reason why it is easy to overlook the incoherence in Quine's attempt to 'Duhemise' the traditional realm of the *a priori* is because one naturally thinks of proof as conferring no more than a conditional warrant upon its conclusion, from premises for which, for this reason, the ultimate ground cannot itself be proof. But that is just an oversight. If we derive B from A using classical propositional logic, then B may be said to be proved conditionally on our acceptance of A; and $A \vdash B$ may be said to have been proved conditionally on our acceptance of classical propositional logic; but $A \vdash_{CPL} B$ has been proved conditionally on nothing at all. A sequence of operations of the relevant sort, taken as a proof that a certain logic does indeed have the materials to yield a specific conclusion from specified premises, can possess complete phenomenological cogency. No coherent methodology of empirical science can avoid recognising that such judgments, proved unconditionally in this way, play an ineliminable part in our conception of what it is for experience to collide with a body of theory. What, it seems to me, is fundamentally unsatisfying about the philosophy of logic of the global pragmatism in 'Two Dogmas' is that it is forced to locate the rationality, or otherwise, of our acceptance of such a judgment quite elsewhere than in the cogency of the operations which constitute its proof – and indeed, if what is said above is correct, winds up giving it no proper location whatever.

III FACTUALITY

6. I wish to carry forward two things from the preceding. First, I shall take it that we do possess some sort of concept of logical necessity (analyticity). Second, the correct account of the basis for the majority of judgments of logical necessity which we are prepared to make must make reference to the utterly convincing, self-contained character of suitable proofs. But the crucial point is that this much luggage is by no means a commitment to the objectivity syndrome adumbrated in section 1. If Quine's doubt about analytic statements may usefully be compared to the contemporary doubt about the existence of witches, the line of thought to be developed now will suggest a doubt about the reality of logical necessity akin to the doubt which Locke had whether anything is *really* red, from an objective point of view, or the doubt which most of us have whether anything is, in the same sense, *really* funny.

It is evident enough that there are uses of declarative sentences which are not aimed at fact-stating. Promises, rules ('The King moves one space in any unobstructed direction'), and commands ('The platoon will be on parade at 6:30 am tomorrow morning') are obvious examples. But a large and important class of philosophical disputes pivot precisely on whether the declarative sentences in a contentious family are apt for fact-stating, whether there is any genuinely factual, or cognisable, subject matter for them to state. Such disputes arise for a variety of reasons. The Logical Positivists' conception of literal significance more or less forced them to deny the factuality of anything but reports of immediate observation. Similarly, the Dialectical Materialism of hard-line Marxists pushes them towards the view that all facts about human society and consciousness are ultimately constituted in the economic sub-structure. A third and perhaps more appealing motive is the thought that any genuine fact ought to be available to the cognitive powers of an appropriately endowed being; and that pure cognition cannot ever require the exercise of anything but intellect and reliable sensory faculties. It would follow that sentences involving terms like 'funny', 'boring', or 'obscene', competence with which requires a subject's capacity for certain sorts of *affective* response, cannot be (purely) fact-stating.

Whatever their motivation, there are unsettled philosophical issues of this general character in ethics, aesthetics, philosophy of science, and the philosophy of mathematics whose resolution would constitute a tremendous advance in our philosophical understanding. Yet what is really in dispute? How can we characterise the needed distinction between *genuine statements*, declarative sentences apt to have truth or falsity conferred upon them by the properties of a real subject matter, and hence suitable for the expression of genuine knowledge, and the rest:[4] those sentences which have all the syntax – the susceptibility to embedding in conditionals and expressions of propositional attitude, etc. – of genuine statements yet which do not play a fact-stating role?

A sound and simple thought is this. If we are concerned with a genuine statement, apt to be rendered true or false by germane aspects of the world, then there must presumably be sense in the comparison between what any particular subject, or group of subjects, takes the truth value of the statement to be and what its truth value actually is. The point can be made vivid by a dilemma. Suppose we are concerned with a type of statement which (in principle) we can come to know. Well, cognition is a relational business: it involves getting one's beliefs, in appropriate ways, into line with the way matters stand. But there is no sense in the idea of securing such a coincidence unless there is a distinction between describing how things stand on one end of it, in the realm of the subjects' opinions, and describing how they stand at the other, in the realm of fact. Suppose on the other hand we are concerned with a type of statement which we cannot (in principle) come to know. Even here we can, presumably, guess at the truth value of the statement, and possibly get it right. So the relevant idea of coincidence must at least make sense. Accordingly we may affirm quite generally that only if:

(i)   it is accepted by such and such a person/group of persons that P;

and   (ii)   it is the case that P;

enjoy an appropriately contrasting content, is it in order to regard P as a genuine statement. 'Appropriately contrasting' leaves lots of scope; but, standardly, we should expect space to be made for the possibility of being in position to assert either (i) or (ii) while being in position to deny, or at least being in no position to assert, the other. (It is the first two possibilities, of course, that provide room, respectively, for a subject's *error* about and for his *ignorance* of the facts.)

These ideas ought to seem uncontentious. But they are not toothless. Wittgenstein's leading idea, as I read him, in *Philosophical Investigations*, §§256–61 is exactly that the requisite contrasting content cannot be made out if the subject in question is to be the 'private linguist' and P is to range over the 'statements' of his private language.[5] Moreover the hesitation which it is natural to feel about the factuality of our judgments concerning what is funny, or what is obscene, surely has something to do with our diffidence that we really understand what it would be to be entitled to regard a majority – or even a large – group as strictly mistaken, or ignorant, in their

---

[4] What Dummett calls 'quasi-assertions' (1981: 353–63).
[5] I pursue this idea in my (forthcoming).

opinion on such a matter. Yet these considerations point, evidently, only to a necessary condition for a class of declarative sentences to count as genuine statements. At any rate, the (i)–(ii) contrast is *in use* in many of the areas – theoretical science, pure mathematics, ethics, aesthetics – where factuality is in dispute. Likewise with the topic of our present concern: if *P* depicts *B* as a consequence of $\{A_1 \dots A_n\}$, or avers that such-and-such a structure is a valid proof in such-and-such a system, nothing seems easier than to understand what it would be to be in a position to make any of the four contrasts adverted to. Rather than find so easily in favour of the realist/cognitivist view we should seek a strengthening of the proposed account. Not only the possibility but, in a sense we have to explain, the *propriety* of practising a distinction between judgment and fact is what is at issue.

One useful suggestion, I think, originates in the idea, touched on above, that knowledge is *dispassionate*. Another is the thought that truth is *coercive*: when a statement expresses a matter of fact, assent to it may, in certain circumstances, be commanded of us. Of course, finding something funny may also be, in context, an irresistible response. The intuitive difference – putting the two suggestions together – is that when a statement of fact commands our assent, it does so independently of any emotional or affective response which we have to the matter. If ever a genuinely factual statement is beyond dispute, it is, properly speaking, for the rational, whose intellects, senses, and memories are functioning properly, that it is beyond dispute.

A bold proposal would now take, as the hallmark of the factual, the appropriateness of an ideal of rational consensus. The idea would be that we should think of a class of statements as expressive of genuine matters of fact only where it can be shown that, if perfectly rational beings were permitted to conduct a sufficiently thoroughgoing investigation, the opinions which they formed about the acceptability, or otherwise, of such statements could not but coincide. Genuine truths, on this view, are what perfectly rational beings would agree to be true on the basis of a sufficiently lengthy and painstaking investigation. Failing better motivation, however, the proposal seems over-contentious: again, too easy a resolution is promised of too many of the controversies in which factuality is pivotal – only this time the verdict goes against the realist/cognitivist. Theoretical science for example, could not qualify as factual under the proposal unless the falsity could be demonstrated of the notorious thesis of the underdetermination of theory by empirical data; and it is, at best, highly controversial whether all ethical, or aesthetic, disagreements may in principle be resolved by rational means alone. More generally, the proposal assumes that there is no such thing as our forming a clear conception of a possible state of affairs for supposing which to obtain, or to fail to obtain, even a perfectly rational, indefinitely extended enquiry might be able to disclose no reason. That is to presuppose the falsity of realism in Dummett's sense. I myself do not regard such a presupposition as an error of substance. But it is certainly a political error: if the right way to draw the distinction between genuine statements and the rest is to eventuate in an objection against realism, the way the distinction is initially drawn should carry an appeal for the realist and anti-realist alike.

The most plausible way, it seems to me, of preserving what seems right about the bold proposal – the idea that fact-stating has somehow to do with an appeal to our rational faculties – while avoiding immediate question-begging against Dummettian realism, is to take the 'tug' on the rational faculties to be exerted not by an idealised enquiry but by the state of information in which we happen to be. A genuine statement will be: not a statement about whose truth value ideally rational investigators could not disagree after a sufficiently thorough-going investigation, but rather a statement about whose assertibility, or otherwise, ideally rational subjects will not disagree *in any particular state of information*. Anti-realistically problematic examples can now qualify: if Goldbach's Conjecture, for example, is utterly 'verification transcendent', then, no matter what their state of information, perfectly rational subjects will presumably agree that there is no basis either for its assertion or for its denial. In contrast, such subjects may disagree – our intuitive feeling is – about whether, say, a particular interview of a leading politician was unintentionally comic without there having to be any suggestion that one enjoys a superior state of information to the other or, if their states of information are the same, that one is being less than ideally rational.

Genuine statements, according to the milder proposal, distinctively command a particular response from the rational, *modulo* a state of information. Contraposing, differences of opinion about such statements – that is, one subject holding an opinion which another does not – will have to be traceable back to some breach of ideal rationality or material difference in the subjects' respective states of information. This proposal should, I believe, commend itself to the reader as intuitively correct; but only in a formal sense, since no condition has so far been imposed on what can qualify as an item of *information*, meet to enter into a state thereof. If we are aiming at the adjudication of controversial cases, the proposal is so far, therefore, entirely powerless. The way to give it some cutting edge is to retain the suggestion that what is distinctive of genuine statements must be sought in the range of possible sources of differences of opinion about them, but to attempt to be more specific about the members of that range. The following more detailed proposal is such an attempt.

Where 'facts of the matter' are concerned, differences of opinion can be rendered fully intelligible to a third party, I suggest, only if he can

(a)   identify a material mistake on the side of one of the parties; or
(b)   identify some material ignorance on the side of one of the parties; or
(c)   identify some material prejudice on the side of one of the parties; or
(d)   disclose some material vagueness in the statement used to express the opinion in question.

Mistake is here to be taken to cover any sort of perceptual, recollective, or intellectual malfunction. More needs to be said, obviously, about when it is satisfactory to explain a difference of opinion by placing it in this category, but the following remarks will serve our immediate purpose. Presumably it should count as satisfactory if the mistake is identifiable independently of any view about the disputed opinion, as in the case of an error made in the course of a calculation, for example, or a misreading of a gauge; or, failing such an identification, if aspects of the condition of the subject, or of the circumstances of his judgment, are known about which, against a background of information, say, concerning the physiology of germane modes of the subject's functioning, would make a mistake of one of the relevant sorts likely. But attribution of mistake will *not* count as a satisfactory explanation so long as the sole ground for the attribution is the subject's view of the disputed statement. Similar points apply to *ignorance*. It will be satisfactory so to explain a difference of opinion whenever some material ignorance is identifiable independently of one's view of the disputed statement; or, failing such identification, when there is at least an explanation of why it was likely, or even inevitable, that the subject should be left in ignorance of the status of that statement. But it will not be satisfactory if the sole ground for attributing ignorance to the subject is that he does not hold a certain view of the disputed statement.

Prejudice would be the appropriate form of explanation in situations where the protagonists agree about the material data but disagree about its supportive strength. However this needs a qualification. Intuitively no compromise of rationality is involved if, for example, X requires that the probability of getting a certain favourable outcome from a change in some policy be at least $0\cdot75$ before he is prepared to implement the change, whereas Y is satisfied with a probability of $0\cdot70$. The question, whether a certain degree of probabilistic support makes it rational to hold a particular belief, does not everywhere admit of a determinate answer. That, however, cannot *always* be the situation so long as the belief does admit in principle of probabilistic confirmation and disconfirmation. If something factual is at issue, it must be possible for the evidence to assume such a shape that only irrationality can explain the refusal, or willingness, of someone who knows of the evidence to accept the belief in question. Prejudice, as the notion is here intended, is what is operative when someone assigns an irrationally high or low supportive force to an agreed body of evidence. Rationally permissible differences in personal probability thresholds, as it were, cannot be the explanation in all possible cases of differences of opinion, concerning genuine statements, for which the only evidence is probabilistic and is agreed on both sides.

The relevant point about *vagueness*, as a quite general possible source of differences in opinion about genuine statements, is similar. To wit, for the statements in question to qualify as factual, it is necessary that not *every* possible difference of opinion about their status, in given circumstances, can be put down to vagueness. Descriptions of colour, for example, if *pace* Locke we regard them as factual at all, so qualify only because, though the borderline between various colours is blurred, some things are, for example, determinately pink and others determinately not.

The proposal, then, comes to this. Statements of a certain class are apt for the expression of genuine matters of fact only if there are contexts – in which vagueness, or permissible differences in personal evidence thresholds, are not to the point – in which it is *a priori* that differences of opinion concerning one of the relevant statements can be fully explained only by disclosing (in a manner which observes the constraints sketched above) some material ignorance, error, or prejudice on the part of some or all of the protagonists. And a particular debate concerns a genuine matter of fact only if the statement(s) which express what is in debate satisfy this condition in the context in question. By contrast, members of a class of apparent statements will not count as apt for fact-stating if, whenever such a statement is in dispute, it can never be ruled out *a priori* that an explanation of the dispute should be of some other kind than those just described. Disputes about 'matters of taste', for example, *may* be traceable to ignorance, error, or prejudice but their intelligibility never *requires* that they be so: X and Y may, for example, just find different things agreeable in matters of interior decoration and design – that may just be the whole of the matter. On the other hand the proposal seems to do justice to our preconceptions concerning the fact-stating character of, for example, statements concerning yesterday's weather, the whereabouts of the cat, or the number of times I have been to Holland. It is, for example, *prima facie* impossible to understand how you and I could have a difference of opinion about the last whose explanation – saving some material misunderstanding like the belief that 'Holland' covers all the Low Countries, or our counting 'trips' differently – would not make good such a claim as that I have forgotten, or dreamed up, a trip; or that you are in no position to know; or that you are for some reason

pleased to think of me as someone with no experience of travel abroad...
and so on.

I commend this proposal only as an outline, in essentials, of (part of) the
inchoate notion of factuality which we actually have. And be it noted that
it is the truth of the proposal, rather than its status as a (complete and
non-circular) analysis, which matters in what follows. If it incorporates at
least a necessary condition for a class of statements to qualify as genuine,
then it will be reasonable to demand of a factualist about ethics, or
aesthetics, or indeed necessity, that difference of opinion about such
matters – if genuine, that is, based on no misunderstanding – must, at least
in the relevant sort of contexts, be explicable in one of the three ways described. Let us say that a dispute is *Humean*[6] provided there is no material
misunderstanding of any concept involved in the formulation of the object
statement, and the source of the dispute is not error, nor ignorance, nor
prejudice. The anti-factualist about a given class of statements will hold that,
whenever there is a difference of opinion about such a statement, it will
always be a possibility, *a priori*, that it is Humean, that is, may be successfully
explained without being placed in any of these three categories. The
factualist, in contrast, must hold that, unless vagueness, or rationally
permissible differences in evidence thresholds, are to be the explanation, it
has to be the case that it is in one of those three areas that the explanation
lies.

7. This proposal, too, may be in tension with Dummettian realism. Only
now, I think, that will constitute an argument, rather than a question
begged. Can any genuine statement – by the lights of the proposal – be
utterly verification transcendent, so that not even the weakest ground for
believing or doubting it can be given? Only if a difference of opinion about
such a statement need not be Humean. But that requires that there are
circumstances in which it is *a priori* that such a difference of opinion has to
be put down to ignorance, error, or prejudice. Now, there might be no
difficulty were it that agnosticism was always the rational attitude to take
up towards such a statement. For then, since any difference of opinion is
always going to involve at least one of the parties not being agnostic, the
explanation would presumably always be either a mistaken belief that
certain data were available or a prejudicial indifference to the total absence

---

[6] At the Lyme Regis Thyssen conference in 1983 at which the original version of this paper
was presented, I called such disputes 'Homeric'. The epithet was meant to convey an
allusion to Sir Peter Strawson's inaugural lecture in which he spoke of the 'Homeric
struggle' between truth conditional and communication-intention approaches to meaning,
urging that the two approaches are in no genuine dispute. But (i) nobody got the allusion;
and (ii) it was not in any case quite felicitous, since disputes with no factual subject matter
can be real enough, and should therefore be contrasted with cases where the protagonists
merely believe they are in dispute.

of data. But agnosticism is not always the favoured realist response to such statements. A good example is provided by Edward Craig's handling of his 'assumption of uniformity' in his contribution to the present volume. The assumption is, as Craig conceives it, one which human beings make quite naturally; it is that

Other members of their species experience inner (that is to say, epistemically private) states which are pretty much like the ones they experience themselves, and that they experience them when the outward circumstances are broadly speaking similar. (p. 175)

It is essential to Craig's argument that this is a genuinely factual assumption, which may be 'frequently correct in particular cases' (p. 176). And Craig evidently thinks that, so far from it being unreasonable to make such an assumption, it is a natural and proper thing to do. Yet to hold that we are indefeasibly within our rights in making such an assumption, in the absence of any possible evidence, and, at the same time, to concede that there is no guarantee that an agnostic need be guilty of any identifiable error, or ignorance, still less a prejudicial response to data, is to bring it about that, by the lights of the proposal, a statement of the assumption fails to qualify as factual. For in that case neither the Craigian nor the agnostic can be brought under any of the three pertinent headings. (The result, I suggest, is that the idea of *consensus* with respect to our description of inner states cannot be elucidated, in the manner Craig suggests, by reference to the possible truth of such an assumption. But I have no space here to engage Craig's argument in further detail.)

There are actually rather a lot of 'assumptions' which seem to be in this category: hypotheses of apparent depth which we are inclined to regard as possessing determinate truth conditions but for which, under sceptical pressure, we seem to be unable to find even the weakest support to corroborate the attraction which they have for us. Familiar examples would be 'there are other consciousnesses besides my own', 'the earth is many millions of years old', 'material objects exist when unperceived', and many more. In each case, of course, we can offer what at first sight appears to be plentiful and powerful supporting evidence; but it is, famously, easy for the sceptic to argue that such evidence is variously question-begging. One issue now is whether it can be coherent to grant so much to the sceptic while retaining the beliefs both that there *are* substantial matters of fact at issue and that it is somehow not improper to retain one's convictions in the teeth of the sceptic's arguments. The threat presented to the Dummettian realist is exactly that the price of saving the factuality of the subject matter in sceptical disputes may turn out to be that the sceptic *wins*: that all our talk about other minds, the past, and the material world turns out to be based on groundless assumptions which, rationally, deserve agnosticism. Of course the belief that such 'assumptions' are misinterpreted if taken to be factual is a leading theme of Wittgenstein's notes (1969). Wittgenstein has a variety of motivations for the idea, none of them exactly coincident, it seems to me, with the train of thought adumbrated. (I defer fuller discussion of the matter to another occasion (cf. Wright 1985).)

IV HUMEAN LOGICAL NECESSITY

8. No doubt the proposal could do with more refined formulation. But it is not, as it stands, too crude to display a problem with the factualist conception of necessity which Quine rejected and to suggest merit in the attitude of those who would have described themselves as 'conventionalists' when the (unresolved) dispute about the nature of logical necessity was in its heyday during the 1930s and 1940s. The problem is simply that it is unclear, on reflection, why it is not *always* possible to have a Humean difference of opinion about the necessity of a statement generally accepted as necessary; in particular, why someone may not always Humeanly stop short of accepting the necessity of such a statement while allowing its truth.

To elaborate briefly by reference to the case of formal proof in logic. Suppose that what is at issue is the *technical* correctness of such a proof – so the sort of disputes which classicists, intuitionists, and relevantists', for example, might want to have about its soundness are not to the point. The issue is to be merely whether what we are presented with is a correct proof in a particular formal system. Now, the concept of logical necessity enters even here, it will be recalled, in so far as the status of such a construction as a proof – rather than, for example, an experiment – depends upon its *essential stability*: it must not be 'logically possible' that the outcome of the proof should vary through successive performances in the way that the outcome of a physical experiment can. Accordingly there will be some description of the successive operations of the proof such that, although the result at each stage is not explicitly given by this description, it is nevertheless necessary, or so we ordinarily think, that if precisely the sequence of described operations is carried out on the starting point of the proof, nothing but the eventual outcome *can* result. To take a trivial example, consider

$$(1) \quad A \to B \vdash A \to B$$
$$(2) \quad A \vdash A$$
$$(3) \quad A \to B, A \vdash B \qquad 1,2 \; MPP$$
$$(4) \quad A \to B, A \vdash B \lor C \qquad 3, \text{vel-I}$$

An appropriate description, given in the form of a conditional, could be something like:

> If any proof commences with a pair of assumption-sequents, $A \vdash A$, and $A \to B \vdash A \to B$, followed by the *modus ponens* step which those two lines furnish, followed in turn by a step of vel-Introduction on the result with C as the right-hand constituent in the then resulting disjunction, then that disjunction will be $B \vee C$, and will depend on A and $A \to B$ as assumptions.

Imagine now a dispute between X who, viewing the structure, accepts it as a proof, and so accepts the necessity of such a conditional as the above, and Y who merely regards the structure as experimentally corroborating the conditional, whose truth he regards as enormously probable. If there is to be a genuinely factual issue whether that structure is a proof, such a dispute cannot always be Humean: there have to be circumstances in which we can say in advance that the only way of rendering the dispute intelligible is if one or each of the parties has committed some specific error, or is ignorant in some material way, or is guilty of prejudice. Moreover, since there is no germane vagueness in the statement at issue and since what is at issue between X and Y is clearly not to be put down to permissibly differing evidence thresholds, we may take it that the envisaged dispute between X and Y takes place in just such circumstances. Given, then, that the factualist will want to regard X as right, how should Y be handled?

A natural thought is that Y's very response to the proof – his treating it as, in effect, a sort of experiment – betrays a misunderstanding of the notion of necessity: that if Y genuinely understands that notion, he *must* see that the necessity of an appropriate conditional is apt to be demonstrated by such a structure. Accordingly, there is no need to view the case as a genuine difference of opinion at all. But there are two obvious drawbacks to this. First, a parallel thought is likely to be available *whenever* it looks as though Humean disputes are always going to be possible in some area, and cherished factualist preconceptions are consequently under threat: were it to appear, for example, that Humean disputes about fundamental moral precepts are always possible, the response will always be available that the agnostic can have no proper grasp of moral notions. So the charge of misunderstanding can be admissible only subject to certain controls; otherwise it becomes a two-edged sword, leaving no clear distinction between responsible forms of factualism and mere crankishness. Second, we can imagine Y elaborating his position in a way which makes it evident enough that he understands pretty well what is at stake. He may grant, for example, that he cannot imagine what it would be like for a structure to seem to him to meet the specification of the antecedent of the conditional and yet have a different outcome. He may grant that this marks an interesting and important contrast with other experiments, where a detailed description of counter-factual outcomes, or even a cine film simulation of them, might be possible. But he sees, he insists, no cause to project aspects of our imaginative powers onto reality, or to dignify them as apprehension of what *must*, or *cannot*, be the case. After all, it surely *is* imaginable that we might somehow, sometime want to describe some structure as indeed a counter-example to the relevant conditional; and that we shall then find it extraordinary that we could have been so blind before....[7]

Given that he explains himself along these lines, the charge that *Y* misunderstands the relevant notion of necessity looks far-fetched. Indeed there seems to be no cause to reproach his understanding of any relevant concept, since he does, after all, show himself aware of the character of the ingredient steps in the construction and of what statement it confirms. The dispute hinges, rather, on the proper interpretation of the nature of this confirmation.

Granted, then, that the difference of opinion is genuine, it must not, for the factualist, be Humean. So *Y* must be guilty of error, ignorance, or prejudice. But the last of these possibilities is not to the point, for it requires that the data be agreed; and if *X* were to admit that the data are just as *Y* describes – that they are constituted by the empirical features of the construction, plus the considerations about imaginability which *Y* acknowledged – then he would be obliged to answer *Y*'s question: what reason do we have to believe that such data are indicative of a genuinely objective *genre* of 'necessities' and 'possibilities'? And it is unclear what response *X* has to that. Yet making *Y* out to be in error, or ignorant of relevant data, looks to be a no more promising prospect. *Y*'s perception of the construction is presumably in order, and he need be guilty of no technical error in working over it. Likewise we may suppose it impossible fairly to interpret him as being ignorant of any relevant consideration, unless it be the necessity of the conditional, and so the status of the construction as a proof, itself. So *X*'s case demands *either* that the facts acknowledged by *Y* actually constitute his – *Y*'s – recognition of the proof, without his realising it; *or* that *Y* is here 'proof blind', as it were – that more is indeed involved than *Y* acknowledges, the extra being precisely intellection of a logical necessity. But, either way, the difficulties are evident. The former line demands an answer to *Y*'s doubts about the warrant for so 'dignifying' features of our imagination. And the latter again faces the reproach that it exemplifies a manoeuvre which is *always* available to factualism, resort to which, without proper controls, will merely erode the very content of the issue.

[7] Cf. Wittgenstein (1964: 3d edn, III §87).

Above, I imposed the condition that it cannot count as satisfactory to attribute a subject's view of a particular statement to a mistake, or ignorance, if the sole ground for doing so is that he takes the view he does. It should now be clearer why this constraint is needed. Unless there is more to be said, we are powerless to defend the distinction between the operations of any genuinely cognitive faculty, affording non-inferentially based knowledge, and the working of something which, like the 'sense' of humour, we do not wish to regard as genuinely cognitive at all. It may be, in certain cases, that there is no *identifying* a subject's mistake/ignorance except by describing his view of the disputed statement, but the *ground* for so describing him cannot stop there. What the dispute between X and Y brings out is that there is a disturbing parallel (at least it ought to disturb the factualist) between judgments of logical necessity and judgment about what is amusing. In both cases, disputants may be in agreement about all features of a situation *except* whether it establishes a logical necessity or is amusing; and all the cards may be on the table – no further consideration need be available which, once apprised of it, would bring the disputants into agreement.

The parallel is not, of course, decisive: there is still space for the claim that the status of the construction as a proof, for example, is a further feature of it, over and above its empirical features, sensitivity to which calls for the operation of a special faculty. But then there has also to be space for the corresponding, highly unattractive claim about amusingness. One thing, accordingly, is clear: the postulation of a special intellectual faculty, sensitive to logical necessity, cannot be justified merely by our propensity – if we have it – non-collusively to agree in our ratification of new proofs, or, more generally, in our judgments about necessity in novel cases. What counts is not the propensity towards non-collusive agreement, however widespread, but whether Humean disputes about necessity are always possible. A universally shared sense of humour would not make issues concerning what is funny any more factual – assuming that they would, on proper analysis, prove not to be so. It is a coherent and competitive view to hold both that the notion of logical necessity is genuine and that the anti-factualist spirit of 'Two Dogmas of Empiricism' should be endorsed.

Why does the suggestion that the sense of humour is a cognitive faculty seem so outlandish? At bottom, it is because our conception of ourselves and of our knowledge-acquiring powers is broadly *naturalistic*. We are content to regard something as a cognitive faculty only so long as there is the promise of a proper explanation of its physiological basis, an account which enables us to see its output as the product of physical interaction between our bodies and the environment. There simply is no such promise in the case of amusingness; we do not have the slightest idea what the amusingness of a situation could physically consist in (contrast redness and the emission of light waves of such-and-such frequency) on the basis of which an account might be built to match the joint achievement of physiologists of the visual system and physicists of light. It is the background supplied by such an account which enables us, ultimately, to substantiate attributions of error, or ignorance, in the manner called for by the earlier constraints.

It is a great question whether naturalism affords the materials for an overall coherent epistemology. But the factualist about logical necessity had better believe that it does not. For everything said in the previous paragraph about amusingness applies to necessity also.

9. Readers familiar with another discussion of mine of this issue (1980: chapter 23) will recall the prominence there given, in the attempt to arrive at a general description of the domain of the factual, to the role of the seemingly ubiquitous possibility of sceptical doubt. Of course the sceptic as an actual human agent – one who resolutely seeks to tailor his corpus of beliefs to those consistent with sceptical standards of justification – is presumably a fiction. But the prototypical sceptical *routine* – the play with the inconclusiveness of available data, the fallibility of our capacities, etc. – looks to be a possible manoeuvre everywhere. This reflection need not be a reason for modifying the account proposed above: a difference of opinion generated by sceptical doubt might prove to be best described as involving 'prejudicial assessment of data', for example.[8] The important point for the anti-factualist about necessity is rather that Y's position in the above dispute must not be best described, in essential respects, merely as a form of scepticism. If it were, the factualist could evade the need to give proper substance to a preferred description of Y as in error, or ignorant, presenting him instead as a familiar animal, occupying a stance which is available everywhere and has no bearing on questions of factuality.

The matter needs a more detailed discussion than I have space remaining to attempt here.[9] Still, one initial consideration suggests that Y's position is not happily described as sceptical. Traditional forms of scepticism – about other minds, or the past, or generalisations inductively arrived at, for instance – never dispute that there is such a thing as getting the truth values of the relevant class of statements right. Their essential claim is rather that, for all the controls which we have at our disposal, success will be a *fluke*: no ground is, or can be, possessed for the reliability of those controls. It is granted that there is an objective subject matter at issue: the challenge of

---

[8] This description would require, to stress, that Y, as sceptic, concurs with X about the data germane to X's judgment that the construction demonstrates necessity. If that is so, the data would have to be empirical features of the construction plus the considerations about imaginability which Y acknowledged – so, it might plausibly be urged, Y's scepticism would be well conceived. Cf. Wright (1980: 464).

[9] The issue is taken up by Edward Craig in his (1984).

the traditional sceptic is that we make good our belief that our epistemic capacities are up to the task of securing reliable beliefs about it. It is clear enough that this is not what Y was depicted as saying. Y did not grant X that *some* descriptive conditional is necessary, and then seek to cast doubt on the effectiveness of our controls – principally, careful attention to the promptings of intuition and meticulous checking of constructions – on attempts to winkle out the right one. Rather, he sought to be persuaded that, in order to do justice to the construction, there was any cause to invoke a special notion of 'necessary' truth. And it is, so far, quite unclear whether, or how, he ought to be persuaded of that. The issue is not the presumed reliability of certain capacities of ours, acknowledged as genuinely epistemic on both sides, but rather whether we are concerned with a genuine epistemic capacity at all.

Two concluding remarks. First, I have recently quite often encountered in conversation the impression that the 'rule following considerations' somehow dispose of this class of questions, teaching us that all our judgments – in ethics, aesthetics, pure mathematics, empirical science, and any other field of human expression you care to consider – are ineliminably conditioned by basic human reactive propensities; that if our nature has a part to play in judgments about what is funny, for example, it has a comparable part to play everywhere. It would be a major task to unpick all the knots of confusion in this notion. But one thing I hope to have made plausible is that a framework remains for discussion of issues to do with factuality which may be utilised even after the global lessons of Wittgenstein's ideas about following a rule have been fully digested. Second, although I believe that the framework described provides a context for many of our raw intuitions on these questions, I cannot pretend to certainty that further work will not disclose that there is no real substance to them. *Quietism*[10] may yet win the day: it may prove impossible to give clear content of the distinction between genuinely fact-stating and non-fact-stating declarative discourse, and Wittgenstein's stress in the *Philosophical Investigations* on the essential multiplicity of language games may prove to be profoundly insightful in just this respect (1953: section 28).

Actually, such a result would itself motivate a kind of anti-factualism, though one defined by its rejection of the basis of the factualist position rather than by its opposition to it. At any rate, the issues are wide open; and if philosophy can legitimately aspire to yield illuminating comparisons between our modes of thought and speech and the way things really are, they are important issues.

[10] The term is Simon Blackburn's (1984: 146).

REFERENCES

Blackburn, S., 1984. *Spreading the Word*, Oxford: Clarendon Press.

Craig, E. J., 1984. Arithmetic and Fact, in *Exercises in Analysis*, ed. I. Hacking, Cambridge: University Press.

Craig, E. J., 1986. Privacy and Rule-Following, this volume.

Dummett, M., 1959. Wittgenstein's Philosophy of Mathematics, *Philosophical Review* 68: 324–48.

Dummett, M., 1981. *Frege: Philosophy of Language*, 2nd edn, London: Duckworth.

Grice, H. and Strawson, P., 1956. In Defence of a Dogma, *Philosophical Review 65*: 141–58.

Quine, W., 1961. Two Dogmas of Empiricism, reprinted in *From a Logical Point of View*, 2nd edn, New York: Harper and Row.

Wittgenstein, L., 1953. *Philosophical Investigations*, ed. G. E. M. Anscombe & R. Rhees, Oxford: Blackwell.

Wittgenstein, L., 1964. *Remarks on the Foundations of Mathematics*, 3rd edn, ed. G. H. von Wright, R. Rhees and G. E. M. Anscombe, Oxford: Blackwell.

Wittgenstein, L., 1969. *On Certainty*, ed. G. E. M. Anscombe and G. H. von Wright, Oxford: Blackwell.

Wright, C., 1980. *Wittgeinstein on the Foundations of Mathematics*, London: Duckworth; Cambridge Mass.: Harvard University Press.

Wright, C., 1985. Facts, Scepticism and Certainty, *Proceedings of the British Academy*, December 1985.

Wright, C., (forthcoming.) Does Wittgenstein have a cogent argument against Private Language? Investigations §§258–61, in *Subject, Thought and Context*, ed. J. McDowell and P. Petitt, Oxford: Clarendon Press.

Intuition in constructive mathematics*

CHARLES PARSONS

I

The most systematically developed constructivist view of mathematics is that originated by L. E. J. Brouwer, which still goes by the name of Intuitionism given to it by him. He used this name even early in his career (1912), because of his view that a certain kind of intuition is basic to mathematical evidence. Brouwer's conception is related to Kant's notion of 'construction in pure intuition', though with important differences. A conception of intuition even more closely related to Kant's occurs in Hilbert's account of the mathematical methods that his programme envisaged for the justification of non-constructive methods in mathematics by proving the consistency of formalized axiomatic theories. Hilbert's 'finitary' mathematical method clearly encompasses a proper subclass of what is admitted by intuitionists. According to Hilbert, the theories that form mathematics proper (particularly classical analysis and set theory) are not evident or justified in any direct way but are rather justified by finitary mathematical arguments establishing the consistency of the theories and their conservativeness with respect to finitary mathematics. Thus, on both Brouwer's and Hilbert's views, intuition in a roughly Kantian sense is a basic and indispensable source of mathematical knowledge.

In the development of intuitionism, already in Brouwer's lifetime, it became clear that the insistence on intuitive evidence, according to a certain conception of intuition, was not the most original or the most distinctive feature of the 'intuitionist' point of view. Implicit in Brouwer's counterexamples to instances of the law of the excluded middle and to many theorems of classical mathematics is what has been called a verificationist conception of the meaning of mathematical statements. When Brouwer's pupil Arend Heyting constructed an intuitionistic logic, his sketch of an intended interpretation was based on the idea that the meaning of a statement in the

* I am much indebted to the discussion at the Thyssen conference for clarifying my ideas. Correspondence with W. W. Tait and discussion with Isaac Levi have also been extremely valuable.

language of mathematics is to be explained by giving the conditions under which a 'construction' is a *proof* of the statement. In the intervening fifty years, this idea has undergone a lot of elaboration in both technical and philosophical work. In recent years, discussion of the foundations of elementary intuitionistic mathematics has concentrated almost entirely on the problems surrounding this conception of the meaning of mathematical statements. A consequence, perhaps intended by no one, is that the role of intuition in intuitionism has become obscured. I shall argue, however, that intuitionism and other constructivist philosophies of mathematics need a notion of intuition.

A symptom of this situation is to be found in the writings of Michael Dummett, where the sort of conception of the meaning of mathematical statements that I am referring to finds the greatest philosophical articulation and widest application. I have not found in the extensive Dummett corpus more than passing reference to Brouwer's conception of intuition (e.g. 1977: 32; 1980: 609). It is clear that according to Dummett it is a certain conception of the meaning of mathematical statements, and in particular of the logical connectives and quantifiers as used in mathematics, that distinguishes intuitionist from classical mathematics. Therefore the theory of meaning is the arena in which issues between the intuitionistic and classical conceptions of mathematics are to be worked out. Where Dummett does give an extended discussion of a conception of mathematical intuition, in his paper 'Platonism' (1978: 202–14), it is a 'platonist' conception, such as might be attributed to Gödel, that is his stalking horse.

In a recent discussion, Dummett analyses Brouwer's case against classical mathematics and sees it as resting on three premises (1980: 610):

(i)   A mathematical statement has a content.
(ii) This content is given in terms of what counts as a proof of it.
(iii) The meaning of any statement must be determined by its composition.

It seems that intuition enters through (i), since according to Brouwer arithmetical statements involve reference to the 'empty form' of a basic temporal experience (e.g. 1952: 141); an earlier remark of Dummett's (1980: 609) indicates that he reads Brouwer in this way. If this were the only bearing of Brouwer's notion of intuition on the matter, it would be hard to see the relevance to the critical case of this rather than another view of the 'content' of arithmetic. Spelling this out (as Dummett does not) leads into considerations under (ii). It has long been obvious that according to Brouwer the infinity of the natural members is potential only, and evidently this is to fall out from this description of temporal experience. The 'original intellectual phenomenon of the falling apart of a life moment into two qualitatively distinct things' (1929: 153), is in a certain way iterable: since we can divide our experience into past and present/future, independently of its objects, we can continue to repeat that division, so that there 'arises by self-unfolding of the original intellectual phenomenon the temporal series of appearances of arbitrary multiplicity' (*ibid.*) The natural numbers are apparently a common form of such a series (1929: 154–5 or 1952: 141); the unfolding in time is a feature of the concrete situation that is preserved when one passes to the abstract form. Dummett expresses this by saying that 'an infinite structure is always to be thought of as something in process of generation, not as something the construction of which can be completed' (1977: 32). This of itself might not have any implications for mathematical reasoning; for example, if one applies classical modal logic to the 'potentialities' of 'generation' of natural numbers, given a predicate 'Fx' assumed to apply truly or falsely to each natural number, either it is necessary that each natural number that is eventually generated is F, or it is possible that a number should be generated that is not.[1] Brouwer presumably thought there was no more basis for such classical reasoning about the possibilities of generation than for direct classical reasoning about what *will* be generated in the infinite future. It is of course at this point that Dummett's premiss (ii) enters: the only basis there can be for the truth of a general statement about such a potential infinity is a proof on the basis of a certain stage of the generating process and the rule on the basis of which it proceeds.

However, ideas about the temporality of experience enter into Brouwer's conceptions about proofs; in particular, proofs are themselves constructions that unfold in time, and the subject is situated in time. The assumptions about *time* may have a truistic character, in contrast to assumptions about the connections between the unfolding of the subject's mathematical knowledge and mathematical truth (as in Brouwer's theory of the 'creative subject'). However, a philosophy of intuitionism does have to have something to say about their status.

In this connection, I might remark that in his mature writings Brouwer does not seem to me especially wedded to any notion of the *a priori*. His taking the 'empty substratum of all two-ities' to be the 'original intuition of mathematics' (1929: 154) is a notion of 'formal intuition' reminiscent of Kant, but the overall theory in which it occurs has pronounced naturalistic features: 'mathematical consideration', of which 'temporal orientation' is an aspect, is an act of *will* undertaken in the service of self-preservation. Because of its subjectivistic and in some respects mystical character, Brouwer's view is quite different from the naturalistic epistemology of our own day, but it is equally different from the apriorism of Kant.[2]

---

[1] See for example Parsons (1971, note 11; expanded in the reprint in Parsons (1983)).

[2] Dummett rightly speaks of Brouwer's philosophy of mathematics as 'psychologistic through and through' (1980: 609); he does not remark how sharply this separates Brouwer's outlook

CHARLES PARSONS

I shall make one further remark about Brouwer. What he calls the 'original intuition of mathematics' is not an intuition *of* iteration or of the natural numbers. I think one can regard Brouwer as holding that any natural number can be given in intuition; iteration and the structure of the natural numbers arise through the 'self-unfolding' of the intuition, but there is no reason to suppose that either is an *object* of intuition. The phrase 'intuition of iteration' does not, so far as I know, occur in Brouwer's writings; it *was* used by Hermann Weyl, who said that on the basis of the intuition of iteration we are convinced that the concept of natural number is 'extensionally definite' (*umfangsdefinit*; 1919: 85), that is, that the natural numbers are a domain over which classical quantification is valid.[3] In my opinion, such a view at best presupposes a different conception of intuition and is at worst confused. In fact, Weyl's conception of intuition seems to derive not from Kant or Brouwer but from Husserl.

It is not my main purpose to interpret Brouwer or Dummett. One might conjecture that Dummett holds that an appropriate analysis of the meaning of mathematical statements will imply a sufficient analysis of the basis of our knowledge of them which will leave no room for intuition. Since a meaning-theoretic approach, in a broad sense, is common to a number of writers on the foundations of constructive mathematics, the thesis that this approach can dispense with intuition is worth examining in its own right, whether or not Dummett holds it. However, I shall confine myself to the kind of analysis that relates the meaning of a mathematical statement to what counts as a proof of it. Thus I shall not be concerned with other philosophies of mathematics that reject mathematical intuition, such as the holistic empiricism of W. V. Quine.

II

It is necessary to be more precise about the concept of intuition than Brouwer is; I shall rely on my own discussion of the notion (1980), which owes more to Kant and Hilbert than to Brouwer. An elementary distinction is that between intuition of *objects* and intuition of *truths*. The former, as I see it, is a relation to objects that is importantly analogous to perception, the latter a kind of propositional knowledge that is analogous to perceptual

from Kant's. Psychologism is even more marked in Brouwer's older contemporary Gerrit Mannoury.

I am inclined to doubt that the Kantian formulation Brouwer gave to his account of the intuition of two-oneness in his inaugural lecture (1913: 85–6) expresses his real view in later years. Even at the time it may have been adopted to make his ideas more intelligible to his audience.

[3] Cf. (1918: 37). In a parallel passage a little later, Weyl is somewhat more cautious: 'Basing ourselves on the generating process of the natural numbers, given to us in intuition, we hold to the view that the concept of natural number is extensionally definite' (1921: 43).

214

knowledge. In ordinary perception, we do not have the latter without the former: perceptual knowledge involves perception of objects. If one does not assume the same about mathematical intuition, that intuitive mathematical knowledge involves intuition of mathematical objects, then it is hard to see how intuition is distinguished from other kinds of non-inferential knowledge, such as whatever the 'obviousness' of the simplest logical truths consists in. For this reason I follow Kant in taking intuition of objects as the primary notion; I shall not call knowledge intuitive unless it rests on intuition of objects. To be sure, this is more restrictive than the most common use of the term 'intuition' in contemporary philosophy, which seems to be for strong inclination to believe that is not accounted for by perception or conscious reasoning, and that is allowed to serve as data at least at the outset of an inquiry; perhaps the primary example is the 'intuitions' a native speaker has about what is grammatical in his language. My not following this usage is of course terminological legislation, but I believe that my usage brings out distinctions that might otherwise be neglected.

The account given of a kind of mathematical intuition in Parsons 1980 would describe the role of intuition in a particular kind of mathematical theory: the theory of strings based on a finite alpha-bet, interpreted in a very concrete way. It is sufficiently illustrated by Hilbert's example where the alphabet contains just one symbol '|', which we call a stroke. On one point concerning the relation of intuition of truths and intuition of objects, the earlier discussion needs amplification. Section IV of the paper was intended to describe the intuition that has these strings of strokes as objects; being thought of as *types*, they are abstract objects and can reasonably be called mathematical objects. Thus, in speaking of intuition of truths in this case (as I did in section V), I claimed that the condition of resting on intuition of objects was met, by mathematical objects.

However, an objection might be made on behalf of my own earlier self (1971, section III) that what we want to say about these strings can be formulated in a 'modal nominalist' language, in which quantifiers range over tokens (i.e. inscriptions), identity of types is replaced by a certain equivalence relation of tokens, and existence of a type by possible existence of a token. Given this possibility, it follows that the data do not have to be described in terms of abstract objects at all, and hence no such objects are given in intuition.

In general, it seems to me that the fact that certain data can be described in different ways with different ontological commitments does not imply that objects that appear in only some of these ontologies are not objects of perception or intuition. Compare a phenomenalistic account of ordinary physical objects: 'S sees O', where O is a physical object, is not false on the phenomenalistic account, but rather reinterpreted. The same holds for 'S

intuits T' where T is an expression-type, on the modal nominalist account. A notion of mathematical intuition would not disappear on this account, at least if one does not reject the claim that simple propositions 'about types' are intuitively known (1980: 155). But this could be a case of intuition of truths that, though it rests on intuition of objects, does not rest on intuition of mathematical objects.

In fact, I have reservations about the modal nominalist formulation. It imports the notion of physical object, with its standards of individuation and actual existence, into the content of the mathematical theory.[4] It may be appropriate to a context in which the latter is incorporated into a larger body of knowledge, but in my view it is not the formulation that best captures the most elementary mathematical evidences.

Its ontological commitment made the theory of strings depend on intuition. But this would raise the question how far the example can be generalized. The question arises with particular sharpness when we remind ourselves of the 'structuralist' understanding of mathematical theories: although on my conception the strings of strokes can have the 'incompleteness' that the structuralist understanding gives rise to (1980: 161–2), their representability in perception is a determination that goes beyond the structure given by the theory itself, which they will not share with the elements of an arbitrary isomorphic copy. If we assume that natural numbers are to be understood in this structuralist way, then it seems to follow that they cannot be objects of intuition, but it will be with the natural numbers that constructive mathematics begins.

It should be evident, however, that the structuralist understanding does not remove the issue of ontological commitment, though it does remove a possible misunderstanding of what this commitment amounts to. If one tries to express the structuralist view by what is called 'if-thenism' or 'deductivism', where the mathematical truth of a statement about, say, natural numbers is identified with the logical truth of the conditional whose antecedent characterizes the structure and whose consequent is the statement in question, then if there is no instance of the structure the statement and its negation will be equally true. Alternatively, following Putnam 1967, we might identify the mathematical truth with the necessary truth of the statement in *any* structure of the required kind; but the same difficulty will arise unless an instance of the structure is *possible*.[5]

---

[4] I do not now consider my earlier attempt to avoid this by speaking of 'perceptible inscriptions' (1971: 45, esp. n. 9) to be successful.

My discussion here is indebted to Stephanie Katz Ordover, who pointed out the unclarity of the position of Parsons 1980 toward the modal nominalist formulation.

[5] Of course the second-order character of a characterization of the structure of natural numbers is a complication for this sort of view. One might try to save if-thenism by saying that the consistency of the structure-characterizing antecedent is presupposed; however, this

One can make out this existence or possibility by presenting an intuitive model such as Hilbert's strings of strokes. If something of this kind is conceded to be necessary for the 'objective reality' of arithmetic, then the effort to eliminate intuition has been given up. Of course there is the empiricist alternative that makes either the possibility or the existence of some particular model a high-level empirical hypothesis. Such a view replaces mathematical intuition by ordinary perception; in Kantian language, it concedes the necessity for intuition in order for mathematics to have objects, but holds that empirical intuition is sufficient. As I have said, in this paper I am leaving empiricism out of account.[6]

III

I now want to consider whether an approach by way of a theory of meaning can solve or bypass this question of ontological commitment in such a way as to make intuition dispensable. In the specific case of the natural numbers, such an enterprise seems very promising, since a gross description of the use of numerals in counting and calculation may indeed relate them to objects counted, but since the relation between numerical expressions that makes them expressions for the same number can be characterized in other terms, without tagging each onto a *number*, it seems that we can give an account of the meaning of 'expressions for numbers' that has no need for intuition. The addition of quantifiers for numbers to the language described seems to change nothing essential, in spite of the influential view that quantifiers are the vehicle of ontological commitment: a statement of the form 'there is a number x such that Fx' can be regarded as true just in case some instance, that is some statement '$F\bar{n}$' with $\bar{n}$ a *numeral*, is true.

As this last remark reveals, the logical core of such an account of the meaning of arithmetical statements is some sort of truth theory in which numerical quantifiers are treated as *substitutional*. It is the availability of this interpretation that makes it possible to avoid identifying numbers with objects given in some other way or simply assuming numbers as given for numerals to denote. In the literature discussing the relevance of the substitutional interpretation of arithmetic to questions of ontology (e.g. Gottlieb 1980), it is presented and discussed as a classical interpretation and belongs to the general circle of ideas in which meaning is a matter of

seems to reintroduce the problem of ontological commitment, since a statement of consistency is a statement of logical syntax.

[6] But cf. Parsons (1983: 21, 184–6). Although an empiricist form of constructivism does not seem inconceivable, I do not know a clear and plausible formulation. But by 'empiricism' I mean primarily a view that rejects mathematical intuition (as well as rejecting anything like Frege's 'logical objects'); as I indicated above, it is not certain that Brouwer in the end regarded mathematical intuition as *a priori*.

truth-conditions. However, it is by no means tied to classical logic, and in fact in my view something like a substitutional conception of quantification underlies some explanations of quantifiers by constructivists; I shall consider this matter further below.

Any attempt by means of formal semantics to argue that certain propositions are true by meaning, or that inferences are valid by meaning, has to look to the commitments of the metalanguage in which the argument is carried out. This is notorious in the case of logic, since much the same logical inferences as those whose validity is being shown are used in semantical arguments for their validity. The classical substitutional interpretation of arithmetic has an advantage in that the metalanguage does not need to speak of numbers as such. Though this is relevant to some ontological problems, it is not a gain relevant to our present concern, since the metalanguage does speak of expressions, just the sort of objects that are offered as an intuitive model of arithmetic. There has been much debate about what ontology a substitutional interpretation attributes to the object language. In view of the occurrence on the right side of the condition for the existential quantifier of a quantifier over expressions, there is a presumption that the commitment is at least comparable to commitment to expressions. This is true on Quine's view of the matter, according to which the commitment can only be assessed when the object language has been translated into a first-order *objectual* language. The same holds on a proposal I have advanced elsewhere (1971a, 1982) that a substitutional theory will in a case like the present one speak of objects that are 'constituted by language', since without language there are no such objects. Since I have discussed the matter elsewhere, I shall not go further into the general question of the ontology of substitutional theories. But I conclude that a substitutional interpretation of arithmetic does not get around the need for intuition.

Admittedly, a substitutional truth theory for arithmetic is superficially quite different from the sort of interpretation offered by constructivists. Rather, the meaning-theoretic approach is worked out formally in what are called 'theories of constructions', in which conditions are laid down for a 'construction' to be a *proof* of a formula. The underlying theory of constructions and the proof-conditions given for formulae of the various logical forms constitute a 'theory of meaning' for portions of constructive mathematical language. Thus an explicit sense in which a statement might be 'true by virtue of meaning' is this: we formalize the statement in the language of some intuitionistic formal theory. We then describe explicitly a construction of which we show that it is a proof of the formula in question.

With respect to the problem that concerns us, we can consider a rather simple example of a theory of this kind, from the discussion of the notions of finitist function and finitist proof in Tait (1981). We can thus avoid most of the complications and conceptual difficulties that arise in theories of constructions. Typed theories of constructions, of which Tait's is an instance, speak of objects that are given as of a certain type, and contain operations forming types from given types as well as operations forming objects from given objects. Often there is parallelism between the two kinds of operations. Thus for types A and B, there is a type $A \wedge B$ of ordered pairs whose first term is of type A and whose second term is of type B. This can be expressed by an introduction rule

$$\frac{a:A \qquad\qquad b:B}{(a,b):A \wedge B}.$$

In the finitist context that directly concerns Tait, the operation of pairing is 'typically ambiguous': it is given for each pair of types rather than in a general way for all 'objects' regardless of type. Moreover, the term 'operation' does not belong to the theory itself but to our own semantic reflection; the function $\lambda xy \, (x,y)$, for given types A and B, is not a finitist object. (It would have to be of type $A \to (B \to (A \wedge B))$.) Though Tait does not say so explicitly, it appears that the general logic of pairing does not belong to finitist mathematics. But the pair construction for the particular types that do belong to finitist mathematics does belong to it.

The purpose of these observations is to point out that these theories contain quite abstract operations for constructing objects, which are instances of operations that do not depend on the nature of the objects entering into them. In classical mathematics, the traditional way of providing for operations of this kind is the adoption of set theory as a general framework. In addition to pairing, particularly important are basic operations concerning functions, such as application of a function to an argument, composition, and either lambda-abstraction or combinatory operations in terms of which it can be defined. Indeed, combinatory logic or the λ-calculus is the basis of another kind of theory of constructions, the type-free theories first suggested by G. Kreisel and worked out by Nicolas Goodman and others.[7] Such a calculus of functions, of course now in its typed version, occurs only in a very restricted way in the construction of Tait (1981), since finitist mathematics as he conceives it rejects the general notion of function.[8]

To return to pairing, in its full generality it is an operation on objects

---

[7] See Goodman (1970, 1973), and, for a clear and penetrating presentation of the philosophical motivation and some difficulties of these theories, Weinstein (1983).

[8] This is of course not true of the non-finitist framework of Tait (1983), which incorporates a typed lambda-calculus. Tait differs from a common constructivist view in holding that even in constructive mathematics the basic conception of function is the same extensional one that prevails in classical mathematics.

CHARLES PARSONS

quite generally: if we recognize a and b as objects we can 'form' their ordered pair (a,b); this construction depends in no way on the nature of the objects paired. In Tait's context, for a and b to be given as objects means that each is given as of a given type.

Now what reason do we have to suppose that, given a and b, (a,b) exists? We might, extending the conception of intuition with which we have been operating, suggest the answer that when a and b are given in intuition, (a,b) can also be given in intuition, given a suitable conceptualization on the part of the subject. Tait suggests this in the analogous case of finite sequences when he writes, 'We discern finite sequences in our experience.... We not only discern such sequences but we see them *as* sequences' (1981: 529). If A and B are types such that any object of each type can be constructed in intuition, we might then see the construction of (a,b) as a construction in intuition. But this answer will not suffice if the construction of (a,b) is of the generality it appears to have, in no way dependent on the possibility that a and b should be given in intuition. Though the answer would be available to a constructivist who holds that all the objects with which he is concerned are intuitable, it is not directly available to a set theorist (at least without an essentially extended conception of intuition) or to a constructivist who admits objects that are not objects of intuition, as seems to be the widely held view about functions and proofs (cf. Gödel 1958: 281). In spite of the above-cited remarks, Tait rejects this kind of answer even within finitism, for reasons that I discuss below.

Is there another answer that the construction theorist gives? If 'existence is what the existential quantifier expresses', he might well reply that the question is wrongly put and should rather have been: When are we entitled to assert $(\exists x)[x = (a,b)]$: that is, what is it for a construction, given $a: A$ and $b: B$, to prove $(\exists x: A \land B)[x = (a,b)]$. Such a construction is given from (a,b) itself. But then this answer appears to be circular.

I think the real answer implicit in at least some work on the theory of constructions, Tait's included, differs from this circular answer and also from the 'intuitionist' answer considered above. It is the same position that in our earlier discussion motivated the substitutional semantics for discourse about numbers: we understand, and have rules for, the form of *language* in which the operator $(,)$ has its part. The 'formation' of the ordered pair (a,b) is represented or expressed in a canonical way by the formation of the expression $(\bar{a},\bar{b})$ when $\bar{a}$ denotes a and $\bar{b}$ denotes b. If this is to be a general conception of reference to mathematical objects, we should suppose a and b to be given in the same way: that is, with their types are associated a canonical form of expression for objects of that type, such that $\bar{a}$ and $\bar{b}$ are also canonical. If (a,b) is given in this way, then the construction of the expression itself represents all that can be asked in the way of an existence proof.

This conception of how mathematical objects are given is worked out in a quite elaborate way in the intuitionistic theory of types of Per Martin-Löf (1975, 1982). To a type of object corresponds a construction of canonical expressions for objects of that type and hence an introduction rule like that given above for $A \wedge B$. Now an arbitrary $c: A \wedge B$ is given as an ordered pair (a,b), where $a: A$ and $b: B$; thus we can write $a = p_1 c$ and $b = p_2 c$ where p_1 and p_2 are the projection operations. But terms of the form $p_i t$ are not canonical, because if t is of the form (r,s) then $p_i t$ will *reduce* to r if $i = 1$, s if $i = 2$. With a type of object goes not only a canonical form of expression for objects of that type, but also a notion of equality, that is, rules determining when expressions for objects of the type are expressions for the *same* object. Following out the present example (which enables us to simplify considerably from Martin-Löf's exposition, and to use notations derived from Tait), and writing $s = t: A$ for 's and t are the same objects of type A', we have in addition to the introduction rule the elimination rules.

$$\frac{c: A \wedge B}{p_1 c: A} \qquad \frac{c: A \wedge B}{p_2 c: B}$$

introduction and elimination rules for quality

$$\frac{a = c: A \qquad b = d: B}{(a,b) = (c,d): A \wedge B} \qquad \frac{c = d: A \wedge B}{p_1 c = p_1 d: A} \qquad \frac{c = d: A \wedge B}{p_2 c = p_2 d: B}$$

and the equality (reduction) rules

$$\frac{a: A \qquad b: B}{p_1(a,b) = a: A} \qquad \frac{a: A \qquad b: B}{p_2(a,b) = b: B} .$$

The underlying ontological conception of objects as given by canonical expressions for them would seem to imply that in a case like the above, an expression of the form (s,t) would be canonical only if s and t are, and that to evaluate such an expression one would first evaluate s and t, that is, reduce them to equivalent canonical expressions. In the present example (though not in Martin-Löf's full theory),[9] there is no obstacle to such an understanding, and it can be carried through in Tait's finitist theory of types, where the only objects are tuples of numbers and certain proofs. Although his theory does not have existential quantification, it does have the notion of

[9] For the type $A \rightarrow B$ of functions with domain A and codomain B, canonical expressions are λ-terms $\lambda x b$; since in general b can be reduced to canonical form only if a value of x is given, (1982: 160), $\lambda x b$ must be counted as canonical in cases where b is not; for example, if A is the type of natural numbers, b might involve primitive recursion. Martin-Löf's solution to this problem, which arises for some other higher types, is to make whether an expression is canonical depend only on its outward form (1982: 157).

a proof of a purely universal proposition; such proofs are operations on syntactic objects or tuples of them (1981: 535–7). The universal quantifier is implicitly substitutional, and syntactic objects enter explicitly into the theory's conception of proof.[10]

The point I have been trying to make, that theories of constructions cannot bypass the question how syntactic objects are given, is thus especially clear for Tait's theory. But it clearly arises in general for a theory, such as Martin-Löf's, for which objects are given by canonical expressions for them. A claim of a theory of constructions to dispense with intuition would have to rest on the claim that these expressions (and for Tait 1981, simple formal derivations) are given in another way. This seems to be Tait's view, as we shall see.

It might seem, however, from his remark (1981: 529) quoted above, that he would admit the point: he makes clear that for him formal expressions are finite sequences (1981: 529, 538–9), and his remark seems to say that there is something like intuition of finite sequences. However, even if such sequences as the string of nineteen '1's that he uses as an example are intuited, it appears that such intuition belongs to the application of the number concept (p. 530). Furthermore, if one considers finite sequences whose terms come from a small collection of objects each of which we can assume to be intuitable or even perceivable, it does not follow that sequences of these objects of any given length are intuitable. Tait does not say this explicitly, but it is an evident consequence of his view (p. 539) that large numbers are not representable in intuition.

IV

It then emerges that the more crucial issue between Tait and me concerns the notion of the *possibility* of intuition. What does it mean to say that such an object as a string of 10^{10} strokes *can* be intuited? Tait understands such statements in a strict finitist way, in terms of the capabilities of actual human

---

[10] But in Martin-Löf's theory, the conception of quantification is not exactly the standard substitutional one. For a statement $(\exists x:A)B(x)$ to be true is for there to be a proof of it. According to Martin-Löf, a proposition is a type, and a proof of it is just an object of that type. But p is of type $(\exists x:A)B(x)$ just in case p is a *pair* (a,b) where a is of type A and b is of type $B(a)$, that is, a proof of $B(a)$. Since a can be given by a canonical expression, this will agree with the substitutional conception. But in the case of higher types, no substitution class is given in advance. For example, what canonical expressions λxt of type $A \to B$ we can construct depends on what other types we have, and this is not determined once and for all. Thus although existential quantification has a certain substitutional character, this is really not true of universal: reasoning about an arbitrary $f:A \to B$ cannot depend on information about the class of such expressions, but only on the assumption that $fx:B$ for arbitrary $x:A$. This accords well with the thesis of Tait (1983) alluded to in note 8 above; see especially Tait (1983: 185–6).

perceivers. Of course such an understanding is available, and taking 'can' in that way one quickly reaches a number, if not 10^{10} then certainly less than 10^{100}, such that it is obviously false that a string of that number of strokes can be intuited.

Many writers have used the word 'can' in a more abstract sense in contexts related to the present one. Indeed, such a use seems to underlie the concept of a computable function as it has traditionally been taken in constructive mathematics: a computing procedure defines a function on a domain D if by means of it a value *can* be computed for any argument in D. If 'can' is understood in terms of actual human capability, this will evidently fail in comparatively simple cases, such as iterated exponentiation, as strict finitist critics of intuitionism have long stressed.[11] In response to this, constructivist writers (and others) have spoken of the possibility *in principle* of carrying out a construction such as a computation. Similarly, in the case at hand it would be natural to say that a string of 10^{10} or even 10^{100} strokes can in principle be intuited.

Such a notion of possibility 'in principle' applied to operations of construction or computation is deeply rooted in the history of mathematical thought. The development of Euclid's geometry implicitly assumed the constructions given by his postulates to be indefinitely iterable; to that extent, ancient mathematics seems to have involved a notion of this kind.[12] In modern mathematics, similar ideas arise even outside the constructive context, most strikingly perhaps in Kurt Gödel's speculation about absolute notions of provability and definability (see Gödel 1946).

In the situation with which we began, the modal notions were connected with an epistemic notion, intuition. Philosophers have connected mathematical notions of construction and computation with epistemic notions, at least since Kant spoke of 'construction of concepts in pure intuition'. A tempting way of understanding the possibility in principle with which we are concerned is as a capacity of the *mind*. The same limitations of actual human capacity, therefore, force us to interpret such a capability as possessed by the mind in abstraction from its embodiment in the human organism. Either transcendental idealism or the solipsistic mysticism of Brouwer could find such a conclusion acceptable.[13] Even a materialistic

[11] E.g. van Dantzig 1955.

[12] The application of a similarly broad notion of possibility to perception, sensation, or 'sensing' is required for the modern phenomenalist construal of statements about the physical world, epitomized by John Stuart Mill's thesis that matter is 'a Permanent Possibility of Sensation' (1865: 183). The issues are not essentially changed if, as the more refined modern formulations do, one relies on counterfactuals rather than modality, since one then faces the problem of interpreting statements about what *would* be perceived under conditions that could not obtain for any real human perceiver.

[13] The 'naturalistic' character we discerned above in Brouwer's philosophy by no means implies materialism. Nevertheless, given the problem of survival that motivates 'mathematical

cognitive psychology might take this line, if the mind is construed as something like a Turing machine, and on the 'functional' level the capabilities of the mind are those of the abstract machine rather than those of its actual physical embodiment. The last version, however, makes explicit a difficulty that was already present in the more traditional ones: the potential infinity that we attribute to the mind's capabilities, by virtue of the indefinite iterability of certain operations, is really being conceived by means of mathematics, rather than its being the case that some independent insight into the mind's capabilities is telling us what is possible by way of mathematical intuition, construction, computation, or proof. The Turing-machine conception makes explicit use of a mathematical model involving the concept of a computable function in order to say what the mind can do. There is thus a kind of circularity.[14]

The first lesson to be drawn from this state of affairs is that the notion of possibility in terms of which it is true, for example, that for a particular computable function a value *can* be computed for any argument is an essentially mathematical one. A number of writers have used the term 'mathematical possibility'.[15] Here, however, it is important to distinguish purely mathematical uses of this notion from those in which it is combined with epistemic or other non-mathematical concepts. The distinction is illustrated by an ambiguity in the above statement about a computable function. We may suppose the function to be given to us by a certain Turing machine programme. To say that a computation can be constructed may mean little more than that there can *be* a computation from this pro-gramme, where a computation is itself a mathematical object. The word 'con-structed' may be taken to be metaphorical, signalling the fact that there is

---

consideration' (1929: 153; see above), there may be a problem whether the iterability of intuitive construction as Brouwer conceives it is compatible with its being a capability of the self. Other intuitionists have taken intuitionism to be concerned with the constructions of an 'idealized mathematician' (e.g. Troelstra 1969: 4).

[14] This is just the problem raised for Kant (with more detailed argument) in Parsons (1964). A Kantian reply might be that Kant need not require that everything that intuition as conceptualized attributes to the objective world be an object of possible intuition in any sense, as opposed to being connected with intuition in definite ways determined by the categories, for example by the analogies of experience. In particular, it is not easy to determine how much Kant relies on a notion of mathematical possibility. (Cf. Parsons 1984, section 1.)

[15] First, I believe, in Putnam (1967). The notion of '"possibility of experience" defined by the form of intuition' (Parsons 1964: 106) is a form of mathematical possibility, which, however, combines mathematical possibility with epistemic notions in the way discussed in the text.

Putnam also uses the notion of mathematical possibility in a material rather than formal way, particularly in interpreting set theory by modal statements about 'standard concrete models' of systems of axioms (p. 57). I doubt that we have any reason to believe that standard models of higher set theories are possible that are in any sense concrete (see Parsons 1983: 192 n. 32).

an order of priority among computations, since longer ones involve or contain shorter ones. It is another matter to say that a value can be computed if this is to mean that some mathematician can arrive at insight as to what the value is. In this case, what is said to be possible is something epistemic or psychological, someone's knowing what the value is, perhaps by intuiting the constructed computation and extracting from it intuition of the value.

It is evidently this second type of application of the notion of mathematical possibility that Tait is committed to rejecting when he says that 10^{10} is 'not any reasonable sense representable in intuition' (1981: 539). But he does not address the notion of mathematical possibility. He is concerned to emphasize the point that in order to understand the notion of number, one has to understand the idea of iteration (or something equivalent to it), and this is 'not found in intuition' (ibid.) With this I agree, and indeed it shows an important limitation of the role of intuition in arithmetic, not adequately attended to by Kant or Brouwer.[16] But however iteration is to be understood, it is clearly a concept or operation, and the question whether certain numbers are representable in intuition, or whether certain strings of strokes can be intuited, is whether certain *objects* can be found in intuition. For this reason Tait's point does not show that a string of 10^{10} strokes is not intuitable 'in any reasonable sense'.

The question of circularity raised above does seem to me a serious matter. But it does not, it should be clear, tell directly against the intelligibility of notions of 'in principle' possibility of the kind we have been considering, unless the theory of the capabilities of the mind that is being used is supposed to be part of a 'first philosophy', prior to mathematics and science. In places Kant seems to have such an intention, in other places not. The manner in which Brouwer rejected much of classical mathematics suggests attributing a similar position to him. A similar problem may arise for the position of Dummett, who attempts to argue from considerations of the philosophy of language to rejection of classical logic in favour of intuitionistic logic.[17]

[16] Cf. Parsons (1964: 108; 1980: 164–5). In my opinion Tait goes beyond the force of his point in another respect in saying, 'But to have this idea [iteration], itself not found in intuition, is to have the idea of number *independent of any sort of representation in intuition*' (ibid.) This concerns not the sufficiency of representation in intuition for the understanding of the idea of number, but its necessity. It seems to imply either that the 'idea of number' is a concept of an abstract structure that does not depend on any manner in which an instance of the structure might be given, or that an instance is given in an essentially non-intuitive way. Tait does not argue for either of these positions, and I am inclined to reject both.

[17] Strict finitism is discussed in more than one of the essays in Dummett (1978). Dummett does not undertake a direct defence of his use of 'in principle' notions of provability, decidability, and computability; he does, however, particularly in (1959) and (1975), criticize the strict finitist rejection of them.

V

What is more important is that the general idea that strings of strokes, or objects constituting some other model of arithmetic, are 'given in intuition' does not strictly require that it be possible to intuit any such object. Physical objects are 'given in perception', but the same sort of difficulties as were raised about the possibility of intuition can be raised about the claim that every physical object can be perceived; it is still true that perception plays a constitutive role in our conceptions of the physical world. Still, there is an important difference: so long as we talk of 'medium-sized' or 'common-sense' physical objects, the obstacles to the practical possibility of our perceiving them lie in our positions in space-time, and not in something more intrinsic to our constitution. When we consider the intuition of very long strings of strokes, the obstacle is of a more structural kind, perhaps analogous to those to the perception of the objects of microphysics. That would suggest that a finitist theory of strings of strokes would already have a theoretical character, going beyond the 'data' of intuition just as physics extrapolates in an essential way from the data of perception.

A reply to this last point is suggested by Hilbert, who required of finitist proof that it should yield *intuitively evident* conclusions. It follows that the intuitively evident must include general propositions. Clearly these propositions are not known by intuiting each object in the range of the variable, and thus coming to know intuitively the relevant instance. It is not even clear at the outset what the connection is supposed to be between intuitive knowledge of a generalization and the intuitability of the objects in its scope.

To consider whether Hilbert's requirement can be satisfied, we need to distinguish two different kinds of cases. The first type are those generalizations that can be seen to be true by imagining an arbitrary object of the required kind. I have argued, for example, that one sees in this way that every string of strokes can be extended (1980: 156–8). This proposition is of particular importance because it is one of the bases of the infinity of the sequence of strings. The imagination involved is a manifestation of the intuition of space. This in turn is an aspect of the manner in which the world is present to us, in particular as extending beyond and within what is more explicitly and immediately present. Imagination of an arbitrary string offers a weak sense in which, even as a practical matter, any string can be intuited. But not, of course, in the sense in which intuition requires taking in all the mathematically relevant articulation of the string. Intuitability in this sense is not required for the evidence of the general proposition, and one can arrive at it only by in one way or another treating the concept of intuition or intuitability mathematically.

The second type of case is generalizations that depend on induction, in

226

particular conclusions of inductive inferences. Induction as a general principle has an essentially higher-order character, and for that reason it seems evident that it cannot be intuitively known. Nonetheless the domain of intuitive knowledge in mathematics will be very impoverished unless some proofs involving induction yield intuitive knowledge. The thesis of Hilbert is that finitist proofs have this character. Finitism regards inductions as evident only one at a time, and then, of course, only when the predicate involved is already clear from a finitist point of view, let us suppose (with Tait) if it belongs to primitive recursive arithmetic. What Hilbert's thesis requires is that such inductions have the property of leading from intuitively evident premisses to intuitively evident conclusions. We may call this property *conservativeness* with respect to intuitive evidence. Given Hilbert's interpretation of arithmetic by the model of strings of strokes, such conservativeness will be sufficient for his thesis if the generalizations needed as initial premisses in inductive proofs are either logical truths, definitions, or generalizations of the first type. This much seems to me to be true, although recursion equations raise issues that I cannot take up here.

But is it true that the inductions of primitive recursive arithmetic are conservative with respect to intuitive evidence? Logical principles seem to have this property, and induction has strong analogies with logical principles (Parsons 1983: 175). This consideration seems to me not to be completely convincing, however, and the question whether elementary inductions have the conservativeness property seems to me not easy to decide. If it were decided affirmatively on the basis of the similarity of induction to a logical principle, however, that would reinforce the observation that even in the most 'intuitive' mathematics, the element of conceptualization or thought is essential. Kant saw this very clearly in understanding mathematical intuition as 'construction of concepts'.

In closing I want to comment on the suggestion that the very idea of mathematical intuition is bound up with one or another form of Cartesian privacy. Brouwer's formulations give every encouragement to such a suggestion. At the Thyssen conference Timothy Smiley proposed that belief in such a connection had led later writers on intuitionism to reject or ignore the concept of intuition. This seems to me a plausible conjecture about the reasons for Dummett's near-silence noted above, and the same considerations may well have influenced others. The connection of mathematical intuition and Cartesian privacy, however, does not seem to me a necessary one. In this respect, mathematical intuition is on quite the same plane as perception. It is communicable and intersubjectively checkable. This should be particularly clear in the cases where intuition is founded on actual perception. No less than perception, mathematical intuition depends for its veridicality on background conditions, in particular the subject's possession of the relevant concepts, and on coherence with other intuitions and deductions from their deliverances. Therefore, the veridicality of intuition on a particular occasion can depend on what happens *subsequently*. That intuitions founded on actual perception and those involved in imaginative thought experiments give rise to workable *theories* is not something that can be obvious before any accumulation of mathematical experience. Nothing I have said here would oblige me to deny the Wittgensteinian thesis that this experience has to be the experience of a community.

REFERENCES

Brouwer, L. E. J., 1912. *Intuitionisme en formalisme*, Amsterdam; translation, Brouwer 1913.

Brouwer, L. E. J., 1913. Intuitionism and Formalism, *Bulletin of the American Mathematical Society 20*: 81–96; reprinted, Brouwer 1975.

Brouwer, L. E. J., 1929. Mathematik, Wissenschaft, und Sprache, *Monatshefte für Mathematik und Physik 36*: 153–64; reprinted, Brouwer 1975.

Brouwer, L. E. J., 1952. Historical Background, Principles, and Methods of Intuitionism, *South African Journal of Science 49*: 139–46; reprinted, Brouwer 1975.

Brouwer, L. E. J., 1975. *Collected Works*, vol. 1. *Philosophy and Intuitionistic Mathematics*, ed. Arend Heyting, Amsterdam: North-Holland.

Dantzig, D. van, 1955. Is $10^{10^{10}}$ a Finite Number? *Dialectica 9*: 272–7.

Dummett, M., 1959. Wittgenstein's Philosophy of Mathematics, *Philosophical Review 68:* 324–48; reprinted, Dummett 1978.

Dummett, M., 1975. Wang's Paradox, *Synthese 30*: 301–24; reprinted, Dummett 1978.

Dummett, M., 1977. *Elements of Intuitionism*, Oxford: Clarendon Press.

Dummett, M., 1978. *Truth and Other Enigmas*, London: Duckworth.

Dummett, M., 1980. Critical Notice of Brouwer, *Collected Works*, vols I and II, *Mind 89*: 605–16.

Gödel, K., 1946. Remarks Before the Princeton Bicentennial Conference on Problems in Mathematics, in *The Undecidable*, ed. M. Davis, Hewlett, NY: Raven Press, 1965.

Gödel, K., 1958. Über eine bisher noch nicht benützte Erweiterung des finiten Standpunktes, *Dialectica 12*: 280–7.

Goodman, N. D., 1970. A Theory of Constructions Equivalent to Arithmetic, in *Intuitionism and Proof Theory*, ed. A. Kino, J. Myhill and R. E. Vesley, Amsterdam: North-Holland.

Goodman, N. D., 1973. The Arithmetical Theory of Constructions, in *Cambridge Summer School in Mathematical Logic, Proceedings 1971*, ed. A. R. D. Mathias and H. Rogers, Jr, Berlin: Springer.

Gottlieb, D., 1980. *Ontological Economy: Substitutional Quantification and Mathematics*, Oxford: Clarendon Press.

Martin-Löf, P., 1975. An Intuitionistic Theory of Types: Predicative Part, in *Logic*

Colloquium '73, ed. H. E. Rose and J. C. Shepherdson, Amsterdam: North-Holland.

Martin-Löf, P., 1982. Constructive Mathematics and Computer Programming, in *Logic, Methodology, and Philosophy of Science VI*, ed. L. J. Cohen, J. Łos, H. Pfeiffer and K. P. Podewski, Amsterdam: North-Holland.

Mill, J. S., 1865. *An Examination of Sir William Hamilton's Philosophy, Collected Works* Vol. IX, Toronto: Univeristy of Toronto Press, 1979.

Parsons, C., 1964. Infinity and Kant's Conception of the 'Possibility of Experience', *Philosophical Review 73*: 182–97; reprinted in Parsons 1983; page references to reprint.

Parsons, C., 1971. Ontology and Mathematics, *Philosophical Review 80*: 151–76; reprinted in Parsons 1983; page references to reprint.

Parsons, C., 1971a. A Plea for Substitutional Quantification, *Journal of Philosophy 68*: 231–7, reprinted, Parsons 1983.

Parsons, C., 1980. Mathematical Intuition, *Proceedings of the Aristotelian Society 80*: 145–68.

Parsons, C., 1982. Substitutional Quantification and Mathematics (Review of Gottlieb 1980), *British Journal for the Philosophy of Science 33*: 409–21.

Parsons, C., 1983. *Mathematics in Philosophy: Selected Essays*, Ithaca and London: Cornell University Press.

Parsons, C., 1984. Arithmetic and the Categories, *Topoi 3*: 109–21.

Putnam, H., 1967. Mathematics without Foundations, *Journal of Philosophy 64*: 5–22; reprinted in H. Putnam, *Mathematics, Matter, and Method: Philosophical Papers*, vol. I, Cambridge: University Press, 1975.

Tait, W. W., 1981. Finitism, *Journal of Philosophy 78*: 524–46.

Tait, W. W., 1983. Against Intuitionism: Constructive Mathematics is Part of Classical Mathematics, *Journal of Philosophical Logic 12*: 173–96.

Troelstra, A. S., 1969. Principles of Intuitionism, Berlin, Springer.

Weinstein, S., 1983. The Intended Interpretation of Intuitionistic Logic, *Journal of Philosophical Logic 12*: 261–70.

Weyl, H., 1918. *Das Kontinuum*, Leipzig: Veit.

Weyl, H., 1919. Der *circulus vitosus* in der heutigen Begründung der Analysis, *Jahresbericht der deutschen Mathematiker-Vereinigung 28*: 85–92.

Weyl, H., 1921. Über die neue Grundlagenkrise der Mathematik, *Mathematische Zeitschrift 10*: 39–79.

Index of names

The Return of Grand Theory in the Human Sciences

Edited by **QUENTIN SKINNER**

A volume of new essays introducing the most influential developments in social and political theory over the last thirty years. Figures discussed include Althusser, Derrida, Foucault, Gadamer, Habermas, Kuhn, Levi-Strauss, Rawls and the *Annales* historians.

Contributors: Barry Barnes, James Boon, Stuart Clark, Anthony Giddens, David Hoy, Susan James, William Outhwaite, Mark Philp, Alan Ryan, Quentin Skinner.

Hard covers
Paperback

Now in paperback

Hegelianism

The Path Toward Dialectical Humanism, 1805–1841

JOHN TOEWS

' ... an impressive scholarly achievement which succeeds at most of the levels which it tackles ... The range of problems and the number of thinkers discussed in the book are remarkable, and the use of first-hand sources and general scholarship are exceptional.' *The Times Higher Education Supplement*

Paperback

The Intellectual Development of Karl Mannheim

COLIN LOADER

Largely inspired by Mannheim's own historical sociology of knowledge, Loader discusses the work of this social theorist and that of his contemporaries. He sets Mannheim's writings in their historical and intellectual context, giving rise to new interpretations of his work, particularly of *Ideology and Utopia*.

Hard covers

An Introduction to Medieval Islamic Philosophy

OLIVER LEAMAN

This book is an introduction to debates within the philosophy of the medieval Islamic world. It discusses a number of themes which were controversial within the philosophical community of that period; the creation of the world out of nothing, immortality, resurrection, the nature of ethics, and the relationship between natural and religious law.

Hard covers
Paperback